INTERNATIONAL BIBLIOGRAPHY OF AIR LAW
SUPPLEMENT 1991-1995

Wybo P. Heere

INTERNATIONAL BIBLIOGRAPHY OF AIR LAW

SUPPLEMENT 1991-1995

KLUWER LAW INTERNATIONAL
THE HAGUE - LONDON - BOSTON

Library of Congress Cataloguing-in-Publication Data is available

Published by Kluwer Law international
P.O. Box 85889
2508 CN The Hague, The Netherlands

Sold and distributed in the USA and Canada by
Kluwer Law International
675 Massachusetts Avenue
Cambridge, MA 02139, USA

Sold and distributed in all other countries by
Kluwer Law International
P.O. Box 85889
2508 CN The Hague, The Netherlands

Printed on acid-free paper

ISBN 90 4110 234 5

Kluwer Law International incorporates the publishing programmes of Graham & Trotman Ltd, Kluwer Law and Taxation Publishers and Martinus Nijhoff Publishers.

Acknowledgments

The supplement for the years 1991-1995 is now ready.

During these years friends and colleagues sent me their information and critical remarks.

Those who kept me regularly up-to-date were, as so often before, Ms. Marietta Sohns, librarian of the Netherlands Civil Aviation Authority: Aart van Wijk, Enrique Mapelli and R.I.R. Abeyratne. My feelings of deep gratitude to them remain unchanged.

Without them this bibliography would be less rich.

As so often before, my wife read and corrected the text. She and I are always surprised at the enormous number of publications that are published in our field: we must be grateful to all those who write their articles or books, for without them there would be no bibliography.

Work on this bibliography involved many personal contacts all over the world. To all these friends and colleagues I am very much indebted.

Wybo P.Heere

Utrecht, February 1996

Preface

In 1990 my last Supplement was published. Since then many developments in the field of air law have taken place, and they can be traced in the multifarious publications which appeared in the last five years.

Owing to these developments the following subjects have been added to my classification scheme: 43.c FIRs; 44.c JAA; 44.d Customs; 48.e Code-sharing; 68 Aviation and automatization; 71.o Homebuilt aircraft; 82.c Spare parts; 115 Handling (the public law aspects); 131.h Liability of the customs; and 196 Sanctions and reprisals.

The 'Directions of use' as presented in the original 1972 Bibliography also apply to this Supplement. Within a certain category publications are listed chronologically - the system preferred by most users of this Bibliography.

The Table of Contents and the Subject Index are published in English, French and Spanish. Where adequate French or Spanish terms for modern developments were not available, English terms have been used.

Closing date of this Supplement was January 1996.

Wybo P.Heere

Institute of Public International Law
Janskerkhof 3
3512 BK Utrecht, The Netherlands

Table of Contents

Chapter IV
The aviation industry

Chapter V
Aircraft

Chapter VI
Aviation personnel

Chapter VII
Airports and air navigation facilities

Chapter VIII
Air transport

Chapter IX
Damage to third parties

Chapter X
Accidents – Towage and salvage

Chapter XI
Insurance

Chapter XII
Criminal law

Chapter XIII
Acts on board aircraft

Chapter XIV
Solution of disputes

Chapter XV
Military aviation. The laws of war and neutrality

Chapter XVI
Miscellaneous

Table des matières

Chapitre III
Organisation de l'aviation nationale et internationale

Chapitre VI
Personnel de l'aviation

Chapitre VII
Aérodromes et autres facilités pour la navigation aérienne

Chapitre VIII
Le transport aérien

Chapitre X
Accidents – Assistance

Chapitre XI
Assurances

Chapitre XII
Droit pénal aérien

Chapitre XIII
Actes survenant à bord des aéronefs

Chapitre XIV
La solution des différends

Chapitre XV
Aviation militaire. Droit de la guerre et de la neutralité

Chapitre XVI
Divers

Índice general

Capítulo IV
La aviación

Capítulo V
Las aeronaves

Capítulo IX
Daños a terceros

Capítulo X
Accidentes – Asistencia y salvamento

Capítulo XI
Los seguros aeronáuticos

Capítulo XII
Derecho penal aeronáutico

Capítulo XIII
Hechos ocurridos a bordo de aeronaves

Capítulo XIV
La solución de controversias

Capítulo XV
La aviación militar. Derecho de guerra y de neutralidad

Capítulo XVI
Varios

Abbreviations

AASL	Annals of Air and Space Law (Montreal, McGill)
ABA	American Bar Association (Chicago IL)
ADMA	Annuaire de Droit Maritime et Aérien (Paris)
AFDI	Annuaire Français de Droit International
AITAL	Asociación Internacional de Transporte Aéreo Latinoamericano
AJIL	American Journal of International Law
ALADA	Asociación Latino Americana de Derecho Aeronáutico y Espacial
ASDA	Association Suisse de Droit Aérien et Spatial (Switzerland)
ATC	Air Traffic Control
AW&ST	Aviation Week & Space Technology (USA)
CIDA-E	Centro de Investigación y Difusión Aeronaútico-Espacial (Uruguay)
CMLR	Common Market Law Review (London)
CNS	Communications, Navigation and Surveillance
DPAC	Diritto e Pratica dell'Aviazione Civile
EALA	European Air Law Association
ETL	European Transport Law (Belgium)
ICC	International Chamber of Commerce
ICLQ	International and Comparative Law Quarterly (UK)
IFAPA	International Foundation of Airline Passengers' Associations
ILA	International Law Association
ILR	International Law Review
ITA	Institut du Transport Aérien (France)
J	Journal
JAL	Journal of Air Law
JALC	Journal of Air Law and Commerce
JIL	Journal of International Law
JILC	Journal of International Law and Commerce
Jornadas	See p. 1
LJ	Law Journal
Lloyd's MCLQ	Lloyd's Maritime and Commercial Law Quarterly (London)
LR	Law Review
NJW	Neue Juristische Wochenschrift (Germany)
RBDA	Revista Brasileira de Direito Aeronáutico
RBDAE	Revista Brasileira de Direito Aeroespacial (Brazil)
RdC	Recueil des Cours de l'Académie de Droit International (The Hague)
Revista European DNMA	Revista Europea de Derecho de la Navegación Marítima y Aeronáutica (Barcelona)
RFDAS	Revue Française de Droit Aérien et Spatial (France)

RGDIP	Revue Générale de Droit International Public
RIDAT	Revista Interamericana de Derecho Aéreo y Turismo (Perú)
Ts	Tijdschrift
ZLW	Zeitschrift für Luft- und Weltraumrecht (Germany)
Zs	Zeitschrift

Chapter I. General subjects

3. The teaching of air law

LARSEN, P.B. – Air law education 1967-91. –
56 *JALC* 1991, pp.705-718

4. Air law conferences

XVI Jornadas iberoamericanas de derecho aeronáutico, del espacio y de la aviación comercial, organizadas por el Instituto peruano de derecho aero-espacial del 10 al 13 de setiembre de 1984. –
Lima [1984], 310 pp.

XVII Jornadas iberoamericanas de derecho aeronáutico y del espacio y de la aviación comercial (Rio de Janeiro – 23-26 de setembro de 1987). Anais. –
[Rio de Janeiro 1987], 82 pp.

La libéralisation du transport aérien dans la CEE: le point de vue des pays voisins. Air transport liberalization in the EEC: the viewpoint of neighbouring countries. –
ITA Études & documents/Studies & reports 88/4, vol. 11, viii-256 pp. Symposium
proceedings Marrakech, 13-14 Oct. 1988

Euroderegulation as seen by Asia. –
ITA Études & documents/Studies & reports 90/2, vol. 19, iv-104 pp. Symposium proceedings Lahore, 11-12 December 1989

Transport aérien 1000 jours pour faire l'Europe? Air transport: 1,000 days to get Europe off the ground? –
ITA Études & documents/Studies & reports 89/5, vol. 17, iv-183 pp. Symposium proceedings Dubrovnik, 9-10 November 1989

EEC air transport policy and regulation, and their implications for North America. Proceedings of a conference held at McGill University, Montreal, Canada, September 1989. Edited by P.P.C.HAANAPPEL, G.PETSIKAS, R.ROSALES, J.THAKER. –
Deventer etc. 1990, ix-216 pp.

Air transport and the European Community. Recent developments. London, 2 November 1989. –
1 EALA Conference papers 1990, 125 pp.

XIX Jornadas iberoamericanas de derecho aeronáutico, del espacio y de la aviación comercial. Madrid 1989. –
Madrid 1990, 248 pp.

KRÄMER, P.M. – East-West aviation conference: 'Opening the skies'. Paris, 19-20 February 1990. –
39 *ZLW* 1990, pp.204-209

MENDES DE LEON, P. – East-West conference 'Opening the skies'. ICC, Paris, 19-20
February 1990. –
15 *Air Law* 1990, pp.167-168

Air transport law and policy in the 1990's. Controlling the boom. Edited by P.MENDES DE LEON and E.ABERSON. Proceedings of an international symposium held in Delft on 4 and 5 October 1990. –
Dordrecht etc. 1991, xiv-160 pp.

Airline mergers and cooperation in the European Community. London 1990. –
2 EALA Conference papers 1991, 122 pp.

HINTZ, M. – International colloquium: The spaceplane and the law. Paris, 14-15 May 1991. –
40 *ZLW* 1991, pp.287-289

JERICHO, E. – History of the Southern Methodist University's air law symposium. –
56 *JALC* 1991, pp.701-703

KRÄMER, P.M. – Conference: Beyond bilaterals, new directions in global air transport negotiations. Brussels, 30-31 May 1991. –
40 *ZLW* 1991, pp.289-293

KRÄMER, P.M. – Deutsche Gesellschaft für Luft- und Raumfahrt (DGLR) und Deutsche Vereinigung für Internationales Recht (DVIR). Gemeinsame Sitzung der Ausschüsse für Luft- und Weltraumrecht, Köln, 30. April 1991. –
40 *ZLW* 1991, pp.284-287

Second annual conference. Brussels 1991. –
3 EALA Conference papers 1991

De Stefani, G. – Il diritto di sciopero nei servizi aerei, aeroportuali e di assistenza
al volo. –
Trasporti 1991, nos 53-55, pp.89-96

SUPANCANA, I.B.R. and KHAN, A.H. – The highways of air and outer space over Asia. Taipeh, 26-31 May 1991. –
16 *Air Law* 1991, pp.195-198

CHENG, Chia-Jui and MENDES DE LEON, P., eds – The highways of air and outer space over Asia. –
Dordrecht etc. 1992, xxxii-364 pp.

VON DER DUNK, F.G. and YAN, L. – The spaceplane and the law – A dream to come true? Colloquium of May 1991. –
17 *Air and Space Law* 1992, pp.20-21

Third annual conference. 15 November 1991 in Berlin. –
4 EALA Conference papers 1992, 137 pp.

Hughes, N. – Eighth annual aviation law operations and claims conference. –
17 *Air and Space Law* 1992, pp.22-24

ICAO. World-wide air transport colloquium, Montreal, 6-10 April 1992. Proceedings. Exploring the future of international air transport regulation. –
ICAO, Montreal 1992

XXI Jornadas iberoamericanas de derecho aeronáutico y del espacio y de la aviación comercial. Lisboa, 6-8 noviembre 1991. –
8 *Revista europea DNMA* 1992, pp.1157-1445

KRÄMER, P.M. – Airport and en-route slot allocation. Brussels, October 28, 1991. –
41 *ZLW* 1992, pp.86-88

KRÄMER, P.M. – Deutsche Gesellschaft für Luft- und Raumfahrt (DGLR) und Deutsche
Vereinigung für Internationales Recht (DVIR). Gemeinsame Sitzung der Ausschüsse für Luft- und Weltraumrecht. Köln, 19. Mai 1992. –
41 *ZLW* 1992, pp.283-287

KRÄMER, P.M. – European Air Law Association. 1991 Annual conference: Recent developments in EC air transport law and policy. Berlin, 15 November 1991. –
41 *ZLW* 1992, pp.89-92

KRÄMER, P.M. – International Civil Aviation Organization. World-wide air transport colloquium: Exploring the future of international air transport regulation. Montreal, 6-10 April 1992. –
41 *ZLW* 1992, pp.275-283

MURRAY, K.I. – 10th Annual Conference of the Aviation Law Association of Australia and New Zealand. –
17 *Air and Space Law* 1992, pp.25-27

Fourth annual conference. 6 November 1992 in Rome. –
5 EALA Conference papers 1993, 192 pp.

International air transport: the challenges ahead. –
OECD, Paris 1993, 94 pp.

XXI Jornadas iberoamericanas de derecho aeronáutico, del espacio y de la aviación comercial. Lisboa, 1991. –
[Lisboa 1993], 109 pp.

KRÄMER, P.M. – Gemeinsame Sitzung der Deutschen Gesellschaft für Luft- und Raumfahrt (DGLR) und der Deutschen Vereinigung für Internationales Recht (DVIR), 'Luft- und Weltraumrecht'. Köln, 20. April 1993. –
42 *ZLW* 1993, pp.291-295

MENDES DE LEON, P. – Conference on the use of airspace and outer space for all mankind in the 21st century. –
18 *Air and Space Law* 1993, p. 291

The new legal framework for aviation in the European Community. Proceedings of the International Colloquium in Paris on 17 June 1993, ed. K.-H. BÖCKSTIEGEL. –
ICC, Paris 1993, 273 pp.

La aviación civil internacional y el derecho aeronáutico hacia el siglo XXI. XVIII Jornadas latinoamericanas de derecho aeronáutico y espacial, Rio de Janeiro, mayo 1994. –
ALADA, Buenos Aires 1994, 218 pp.

Fifth annual conference. 5 November 1993 in Paris. –
6 EALA Conference papers 1994, 138 pp.

WASSENBERGH, H. – A seminar on air transport in Asia; legal and regulatory challenges. Colombo, Sri Lanka, 20-24 June 1994. –
19 *Air and Space Law* 1994, pp.238-239

ABEYRATNE, R.I.R. – The world-wide air transport conference and air traffic rights. – A commentary. –
30 *ETL* 1995, pp.131-147

CHENG, C.-J. – The use of airspace and outer space for all mankind in the 21st century. Proceedings of the international conference on air transport and space application in a new world held in Tokyo from 2-5 June 1993. –
The Hague 1995, xxiii-353 pp.

VAN FENEMA, H.P. – The Beijing symposium. –
20 *Air and Space Law* 1995, pp.294-296

XXIV Jornadas iberoamericanas de derecho aeronáutico y del espacio y de la aviación comercial. Salamanca, 19-21 de octubre de 1994. –
Instituto iberoamericano, Madrid 1995, 473 pp.

KRÄMER, P.M. – Chicago Convention. 50th Anniversary convention. –
44 *ZLW* 1995, pp.57-60

KRÄMER, P.M. – Gemeinsame Sitzung der Deutschen Gesellschaft für Luft- und Raumfahrt – Lilienthal-Obert e.V. (DGLR), Fachbereich S6 'Luft- und Weltraumrecht' und der Deutschen Vereinigung für Internationales Recht (DVIR), Ausschuss 'Luft- und Weltraumrecht', Köln 7.Juni 1995. –
44 *ZLW* 1995, pp.444-450

LABES, H.W. – International colloquium 'Perspectives of Air Law, Space Law, and International Business Law for the Next Century' to celebrate 70 years Institute Air and Space Law and 20 years Chair for International Business Law, Cologne, 7 to 9 June 1995. –
44 *ZLW* 1995, pp.450-458

MAPELLI, E. – XXIII Jornadas iberoamericanas de derecho aeronáutico y del espacio y de la aviación comercial, 1993. -.
11 *Revista europea DNMA* 1995, pp.1663-1671

MAPELLI, E. – XXIV Jornadas iberoamericanas de derecho aeronáutico y del espacio y de la aviación comercial celebradas en la Universidad de Salamanca los días 19, 20 y 21 de 1994. –
11 *Revista europea DNMA* 1995, pp.1672-1676

POONOOSAMY, V. – The ICAO world-wide air transport conference. 23 November – 6 December 1994. –
30 *ETL* 1995, pp.115-130

WASSENBERGH, H.A. and MENDES DE LEON, P. – Impressions from the fourth ICAO world-wide air transport conference, Montreal, 23 November – 6 December 1994. –
20 *Air and Space Law* 1995, pp.22-31

5. The history of air law

ELEIZALDE PETITT, G. – Actas de entendimiento: naturaleza y valor de las relaciones internacionales sobre aviación civil. –
XVI Jornadas iberoamericanas, Lima 1984, pp.115-131

6. Codification and unification of air law

BELCHIOR, St. BASTOS – Fontes do direito aéreo. Acordos. Leis. Costumes. Jurisprudência e doutrina. –
25 *RBDA* 1987, no. 42, pp.7-11

MAPELLI, E. – De la internacionalidad a la uniformidad del derecho aeronáutico. –
12 *ADMA* 1993, pp.405-419. *Aviación comercial, turismo, etc.* (Buenos Aires) 1994, pp.137-142

MAPELLI, E. – Las fuentes del derecho aeronáutico con especial consideración de los usos y costumbres de la actividad aeronáutica. –
10 *Anuario hispano-luso-americano de derecho internacional* 1993, pp.291-312

CLETON, R. – Internationale unificatie van het vervoerrecht, vooruitgang of stilstand? –
Afscheidscollege Rotterdam, 2 december 1993. Zwolle 1994, 38 pp.

CHENG, C.-J. – New sources of international air law. –
In: The use of airspace and outer space, The Hague 1995, pp.277-295

7. Autonomy of air law

MAPELLI, E. – Autonomía del derecho aeronáutico. –
Actualidad Civil (Madrid) 1991, no. 14, pp.189-196

8. Air law as compared with maritime law

ABRAHAM, H.J. – Das Seerecht. Ein Grundriss mit Hinweisen auf die Sonderrechte anderer Verkehrsmittel, vornehmlich das Binnenschiffahrts- und Luftrecht. –
Berlin 1974, 4th ed., xv-284 pp.

BRIANT, A.M. – International carriage of cargo: a comparative study of the liability of the carrier in maritime and air transport law. –
18 *AASL* 1993, pp.45-77

BROWN III, W.C. – Problems arising from the intersection of traditional maritime law and aviation death and personal injury liability. –
68 *Tulane LR* (New Orleans LA) 1994, pp.577-594

Litigation with a foreign flavor: a comparison of the Warsaw Convention and the Hamburg Rules. –
59 *JALC* 1994, pp.907-942

11. Air law and private international law

POLAK, M.V. – Conflict of laws in the air. Some legal issues of international aircraft financing and leasing. –
17 *Air and Space Law* 1992, pp.78-86

AUSTIN, J.B. – A general framework for analyzing choice-of-law problems in air crash litigation. –
58 *JALC* 1993, pp.909-980

12. Literature on air law

a. Manuals

MAYORGA, R. – Elementos de derecho aéreo. –
León (Nicaragua) 1952

LIU, T. – Selected essays on aviation law. –
Taipei, Graduate School of Law, National Cheng-Chi University, 1985, 334 pp.

RODRÍGUEZ JURADO, A. and SUÁREZ DE ARNEDO, M.E. – Teoría y práctica del derecho aeronáutico. –
Buenos Aires, 2nd ed., tomo I, 1986, xvi-330 pp.; tomo II, 1990, ix-433 pp.

LANZA BORJA, C.E. – Fundamentos del derecho aeronáutico. –
La Paz 1987, 413 pp.

ROBERSON, C. – Aviation: a complete legal guide. –
Shrewsbury 1987, x-197 pp.

TAYLOR, S.E.T. and PARMAR, H.A.; revised by UNDERDOWN, R.B. – Aviation law for pilots. –
Oxford 1989, 7th ed., 169 pp.; 1st ed. 1953

MALEEV, J.N. – Internationales Luftrecht. Fragen der Theorie und Praxis. –
Veröffentlichungen des Instituts für Int. Recht an der Universität Kiel, No. 110.
Berlin 1990, 221 pp.

RODIÈRE, R. and MERCADAL, B. – Droit des transports terrestres et aériens. –
Paris 1990, 5th ed., 502 pp.

DIEDERIKS-VERSCHOOR, I.H.Ph. – An introduction to air law. –
Deventer 1991, 4th ed., xxv-226 pp.

BLACKSHAW, C. – Air law and regulation; a framework for the civil aviation industry. –
London 1992, xiv-304 pp.

DEMPSEY, P.S.; HARDAWAY, R.M. and THOMS, W.E. – Aviation law regulation. –
Butterworth 1992, 2 vols, loose-leaf

ŻYLICZ, M. – International air transport law. –
Utrecht Studies in Air and Space Law, vol. 12; Dordrecht etc. 1992, xxi-230 pp.

TAPIA SALINAS, L. – Derecho aeronáutico. –
Barcelona 1993, 2nd ed., xxxi-823 pp.

Aviación comercial, turismo, derecho aeronáutico y espacial. –
ALADA, Buenos Aires 1994, vi-352 pp.

SALAZAR, L.R. – Manual del derecho aeronáutico y del espacio. Vol. I. –
Quito 1994, 210 pp.

ABEYRATNE, R.I.R. – Legal and regulatory issues in international aviation. –
Irvington-on-Hudson (NY) 1995, 350 pp.

b. General articles

CASTELLI, L. – Las mil y una normas del derecho aeronáutico. –
La Ley (Buenos Aires) 1989 C, pp.996-1009

PERUCCHI, H.A. – Problemas jurídicos de la aviación del futuro. –
XIX Jornadas Iberoamericanas, Madrid 1989, pp.41;53

TOSI, J.-P. – L'actualité en droit aérien. –
25 *ETL* 1990, pp.816-830

VIDELA ESCALADA, F. – Considerations on the legal regulation of air transport in the near future. –
15 *Air Law* 1990, pp.140-148

DONATO, M. – Tendencias contemporáneas del transporte aéreo con especial referencia al campo jurídico. –
15 *Revista del CIDA-E* 1991, pp.11-26

MAPELLI, E. – Una nueva etapa del derecho aeronáutico. –
9 *Anuario del Instituto Hispano-Luso-Americano de Derecho Internacional 1991, pp.297-321*

CHENG, B. – Air law. –
In: Encyclopedia of Public Int. Law, Amsterdam 1992, vol. I, pp.66-72

KEAN, A. – Air law past and future: the challenges of the XXIst century. –
17 *AASL* 1992-I, pp.7-13

KOTAITE, A. – El desarrollo del derecho aéreo internacional en los 50 años de vida de la OACI. –
RBDAE, May-Sept. 1994, no. 66, pp.20-24

c. Festschriften

MASSON-ZWAAN, T.L. and MENDES DE LEON, P.M.J., eds – Air and space law: De lege ferenda. Essays in honour of Henri A. WASSENBERGH. –
Dordrecht etc. 1992, xxxiv-305 pp.

El comandante de aeronave. En homenaje a D. Indalecio REGO. –
Instituto Iberoamericano, Madrid 1993,

d. Collected works

PELÁEZ, M.J. – Historia del derecho de la navegación I. –
Barcelona 1994, 799 pp.

e. Dictionaries

TAPIA SALINAS, L. and MAPELLI, E. – Ensayo para un diccionario de derecho aeronáutico. –
Instituto Iberoamericano, Madrid 1991, 650 pp.

CAMBOURNAC, P., ed. – Dictionnaire de transport aérien. –
ITA, Paris 1993, 136 pp.

f. Bibliographies

RODINÒ, W. and HOWARTH, P. – Repertorio bibliografico di diritto dei trasporti: 1988. Trasporti aerei. –
Trasporti 1989, no. 48/49, pp.250-270, at pp.251-258

WISE, S.H. and ANDRUS, K.L. – Bibliography. Current literature on aerospace law. –
55 *JALC* 1990, pp.1219-1224

HEERE, W.P. – Bibliography of air law 1990. –
16 *Air Law* 1991, pp.207-248

HEERE, W.P. – International bibliography of air law. Supplement 1985-1990. –
Deventer 1991, xxxiv-314 pp.

RODINÒ, W. and HOWARTH, P. – Repertorio bibliografico di diritto dei trasporti: 1989. Trasporti aerei. –
Trasporti 1991, no. 53/55, pp.145-169, at pp.147-155

HEERE, W.P. – Bibliography of air law 1991. –
17 *Air and Space Law* 1992, pp.239-284

KAYSER, V. – Air and space law bibliography. B. Air law. –
17 *AASL* 1992, vol. II, pp.597-618, at pp.606-616

LANDRY, Ch. and MARLOWE, A.N. – Bibliography. –
58 *JALC* 1992, pp.643-655

RODINÒ, W. and HOWARTH, P. – Repertorio bibliografico di diritto dei trasporti: 1990. Trasporti aerei. –
Trasporti 1992, no. 56/58, pp.157-178, at pp.158-166

BROADWAY, M.C. and JENKINS, J. – Bibliography. –
58 *JALC* 1993, pp.1225-1231

HEERE, W.P. – Bibliography of air law 1992. –
18 *Air and Space Law* 1993, pp.205-260

RODINÒ, W. and HOWARTH, P. – Repertorio bibliografico di diritto dei trasporti: 1991. Trasporti aerei. –
Trasporti 1993, no. 61, pp.237-253, at pp.239-243

HEERE, W.P. – Bibliography of air law 1993. –
19 *Air and Space Law* 1994, pp.240-286

RODINÒ, W. and HOWARTH, P. – Repertorio bibliografico di diritto dei trasporti: 1992. Trasporti aerei. –
Trasporti 1994, no. 64, pp.199-218, at pp.201-207

HEERE, W.P. – Bibliography of air law 1994. –
20 *Air and Space Law* 1995, pp. 214-267

g. Biographies. Obituaries

PONTAVICE, E. DU – Michel DE JUGLART (1911-1990). –
44 *RFDAS* 1990, no. 4

PÉREZ SAN EMETERIO, C. – Indalecio REGO, in memoriam. –
El comandante de aeronave, Madrid 1993, pp.17-30

PONTAVICE, E. DU – In memoriam. Le professeur Paul DE LA PRADELLE. –
46 *RFDAS* 1993, pp.285-287

DIEDERIKS-VERSCHOOR, I.H.Ph. and WASSENBERGH, H.A. – Dr J.F. LYCKLAMA À NIJEHOLT (1876-1947). –
19 *Air and Space Law* 1994, pp.8-14

DIEDERIKS-VERSCHOOR, I.H.Ph. – R.H.MANKIEWICZ (1905-1993). –
19 *Air and Space Law* 1994, p.30

13. Air law journals

Korean Journal of Air Law, vol. 1, 1989 –

15. International air law conventions

a. General

CONDE ASOREY, L.A. and POYO-GUERRERO SANCHEZ, J. – Convenios internacionales multilaterales de aviación civil: notas y comentarios. – Valencia 1991, 237 pp.

VON DER DUNK, F.G. – Jus cogens sive lex ferenda: jus cogendum? 7. Jus cogens and air law. –
In: Essays in honour of Henri A. WASSENBERGH, Dordrecht 1992, pp.219-239, at pp.233-237

RODRÍGUEZ JURADO, A. – Código aeronáutico internacional anotado. –
Buenos Aires 1992, 190 pp.

BRASIL, S.M. – Tratados e convenções internacionais no direito constitucional brasileiro. –
RBDAE, July-Dec. 1993, no. 64, pp.14-17&

MAPELLI, E. – Código de leyes internacionales de aviación civil. –
Dirección General de Aviación Civil, Madrid 1995, 302 pp.

h. The Chicago Convention with Annexes, 1944

SANES, M.L. and PERUCCHI, H.A. – Las enmiendas a la Convención de Chicago. –
XIV Jornadas Iberoamericanas, Lima 1984, pp.191-237

ALBANO DE SILVEIRA, E. – A importância da Convenção de Chicago para o desenvolvimento da aviação civil internacional. –
25 *RBDAE* 1987, no. 42, pp.80-82

PEREIRA, M. DOS SANTOS – Os anexos técnicos da OACI e o controle integrado de aviação civil e militar. –
25 *RBDAE* 1987, no. 42, pp.145-155

PRESTO DE GONZÁLEZ, A. and GAGGERO MONTANER, M. – A casi medio siglo de la firma del Convenio de Chicago. –
14 *Revista del CIDA* 1989-1990, pp.49-64

DENZA, E. – The interface between the Chicago Convention and the European Community. –
2 EALA Conference papers 1991, pp.15-26

WEBER, L. – EEC liberalization policy and the Chicago Convention. –
3 EALA Conference 1991, pp.17-30

ESPINOLA, S. – Atos de Chicago. –
RBDAE, July-Dec. 1991, no. 55, pp.16-19

DIERIKX, M.L.J. – Shaping world aviation: Anglo-American civil aviation relations, 1944-1946. –
57 *JALC* 1992, pp.795-840

WEBER, L. – EEC air transport liberalization and the Chicago Convention. –
17 *AASL* 1992, vol. I, pp.245-262

ABEYRATNE, R.I.R. – The legal status of the Chicago Convention and its Annexes. –
19 *Air and Space Law* 1994, pp.113-123

The Chicago Convention.

POGUE, L.W.	The International Civil Aviation Conference (1944) and its sequel the Anglo-American Bermuda Air Transport Agreement (1946), pp.1-54
DAVID, P.T.	A review of the work at the Chicago Conference (from a secretariat point of view), pp.55-107
RINALDI BACCELLI, G.	50 Années d'expérience depuis la Convention de Chicago: l'effort italien pour atteindre l'uniformité internationale dans le respect des droits fondamentaux visés par la Constitution, pp. 109-125
BÖCKSTIEGEL, K.-H. and KRÄMER, P.M	Filling in the gaps of the Chicago Convention: main features of the new legal framework for aviation in the European Community, pp.127-143
MATTE, N. MATEESCO	The Chicago Convention – Where from and where to, ICAO?, pp.371-399
MILDE, M.	The Chicago Convention – Are major amendments necessary or desirable 50 years later?, pp.401-452
VÁSQUEZ ROCHA, E.	Toward a new international civil aviation convention?, pp.477-490

19 *AASL* 1994, vol. I

The Chicago Convention.

ABEYRATNE, R.I.R.	The economic relevance of the Chicago Convention – a retrospective study, pp.3-80
COCCA, A.A.	The Chicago Convention and technological development in air and space, pp.135-161
GIALLORETO, L.	A retrospective on the reinvention of international civil air transport economic regulation: circa 1994-2004, pp.327-346
GULDIMANN, W.	The Chicago Convention revisited: possible improvements after fifty years, pp.347-362
JASENTULIYANA, N.	Celebrating fifty years of the Chicago Convention twenty-five years after the moon landing: lessons for space law, pp.429-450

MENDES DE LEON, P. Air transport as a service under the Chicago Convention: the origins of cabotage, pp.523-565
19 *AASL* 1994, vol. II

MAPELLI Y LÓPEZ, E. – Los anexos de la OACI en el derecho interno. –
RIDAT (Lima), August 1994, no. 51, pp.46-51. La aviación civil internacional, XVIII Jornadas latinoamericanas, Buenos Aires 1994, pp.46-51

MATTE, N.M. – The Chicago Convention – Where from and where to, ICAO?
29 *ETL* 1994, pp.535-552

MÜNZ, R. – 50 Jahre Abkommen über die internationale Zivilluftfahrt. Rückschau und Ausblick. –
43 *ZLW* 1994, pp.383-387

PAPKIN, R.D. – El tratamiento de la Convención de Chicago en los tribunales de Estados Unidos. –
RBDAE, May-Sept. 1994, no. 66, pp.26-30. La aviación civil internacional, XVIII Jornadas latinoamericanas, Buenos Aires 1994, pp.47-52

PRIMAVERA, J. – Na data do 50 aniversário da convenvção de Chicago de 1944. Uma questão prévia: Vigoram os Anexos na ordem jurídica interna portuguesa? –
XXIV Jornadas iberoamericanas, Salamanca 1994, pp.429-444

WEBER, L. – The European Union and the Chicago Convention of 1944. –
19 *Air and Space Law* 1994, pp.179-184

KOTAITE, A. – Is there a lessening of State sovereignty or a real will to co-operate globally? –
20 *Air and Space Law* 1995, pp.288-293

SEKIGUCHI, M. – The need to revise the Bermuda capacity principle. The need to update the Chicago Convention. –
In: The use of airspace and outer space, The Hague 1995, pp.23-34

KRÄMER, P.M. – Chicago Convention. 50th Anniversary Conference. –
44 *ZLW* 1995, pp.57-60

16. Air law in different countries

Austria

STERNS, G.C. – The law of products liability in the United States and Europe.
–
Brussels symposium, April 1992, 14-38 pp.

MORSCHER, S. – Zu den Grenzen der Bundeskompetenzen 'Verkehrswesen bezüglich der Eisenbahnen und der Luftfahrt' (Art. 10 Abs. 1 Z 9 B-VG). –

In: Für Staat und Recht. Festschrift für Herbert SCHAMBECK. Berlin 1994, pp.527-547

Belgium

GODFROID, M. – Les transports à titre onéreux et gratuit dans la Convention de Varsovie et en droit belge. –
Mélanges offerts à Robert PIRSON, Brussels 1989, pp.131-141

GODFROID, M. – L'application en Belgique de la Convention de Varsovie et du Protocole de La Haye (1983-1988). –
44 *RFDAS* 1991, pp.209-238

GROSBOIS, Th. – Liberté du trafic et intégration aérienne. La première tentative de rapprochement entre la KLM et la SABENA (1946-1950). –
6 *Lettre d'information des Historiens de l'Europe contemporaine* (Louvain), Dec. 1991, no. 3/4, pp.84-148

GORIS, W. and JAKHIAN, G. – Security rights in aircraft under Belgian law. –
17 *Air and Space Law* 1992, pp.61-67

WOOD, B. – The ownership of international airlines: a European view. Belgium. –
In: The highways of air and outer space, 1992, pp.311-327, at pp.321-323

VAN BAREN, W.H. – Recent aviation case law from the Benelux. –
18 *Air and Space Law* 1993, pp.29-35

NAVEAU, J. – La Belgique fédérale et l'espace aérien. –
27 *Revue belge de droit international* 1994, pp.233-243

GORIS, W. – Security rights in aircraft under Belgian law. –
In: Aircraft finance, The Hague 1995, pp.127-138

Czechoslovakia

DAVIDSON, G.E. – United States' use of economic sanctions, treaty bending, and treaty breaking in international aviation. Czechoslovakia. –
59 *JALC* 1994, pp.291-356, at pp.307-312 and 337-339

France

GUILLAUME, G. – Finanziamento e responsabilità civile dei servizi di assistenza alla navigazione aerea. –
12 *DPAC* 1988, pp.21-31

DE LA VERPILLIÈRE, Ch. – La loi du 10 juillet 1989. –
43 *RFDAS* 1990, pp.323-328

BASTIER, J. – L'administration de l'aéronautique militaire française septembre 1915-mars 1917. –
11 *ADMA* 1991, pp.293-336

FOLLIOT, M.G. – La libéralisation de la politique aéronautique française. –
44 *RFDAS* 1991, pp.359-372

GDANSKI, M. – The French tax lease. –
Airfinance J., July 1991, no. 128, pp.30-32

GUILLAUME, G. -Responsabilité pénale du commandant de bord en droit français. –
16 *AASL* 1991, pp.79-92

GUILLERM, J. – Problèmes liés à la circulation des aéronefs militaires. –
44 *RFDAS* 1991, pp.27-43

VUILLERMET, P. and BRIOT, J.L. – Französische Vorschriften für Massnahmen zur Vogelschlagverhütung auf Flughäfen. –
11 *Vogel und Luftverkehr* 1991, pp.27-33

LE GALL, J.-P. and REEB, S. – Highlighting various tax and security law aspects of aircraft financing – France. –
17 *Air and Space Law* 1992, pp.87-91

KUZNICKI, Th. – Terrorismus und luftspezifische Gefahr in Bezug auf eine Haftung des Luftfrachtführers gemäss Artikel 17 des Warschauer Abkommens. Frankreich. –
41 *ZLW* 1992, pp.360-376

WOOD, B. – The ownership of international airlines: a European view. France. –
In: The highways of air and outer space, 1992, pp.311-327, at pp.316-318

BASTIER, J. – La création du sous-secrétariat d'Etat à l'aéronautique civile et les débuts de la législation aérienne française (1919-1920). –
12 *ADMA* 1993, pp.445-467

FOLLIOT, M.G. – Les grandes tendances du transport aérien en France. Ouverture du ciel et évolution de la responsabilité du transporteur. –
46 *RFDAS* 1993, pp.7-14

LE GALL, J.-P. and REEB, S. – Financial crisis in the aviation industry – France. –
18 *Air and Space Law* 1993, pp.183-191

SCHUBERT, F. – La responsabilité des services de la circulation aérienne. France. –
ASDA Bulletin 1993-2, no. 115, pp.5-34, at pp.17-19 and 25-27

SUEL, M. – Essai sur la codification à droit constant. –
Paris 1993

BENADON, D. – The view of France on the third package. –
6 EALA Conference papers 1994, pp.133-138

MESMIN, O. – La satisfaction des besoins de l'Etat au regard de la nouvelle donne du transport aérien. –
47 *RFDAS* 1994, pp.117-126

VEAUX, D. and VEAUX-FOURNERIE, P. – La pénétration en droit français de la théorie de la faute inexcusable en matière aérienne et maritime sous l'influence des conventions internationales. –
In: L'internationalisation du droit. Mélanges en l'honneur de Yvon Loussouarn, Paris 1994, pp.391-403

LE GALL, J.-P. and REEB, S. – Highlighting various tax and security law aspects of aircraft financing – France. –
In: Aircraft finance, The Hague 1995, pp.109-115

German Democratic Republic

SCHWENK, W. – Rechtliche Auswirkungen aus dem Verhältnis beider deutscher Staaten auf den zivilen Luftverkehr. –
39 *ZLW* 1990, pp.147-164

RIEGER, T. – Steuerhoheit der DDR in den ehemaligen Luftkorridoren zwischen der Bundesrepublik Deutschland und Berlin (West). –
42 *ZLW* 1993, pp.29-34

Germany

BLACKLOCK, M. – Berlin where the Allies still rule. –
131 *Flight International*, 31 January 1987, pp.21-23

KNEIFEL, J.L. – Bilateral aviation agreements of Mauritius and a comparison between the Mauritian Civil Aviation Act of 1974 and the Civil Aviation Regulations of the Federal Republic of Germany. –
Nördlingen 1989, 289 pp.

CZYBULKA, D. and WANDRES, Th. – Rechtsschutz gegen zivilen Fluglärm bei der Festlegung von 'Flugrouten'. –
43 *Die öffentliche Verwaltung* 1990, pp.1033-1040

FRIESE, F.-J. and WERNER, J. – Die Haftung des Bundesluftfahrtamtes aus der Anerkennung und Überwachung luftfahrttechnischer Betriebe. –
Frankfurt am Mian 1990, 55 pp.

GAEBEL, C. – Slots als Eigentum. Verfassungsrechtlicher Eigentumsschutz von Start- und Landezeiten. –
13 *Transportrecht* 1990, pp.407-413

GIEMULLA, E. and MOST, J. – Zur Verletzung luftverkehrsrechtlicher Bestimmungen durch Luftfahrzeuge der Bundesluftwaffe. Materielle und kompetenzrechtliche Frage. –
105 *Deutsches Verwaltungsblatt* 1990, pp.508-511

HORN, W. – Genehmigungsfreie 'Luftfahrtveranstaltungen'? Zu §24 LuftVG. –
Verwaltungsblätter für Baden-Württemberg 1990, pp.321-325

KIM, H.-R. – Das Planungsverfahren umweltrelevanter Grossvorhaben in der Bundesrepublik Deutschland und der Republik Korea am Beispiel der Flughafenplanung. –
Diss. Speyer. Speyer 1990, 349 pp.

KRIEG, J. – Security fee in the Federal Republic of Germany. –
15 *AASL* 1990, pp.145-151

SCHWENK, W. – Rechtliche Auswirkungen aus dem Verhältnis beider deutscher Staaten auf den zivilen Luftverkehr. –
39 *ZLW* 1990, pp.147-164

SONN, J-C. – Liability of the air carrier under West German air law and the limits of liability in different countries. –
2 *Korean JAL* 1990, pp.7-29 (in Korean)

CZYBULKA, D. – Verwaltungsprozessuale Probleme bei der Klage gegen die Festlegung von 'Flugrouten'. –
44 *Die öffentliche Verwaltung* 1991, pp.410-415

HERBER, R. – Das Transportrecht im vereinten Deutschland. –
14 *Transportrecht* 1991, pp.1-6

HIRT, M. The constitutions of Italy, the Federal Republic of Germany and the United States in relation to Article 22 of the Warsaw Convention. –
Diss. McGill. Montreal 1991

KAISER, St.A. – Two recent German cases of privatization: air traffic control and the space agency. –
16 *Air Law* 1991, pp.125-132

KISTOWSKY, Th. von – Ausländische Mehrheitsbeteiligung an einem deutschen Luftfahrtunternehmen. –
40 *ZLW* 1991, pp.132-136

Luftverkehrsrecht, Luftverkehrsgesetz, Luftverkehrsordnung, Luftverkehrs-Zulassungsord-nung sowie andere Bestimmungen. –
Beck'sche Textausgaben, München 1991, 394 pp.

MECHLEM, H.P. – Rechtsgrundlagen für Sicherungsmassnahmen von Luftfahrtbehörden und Luftfahrtunternehmen gegen Angriffe auf den Luftverkehr. –
Diss. Augsburg 1991. Augsburg 1991, 176 pp.

MÜLLER-ROSTIN, W. – German unification and civil aviation. –
16 *Air Law* 1991, pp.9-12

MÜLLER-ROSTIN, W. – Recent developments in German aviation law. –
16 *Air Law* 1991, pp.13-18

QUAAS, M. – Der Schutz vor unzumutbarem Fluglärm in der Planfeststellung: rechtliche Anwendungsprobleme nach dem Luftverkehrsgesetz. –
10 *Neue Zs für Verwaltungsrecht* 1991, pp.16-22

RIEDEL, N.K. and SCHMIDT, A. – Die Nichtausfertigung des Gesetzes zur Privatisierung der Flugsicherung durch den Bundespräsidenten. –
44 *Die öffentliche Verwaltung* 1991, pp.371-375

SCHWEINSBERG, R. – Ensuring aviation security in the Federal Republic of Germany. –
RBDAE, March-April 1991, no. 53, pp.15-17

TSCHENTSCHER, T. and KOENIG, C. – Rechtsqualität, Vergabe und Übertragbarkeit sogenannter 'Slots' nach dem deutschen Verkehrsrecht. –
10 *Neue Zs für Verwaltungsrecht* 1991, pp.219-236

VITT, E. – Rechtsfragen bei der Übermittlung von Radar-Daten durch die Bundesanstalt für Flugsicherung an einen Flughafen-Betreiber. –
40 *ZLW* 1991, pp.123-131

WENZLER, Th. – Die Registrierung von Luftfahrzeugen in der Luftfahrzeugrolle nach dem 'Leasingerlass' des Bundesministers für Verkehr vom 12. Februar 1991. –
40 *ZLW* 1991, pp.276-277

ZUCK, H. – Die Grenzen des behördlichen Versagungermessens bei §25 LuftVG. –
Neue Zs für Verkehrsrecht 1991, pp.218-223

BECHTLOFF, G. – Die Auswirkungen des ÖTV-Streiks 1992 auf den Luftverkehr. Zur Rechtmässigkeit der Streikmassnahmen der Bediensteten des öffentlichen Dienstes auf den Flughäfen. –
41 *ZLW* 1992, pp.226-239

BENTZIEN, J. – Die Lufthoheit nach Herstellung der staatlichen Einheit Deutschlands. –
41 *ZLW* 1992, pp.3-16

FOCKE, K. – Wem dient die Sicherheitsüberprüfung der Flugpassagiere? Einige Anmerkungen zur Zulässigkeit der Luftsicherheitsgebühr. –
41 *ZLW* 1992, pp.240-247

GIEMULLA, E. and SCHMID, R. – Wem gehört die Zeit? Rechtsprobleme der Slots-Zuteilung. –
41 *ZLW* 1992, pp.51-62. In English: 17 *Air and Space Law* 1992, pp.9-16

GIEMULLA, E. and SCHMID, R. – Who owns the time? Legal problems regarding slots. A German view. –
17 *Air and Space Law* 1992, pp.9-16. In German: 41 *ZLW* 1992, pp.51-62

GÜNTHER, K. and ERBACHER, P. – Aspects of aircraft leasing in Germany. –
17 *Air and Space Law* 1992, pp.92-103

HOBE, St. – Zur gerichtlichen Überprüfbarkeit behördlicher Planungsentscheidungen, dargestellt am Urteil BVerwGE 87, 332 zum Flughafen München II. –
41 *ZLW* 1992, pp.248-254

HOFMANN, M. and GRABHERR, R. – Luftverkehrsgesetz. –
München 1992, 2nd ed., loose-leaf

HORN, W. – Sind Verkehrslandeplätze als öffentliche Einrichtungen des Kommunalrechts zu qualifizieren? –
Verwaltungsblätter für Baden-Württemberg 1992, no. 1, pp.5-9

JUTZI, S. – Organisationskompetenz des Bundes für Bahnpolizei und Luftverkehrssicherung. –
45 *Die öffentliche Verwaltung* 1992, pp.650-656

KNITTEL, W. – EC air transport policy: the German view. –
4 EALA Conference papers 1992, pp.131-137

KUZNICKI, Th. – Terrorismus und luftspezifische Gefahr in Bezug auf eine Haftung des Luftfrachtführers gemäss Artikel 17 des Warschauer Abkommens. Deutschland. –
41 *ZLW* 1992, pp.360-376

MÜLLER-ROSTIN, W. – Die politischen Veränderungen in Deutschland und ihre Auswirkungen auf den Luftverkehr. –
ASDA Bulletin 1992-1, no. 112, pp.10-14

PFAFF, M.J. – Die Beschaffung von Verkehrsflugzeugen. –
Diss. Erlangen, Nürnberg 1991. Heidelberg 1992, xvi-299 pp.

REIMER, G. – Deutsche Flughafenpolitik ohne europäische Dimension? –
41 *ZLW* 1992, pp.142-153

STERNS, G.C. – The law of products liability in the United States and Europe.
Brussels symposium, April 1992, 14-38 pp.

WOOD, B. – The ownership of international airlines: a European view. Germany. –
In: The highways of air and outer space, 1992, pp.311-327

ACHTNICH, H. – Neues Flugpreisrecht: Anwendungsvorrang der EWG-VO 2409/92 vor LuftVG, RabG, Zugabe VO. –
39 *Wettbewerb in Recht und Praxis* 1993, pp.731-736

ANN, Chr. – Deregulierung in der Luft, Monopole auf dem Boden. Zur kartellrechtlichen Situation und Problematik der Märkte für Bodendienste auf deutschen Verkehrsflughäfen.
48 *Betriebsberater* 1993, Beilage 16 zu Heft 23, 12 pp.

BÖCKSTIEGEL, K.-.H. and KRÄMER, P.M. – Die luftfahrtbehördliche Erlaubnis zu Aussenstarts und Aussenlandungen. –
42 *ZLW* 1993, pp.343-356

CHUN, S.-H. – A case study of German air law. –
5 *Korean JAL* 1993, pp.385-430 (in Korean)

GÜNTHER, K. – Financial crisis in the aviation industry – Germany. –
18 *Air and Space Law* 1993, pp.192-198

HEESEN, D. – Luftsicherheit – eine neue Aufgabe des Bundesgrenzschutzes. –
Die Polizei 1993, pp.105-117

HEINZE, Chr. – Benutzungs- und Entgeltordnungen für Flughäfen unter Berücksichtigung der Kartellrechtsnovelle von 1989/90. –
12 *Neue Zs für Verwaltungsrecht* 1993, pp.1145-1150

HOBE, St. – Zu den rechtlichen Grundlagen der Änderungen von Schutzauflagen im Planungsrecht und ihrer Relevanz für die Flughafenplanung. –
42 *ZLW* 1993, pp.258-262

KAISER, S.A. – Stolpersteine beim Flugplatzausbau in den neuen Bundesländern. –
42 *ZLW* 1993, pp.151-161

LÜBBEN, N. – Das Recht auf freie Benutzung des Luftraums. –
Diss. Berlin F.U., 1992. Schriften zum öffentlichen Recht 638, Berlin 1993, 166 pp.

SCHUBERT, F. – La responsabilité des services de la circulation aérienne. Allemagne. –
ASDA Bulletin 1993-2, no. 115, pp.5-34, at pp.19-21

STEINBERG, R. and BIDINGER, R. – Kapazitätsbeschränkungen in der luftverkehrsrechtlichen Genehmigung und Planfeststellung? –
Umwelt- und Planungsrecht 1993, pp.281-285

TRAMPLER, H.-P. – Verfassungs- und unternehmungsrechtliche Probleme der bundesdeutschen Flugsicherung. –
Diss. Erlangen, Nürnberg 1992. Berlin 1993, 197 pp.

BARTL, H. – Das neue Reisevertragsrecht. –
17 *Transportrecht* 1994, pp.409-420

BOCKSTHALER, K.B. – Der Sicherheitspilot: wer hat die Entscheidungsgewalt im Cockpit?
38 *Aerokurier*, Febr. 1994, pp.31-32

GIEMULLA and SCHMID – Recht der Luftfahrt. Textsammlung. –
Neuwied/Kriftel/Berlin 1994, viii-647 pp.

GRAUMANN, H. – Die Luftverkehrsbeziehungen Deutschland/USA nach dem Stand vom September/Oktober 1993: ein kurzer Überblick. –
43 *ZLW* 1994, pp.3-10

GREINER, H.W. – Die Betriebspflicht von Flugplätzen. Rechtliche Grundlagen und 'Kleinflieger-Problematik'. –
Bayerische Verwaltungsblätter 1994, pp.449-457

DE GROOT, J.E.C. – Code-sharing. United States' policies and the lessons for Europe. [Germany] –
19 *Air and Space Law* 1994, pp.67-74, at pp.67-69

HERMANN, M. – Schutz vor Fluglärm bei der Planung von Verkehrsflughäfen im Lichte des Verfassungsrechts. Zur Auslegung des §9 Abs.2 LuftVG. –
Diss. Regensburg 1993. Studien zum Umweltrecht Bd 40. Berlin 1994, 378 pp.

KRÄMER, P.M. – Kapazitätsengpässe im Luftraum. –
Diss. Köln 1993. Schriften zum Luft- und Weltraumrecht Bd 12. Köln 1994, xviii-225 pp.

KRÄMER, P.M. – Les répercussions de la réunification allemande en droit aérien. –
47 *RFDAS* 1994, pp.229-244

MÜLLER-ROSTIN, W. – Erfordernis der Novellierung der frachtrechtlichen Vorschriften des Warschauer Abkommens durch eine Ratifikation des Montrealer Protokolls Nr. 4. –
17 *Transportrecht* 1994, pp.321-326

RONELLENFITSCH, M. – Der Militärflugplatz. Merkmale und Kriterien. –
47 *Die öffentliche Verwaltung* 1994, no. 2, pp.45-52

SCHMID, R. – Rechtsprobleme bei der Luftbeförderung im Rahmen von Flugpauschalreisen. –
38 *NJW* 1994, pp.2451-2456

SCHMID, R. – Das Zusatz-Abkommen von Guadalajara und seine Bedeutung für das deutsche Reisevertragsrecht. –
17 *Transportrecht* 1994, pp.420-425

SCHOCH, F. – Haftungsfragen bei der Fluggastbeförderung im nationalen Binnenluftverkehr. –
49 *Betriebs-Berater* 1994, pp.1513-1516

SCHWENK, W. – Luftsportgerät, Luftfahrzeug und Luftfahrtgerät – eine Standortbestimmung. –
43 *ZLW* 1994, pp.143-155

BÖCKSTIEGEL, K.-H. and KRÄMER, P.M. – Völkerrechtliche Gestaltungsvorgaben für die Einführung einer wettbewerbsorientierten Allokation von Start- und Landeslots. –
44 *ZLW* 1995, pp.269-283 und 371-386

BURCKHARDT, Th. – Aus der deutschen Rechtsprechung zum Warschauer Abkommen. –
ASDA Bulletin 1995-1, no. 118, pp.4-27

CZAJA, F. – Eigensicherungspflichten von Verkehrsflughäfen. –
Diss. Köln. Schriften zum Luft- und Weltraumrecht Bd. 13. Köln 1995, xvii-191 pp.

ELBING, G. – Sind Triebwerke wesentliche Bestandteile von Flugzeugen? –
44 *ZLW* 1995, pp.387-395

GIEMULLA, E. and SCHMID, R. – Nochmals – Wem gehört die Zeit? –
44 *ZLW* 1995, pp.259-268

GÜNTHER, K. and ERBACHER, P. – Aspects of aircraft leasing in Germany. –
In: Aircraft finance, The Hague 1995, pp.33-51

SCHWENK, W.; NIESTER, W. and STUKENBERG, D. – Handbuch des Luftverkehrsrechts. –
Köln 1995, 2nd ed., xxxx-760 pp.

Greece

CHRONAS, A.D. – Certain recent developments in Greek aviation law under a Community law perspective. –
17 *Air and Space Law* 1992, pp.297-309

Hungary

MOLNÁR, E. – Options for civil aviation in Hungary, a Central European country. –
19 *Air and Space Law* 1994, pp.164-166

Italy

GUSTAVO, R. – Contributo della dottrina italiana all'unificazione del diritto della navigazione aerea. –
206 *Archivio giuridico 'Filippo Serafini'* 1986, pp.261-287

La Comunità Economica Europea e la struttura del trasporto aereo italiano. –
12 *DPAC* 1988, pp.319-385

FASSINA, G. – Riflessioni su problemi vecchi e nuovi dell'azienda aeroporto. –
13 *DPAC* 1989, pp.361-368

MARCHETTI, M. – L'infrastruttura aeroportuale. Accelerazione dei lavori e programmazione degli interventi. –
13 *DPAC* 1989, pp.322-348

Schema di decreto legge concernente nuove attribuzioni delle società concessionarie delle gestioni aeroportuali e le modalità del loro esercizio. –
13 *DPAC* 1989, pp.349-360

SILINGARDI, G. – Limite di risarcimento nei trasporti aerei internazionali di persone. –
12 *Le nuove leggi civili commentate* (Padova) 1989, pp.773-

FOGLIANI, E. – Recenti vicende del limite di responsabilità del vettore internazionale aereo nella legislazione aerea. –
Diritto dei trasporti 1990, pp.212-

GRIGOLI, M. – L'aeromobile nella giurisprudenza. –
14 *DPAC* 1990, pp.154-198

LOPEZ, C. – La riforma legislativa italiana della responsabilità del vettore aereo nel trasporto interno ed internazionale. –
14 *DPAC* 1990, pp.239-248

MORINI, A. – Qualche riflessioni su di un provvedimento in materia di concorrenza sleale nel trasporto aereo di linea. –
92 *Il Diritto marittimo* 1990, pp.1116-

PIZZINO, A. – EEC air transportation law and its implications for the member States: focus on Italy. –
Diss. McGill, Montreal 1990

ROMANELLI, G. – Giurisprudenza costituzionale. –
14 *DPAC* 1990, pp.234-238

L'esercizio del diritto di sciopero nei servizi aerei, aeroportuali e di assistenza al volo. La tutela del servizio pubblico essenziale di trasporto aereo in Italia ed in Europa. –
15 *DPAC* 1991, pp.1-31 and 32-65

GUERRERI, G. – Seizure and arrest of aircraft in Italy: unique protection for the airline. –
16 *AASL* 1991, pp.460-462

HIRT, M. – The constitutions of Italy, the Federal Republic of Germany and the United States in relation to Article 22 of the Warsaw Convention. –
Diss. McGill, Montreal 1991

RINALDI BACCELLI, G. – La réglementation du droit de grève et le transport aérien en Italie. Considérations sur la Loi 194 sur la grève dans les services publics essentiels. –
16 *AASL* 1991, pp.3-10

Rumore degli aerei e tutela dell'ambiente. I. Il quadro normativo internazionale. II. La situazione italiana ed il quadro normativo. –
15 *DPAC* 1991, pp.67-118 and 119-147

DELUCA, H.O. – El derecho de huelga: alcances. Los servicios públicos esenciales. Situación en la República Argentina, España e Italia. –
8 *Revista europea DNMA* 1992, pp.1411-1418, at pp.1414-1415

ANTONINI, A. – I sinistri aeronautici. –
Trasporti 1993, no. 61, pp.51-70

BUSTI, S. – Il trattamento del passeggero nelle condizioni generali del contratto aereo. –
17 *DPAC* 1993, pp.41-69

CAVALLI, M. – Rifiuto all'imbarco e overbooking: problemi di diritto interno e di diritto comunitario. –
32 *Diritto comunitario e degli scambi internazionali* 1993, pp.377-379

CURSO, C. – Riflessioni sul quadro giuridico amministrativo dell'aviazione civile. –
17 *DPAC* 1993, pp.5-13

FOGLIANI, E. – Il controllo della R.a.i. sulla costruzione di aeromobile e cooperazione internazionale. –
Diritto dei trasporti 1993, pp.505-

MASINI, L. – Brevi considerazioni sull'ammissibilità della stipulazione di contratti a tempo determinato per il personale di volo. –
95 *Il Diritto marittimo* 1993, pp.63-67

MASINI, L. – Problematiche attinenti all'applicazione della legge 156/90 relative all'esercizio del diritto di sciopero nei servizi pubblici essenziali. –
95 *Il Diritto marittimo* 1993, pp.464-473

MIRABELLI, Ph. and PHIPPARD, S. – Rights and remedies open to airlines and other operators for non-payment of route navigation charges, with particular reference to the position in Italy. –
18 *Air and Space Law* 1993, pp.141-147

ROMANELLI, G. – I contratti di utilizzazione della nave e dell'aeromobile nel Codice della navigazione italiano. –
12 *ADMA* 1993, pp.59-70

SPANÒ, A. – Considerazioni in tema di ipoteca aeronautica. –
Diritto dei trasporti 1993, pp.854-

RINALDI BACCELLI, G. – 50 Années d'expérience depuis la Convention de Chicago: l'effort italien pour atteindre l'uniformité internationale dans le respect des droits fondamentaux visés pour la Constitution. –
19 *AASL* 1994, vol. I, pp.109-125

GUERRERI, G. – An overview of Italian product liability law. –
44 *ZLW* 1995, pp.21-28

The Netherlands

DE ROODE, A.A. – Luchtverkeersbeveiliging. De geschiedenis van de luchtverkeersbeveiliging in Nederland 1910-heden. –
Houten 1988, 160 pp.

SCHNITKER, R.M. – Overheidsoptreden bij luchtvaartongevallen in wetstechnisch perspectief. –
Handboek ongevallen- en rampenbestrijding, aanvulling 38, sept. 1990, pp.A1550-1 – A1550-33

VAN BAKELEN, F.A. – De financiering van luchtvaartuigen en het NBW. – In: 85 jaar Nederlandse Vereniging van Hypotheekbanken, Deventer 1991, pp.207-238

BAKKER, H. – De zware bevalling van een akkoord over Schiphol: luchtvaart mag groeien, maar alleen beheerst. –
9 *Ruimtelijke ordening en milieubeheer*, juni 1991, pp.4-10

GROSBOIS, Th. – Liberté du trafic aérien et intégration aérienne. La première tentative de rapprochement entre la KLM et la SABENA (1946-1950). –
6 *Lettre d'information des Historiens de l'Europe contemporaine*, déc. 1991, no. 3/4, pp.84-148

HOBMA, F.A.M. – Het beleidsconvenant plan van aanpak Schiphol en omgeving. –
28 *Bouwrecht* 1991, pp.829-836

HOOGEVEEN, J.P.; NOORDZIJ, A.S.; DE VOS, M. and VROLIJK, R. – Geluidshinder rondom Schiphol. –
's Gravenhage 1991, 108 pp.

ROODZANT, R.W. – Het complexe politiebestel op Schiphol. –
53 *Het Tijdschrift voor de Politie* 1991, pp.255-260

TAN, T.G. and others – Het plan van aanpak Schiphol. –
Vereniging van Milieurecht 1991-92, Zwolle 1991, vi-80 pp.

Aircraft financing: recent developments and prospects.
CRANS, B.J.H. – Selected pitfalls and booby-traps in aircraft finance, pp.43-52
HOFLAND, D. – Tax aspects of aircraft leasing in The Netherlands, pp.53-60
POLAK, M.V. – Conflicts of law in the air, pp.78-86
VAN MIERLO, T.I.M.- Dutch security rights in aircraft and engines, pp.11-117
CLUMPKENS, R.W. – The role of the notary under the laws of The Netherlands with respect to the transfer of title and encumbrance of registered aircraft, pp.118-124
17 *Air and Space Law* 1992

DUTHEIL DE LA ROCHÈRE, J. – La libéralisation du transport aérien communautaire et les relations avec les pays tiers. L'accord de 'ciel ouvert' Pays-Bas/États-Unis, un contre-exemple? –
38 *AFDI* 1992, pp.983-988

WOOD, B. – The ownership of international airlines: a European view. The Netherlands. –
In: The highways of air and outer space, 1992, pp.311-327, at pp.323-324

BANGMA, K.L. and BONESCHANSKER, E. – Steunverlening aan de luchtvaart. –
25 *Openbare Uitgaven* 1993, pp.143-152

VAN BAREN, W.H. – Recent aviation case law from the Benelux. –
18 *Air and Space Law* 1993, pp.29-35

BUNJES, H.J. – Aansprakelijkheid vaststellen is lastig en moeizaam karwei. –
23 *Welwezen*, juli 1993, pp.12-17

CLETON, R. – Aansprakelijkheid en schadevergoeding als nasleep van luchtvaartongevallen. –
68 *Nederlands Juristenblad* 1993, pp.621-629

CORDES, J.H. – Flying the open skies: an analysis and historical perspective of the U.S.-Netherlands bilateral air transport agreement of September 4, 1992. –
6 *The Transnational Lawyer* (Sacramento CA) 1993, pp.301-327

DIEDERIKS-VERSCHOOR, I.H.Ph. – Air law. –
In: Introduction to Dutch law for foreign lawyers, edited by J.M.J.CHORUS and others, Deventer/Boston 1993, pp.185-192

HILLESTAD, R. and others – Airport growth and safety: a study of the external risks of Schiphol Airport and possible safety-enhancement measures. –
Santa Monica 1993, Rand European-American Center for Policy Analysis, xxx-181 pp.

DE KRAMER, T. and VAN DEN BERG, C. – Rechtsbescherming en luchtvaartlawaai. Juridische instrumenten ter bescherming van de burger tegen luchtvaartlawaai, in het bijzonder tegen dat van militair vliegveld Soesterberg. –
Wetenschapswinkel Rechten Utrecht, mei 1993, 131 pp.

LEFFERTS, A. – De stand van zaken rond de militaire luchtvaartterreinen. –
16 *Geluid*, juni 1993, pp.60-63

MENDES DE LEON, P. and MIRMINA, S. – The international and American law implications of the Bijlmer air disaster. –
6 *Leiden JIL* 1993, pp.111-122

MOELKER, C. – De invloed van afdeling 6.5.3 NBW op standaardvoorwaarden in het vervoer. –
Mededelingenblad van de Nederlandse Vereniging voor Zee- en Vervoersrecht, februari 1993, no. 8, pp.1-3

VAN WIJNGAARDEN, P. – Veertig jaar luchtvaartpolitie. –
9 *Vliegwereld* 1993, no. 2, pp.8-9 and 12-13

CLUMPKENS, R. – The role of the notary under the law of the Netherlands with respect to the transfer of title and encumbrance of registered aircraft. –
In: Aircraft finance, The Hague 1995, pp.139-147

HOFLAND, D.A. – Recent developments in tax law. –
In: Aircraft finance, The Hague 1995, pp.95-101

VAN MIERLO, T.I.M. – Security rights in aircraft and engines under Netherlands law. –
In: Aircraft finance, The Hague 1995, pp.71-82

Norway

GRAVER, H.P. – Flyhavarikommisjonen for sivil luftfart – oppgaver og saksbehandling. –
103 *Tidsskrift for Rettsvitenskap* (Norway) 1990, pp.592-624

HEFFERMEHL, J.S. and MUSAEUS, L. – Aircraft finance in Norway. –
Legal aspects of aviation finance, supplement of *Airfinance J*, Sept. 1992, pp.13-15

LUDVIGSEN, J. – Liberalization of market entry for Norwegian regional airlines.
32 *Transportation J*, summer 1993, pp.41-55

Poland

DAVIDSON, G.E. – United States' use of economic sanctions, treaty bending, and treaty breaking in international aviation. –
59 *JALC* 1994, pp.291-356, at pp.300-307 and 341-348

Portugal

PRIMAVERA, J. – Na data do 50 aniversário da convenção de Chicago de 1944. Uma questão prévia: Vigoram os Anexos da ICAO na ordem jurídica portuguesa? –
XXIV Jornadas iberoamericanas, Salamanca 1994, pp.429-444

Romania

GUINCHARD, M. – Le droit aérien roumain: situation et perspectives (mars 1995). –
48 *RFDAS* 1995, pp.173-186

Russia – USSR

BUTLER, W. – Legal considerations to aircraft financing in the USSR. –
Airfinance J, April 1990, no. 113, pp.40-41

The Air Code of the USSR 26 December 1961 (as amended). –
3 *Korean JAL* 1991, pp.285-318

GIEMULLA, E. and SCHYNDEL, H. VON – Rechtliche Aspekte des Luftverkehrs nach den Veränderungen in der ehemaligen Sowjetunion. –
42 *ZLW* 1993, pp.239-249

BORDUNOV, V.D. – Air law developments in the GIS: modern trends. –
19 *AASL* 1994, vol. II, pp.107-124

DAVIDSON, G.E. – United States' use of economic sanctions, treaty bending, and treaty breaking in international aviation. The USSR. –
59 *JALC* 1994, pp.291-356, at pp.294-300 and 339-341

CANNING, R. – Climbing steppes. –
Airfinance J, July-Aug. 1995, no. 175, pp.14-16, 18-19

GIEMULLA, E. and VON SCHYNDEL, H. – Transport sector privatisation in the Russian Federation. –
23 *Transportation LJ* 1995, pp.99-117

KASYANENKO, V. – The current development of civil aviation in Russia. –
20 *Air and Space Law* 1995, pp.87-91

SAPRIKIN, F.I. – The civil aviation authorities within the CIS. (in Russian) –
Moscow JIL 1995, pp.104-115

SAPRYKIN, Ph. – The legal status of the airspace above the Commonwealth of Independent States. –
20 *AASL* 1995, vol. II, pp.325-335

Scandinavia

WISSUM, C. and ASKERUD, T. – Tax leasing favours the few. –
Airfinance J, May 1991, no. 126, pp.33-34

SVERNLÖV, C. – Security in aircraft: the Scandinavian systems. –
17 *AASL* 1992, vol. II, pp.369-401

The (former) Socialist countries of Europe

NATOV, N.S. – The contractual carrier's liability in passenger carriage between the Socialist countries. (in Bulgarian) –
78 *Annuaire de l'Université de Sofia* 1985, pp.306-

FLINT, P. – A riddle wrapped in a mystery. –
27 *Air Transport World*, June 1990, pp.67-68

WASSENBERGH, H.A. – The future of East-West civil aviation in Europe. –
15 *Air Law* 1990, pp.149-156

Spain

MAPELLI, E. – La Organización de la Aviación Civil Internacional y la cuestión española. –
VII *Revista europea DNMA* 1991, pp.1061-1077

DELUCA, H.O. – El derecho de huelga: alcances. Los servicios públicos esenciales. Situación en la República Argentina, España e Italia. –
VIII *Revista europea DNMA* 1992, pp.1411-1418, at p.1415

LÓPEZ ANTÓN, F. and FALCÓN RAVELO, J.F. – Aircraft financing in Spain. –
17 *Air and Space Law* 1992, pp.104-110

MAPELLI, E. – Limitación de propiedad por la navegación aérea, según el derecho español. –
Boletín del Ilustre Colegio de Abogados de Madrid, mayo-junio de 1992, no. 3, pp.43-55

PELÁEZ, M.J. – Notas para una historia del derecho laboral aeronáutico español (1911-1946): régimen jurídico y jurídico-laboral del personal de vuelo y tierra. VIII *Revista europea DNMA* 1992, pp.1165-1176. Also in: Historia del derecho de la navegación I, Barcelona 1994, pp.601-614

WOOD, B. – The ownership of international airlines: a European view. Spain. In: The highways of air and outer space, 1992, pp.311-327, at pp.320-321

MORILLAS JARILLO, M.J. – Algunos aspectos del leasing de aeronaves en España. –
Revista de Derecho Mercantil 1993, no. 208, pp.471-586

APARICIO GALLEGO, J. – Aeropuertos españoles y navegación aérea: el nuevo ente público de la organización jurídico administrativo española. –
Aviación comercial, turismo, etc., Buenos Aires 1994, pp.195-199

LIZARRAGA LACALLE, M.D. – Comentario sobre el procedimiento de evaluación de impacto ambiental. –
XXIV Jornadas iberoamericanas, Salamanca 1994, pp.341-357

MAPELLI, E. – Consideraciones jurídicas sobre el accidente aéreo. –
Revista General de Derecho (Valencia), mayo de 1994, no. 596, pp.5291-5308

FALCÓN RAVELO J.F. – An overview on aircraft leasing in Spain. –
In: Aircraft finance, The Hague 1995, pp.83-94

PELÁEZ, M.J. – Notas sobre la conceptualización jurídica de la aeronave. Perspectiva histórica y regulación normativa en derecho común y comparado, preferencialmente italiano y francés, en relación al derecho español. –
Historia del derecho de la navegación, Barcelona 1994, pp.633-721. 11 *Revista europea DNMA* 1995, pp.1655-1660

Sweden

MALMBERG, L.-G. – Rätt till luftfart. –
Diss. Lund. Acta Societatis Juridicae Lundensis Nr 108. Lund 1990, 494 pp.

NELMS, D.W. – Competition, Swedish style. –
28 *Air Transport World*, Jan. 1991, pp.94-97

PILLING, M. – The cost of fair play. –
46 *Interavia Aerospace Review*, Jan. 1991, p.36

EKBOM, P.G. – Legal aspects of aircraft finance in Sweden. –
In: Aircraft finance, The Hague 1995, pp.103-108

Switzerland

STAEHELIN, B. – Gewerbsmässiger Luftverkehr und Konsumentenschutz. –
ASDA Bulletin 1991-1, no. 110, pp.5-46

DETTLING-OTT, R. – Zulassungszwang auf schweizerischen Flughäfen. –
ASDA Bulletin 1992-2, no. 113, [6]-50-[4] pp.

HEUBERGER, G. – Die Luftverkehrsabkommen der Schweiz. –
Diss. Zürich. Schweizer Studien zum internationalen Recht Bd. 75. Zürich 1992, xlvi-665 pp.

DETTLING-OTT, R. – Internationales und schweizerisches Lufttransportrecht. –
Zürich 1993, xxxix-315 pp.

KUNZ, D. – Rechtliche Aspekte der neueren Luftraumorganisation und der internationalen Flugsicherungszusammenarbeit. –
ASDA Bulletin 1993-1, no. 114, pp.19-44

SCHUBERT, F. – La responsabilité des services de la circulation aérienne. Suisse. –
ASDA Bulletin 1993-2, no. 115, pp.5-34, at pp.22 and 27-28

SPOENDLIN, K. – Schweizerische Lufthoheit und Fluglärm um den Flughafen Basel-Mulhouse. –
94 *Schweizerisches Zentralblatt für Staats- und Verwaltungsrecht* 1993, pp.285-297

AUER, A. – Das Verhältnis der Schweiz zur Europäischen Gemeinschaft im Bereich des Luftverkehrs. –
ASDA Bulletin 1994-2, no. 117, pp.11-17 and in: *Jahrbuch der Schweizerischen Verkehrswirtschaft* 1993/4

GRIESSHAMMER, E.R. – Ausländische Fluggesellschaften: Mehrwertsteuerpflichtig! –
ASDA Bulletin 1994-2, no. 117, pp.5-10

VON SCHULTHESS, H.C. – Rechtsfragen zur Abfertigung von Passagieren und ihrem Gepäck auf den Schweizer Flughäfen, insbesondere auf dem Flughafen Zürich. –
ASDA Bulletin 1994-1, no. 116, pp.4-16

GULDIMANN, W. – Luftrecht. Texte und Tafeln. –
Zürich 1995, 87 pp.

Turkey

SÖZER, B. – Aircraft registration in Turkey. –
18 *Air and Space Law* 1993, pp.76-84

United Kingdom

RUFF, A. – The Immigration (Carriers' Liability) Act 1987: its implications for refugees and airlines. –
1 *International J of Refugee Law* 1989, pp.481-500

FELDMAN, J.M. – The bilateral shuffle. –
27 *Air Transport World*, Dec. 1990, pp.26-29, 32

GARDINER, R. – Air law's fog: the application of international and English law. –
43 *Current Legal Problems* (London) 1990, pp.159-184

MCBAIN, G.S. – Aircraft liens under English law. –
15 *Air Law* 1990, pp.79-86

MONTLAUR-MARTIN, E. DE – Réglementation des enquêtes-accidents en Grande-Bretagne. 44 *RFDAS* 1990, pp.123-125

NEVE, E.C. – The British Government's position. –
2 EALA Conference papers 1991, pp.11-14

THORNE, P. and FARRELL, P. – Salvage or survival when an airline crashes. –
Legal aspects of aircraft finance, supplement to *Airfinance J*, Febr. 1990, no. 111, pp.2-7

BRIGGS, M. – The English summer of 1990 – further progress towards deregulation of the aviation and travel industry. –
16 *Air Law* 1991, pp.50-62

British competition policy: an interventionist policy to ensure competition. –
8 *The Avmark Aviation Economist*, Jan. 1991, pp.3-6

CAVES, R. and HIGGINS, Chr. – A comparison between the consequences of the liberal and the non-liberal UK-Europe bilaterals. –
Loughborough, Univ. of Technology, Dept. of Transport Technology, 1991, 33 pp.

DOBSON, A.P. – Peaceful air warfare. The United States, Britain, and the politics of international aviation. –
Oxford 1991, xiii-307 pp.

HALLAM, R. – Keeping out of bankruptcy courts. –
In: Legal aspects of aircraft finance, supplement to *Airfinance J*, May 1991, no. 126, pp.17-19

PLANT, G. – The Aviation and Maritime Security Act 1990. –
Lloyd's MCLQ 1991, pp.44-51

BLACKSHAW, C. – Air law and regulation: a framework for the civil aviation industry. –
London 1992, xiv-304 pp.

BRYMER, T.R. – Le 'forum shopping' ou la course à la compétence: la réponse des tribunaux anglais. –
45 *RFDAS* 1992, pp.9-23

CHRISTOPHERSON, T. and BAX, J.-H. – Eurocontrol: U.K. detention rights. –
17 *Air and Space Law* 1992, pp.2-8

DIERIKX, M.L.J. – Shaping world aviation: Anglo-American civil aviation relations, 1944-1946. –
57 *JALC* 1992, pp.795-840

GOH, J. – Fear and loathing in the air. –
142 *New LJ* (UK) 1992, pp.822 and 868

KEAN, A. – Self-incrimination and accident investigation. –
J. of Business Law 1992, pp.319-322

DE MONTLAUR-MARTIN, E. – Récentes mesures prises aux États-Unis et en Grande-Bretagne contre le terrorisme aérien. –
45 *RFDAS* 1992, pp.81-83, at p.83

STERNS, G.C. – The law of products liability in the United States and Europe. –
Brussels symposium, April 1992, 14-38 pp.

WEBB, R.S. – Significant legal developments in aviation and insurance law in the United Kingdom and Europe. –
Brussels symposium, April 1992, 8 pp.

WOOD, B. – The ownership of international airlines: a European view. United Kingdom. –
In: The highways of air and outer space, 1992, pp.311-327, at pp.314-316

Carriage by air: private rights and liabilities. –
Clyde & Co., London 1993, 34 pp.

FARRELL, P. – Financial crisis in the aviation industry – United Kingdom. –
18 *Air and Space Law* 1993, pp.153-167

GARDINER, R. – Treaty interpretation in English courts. Antwerp United Diamond v. Air Europe. –
Lloyd's MCLQ 1994, pp.184-189

HABIB, P.B. – ATC privatisation: how far can you go? –
11 *The Avmark Aviation Economist*, Nov. 1994, pp.11-14

MURIEL, A. and CLARK, D. – Security assignments and the lessee. –
Airfinance J, March 1994, no. 160, pp.40-41

United States-United Kingdom arbitration. Heathrow Airport user charges. –
88 *AJIL* 1994, pp.738-744

GARDINER, R. – Treaty interpretation in the English courts since Fothergill v. Monarch Airlines. –
44 *ICLQ* 1995, pp.620-628

VAN HAERSOLTE-VAN HOF, J.J. – US/UK arbitration concerning Heathrow Airport user charges. Some procedural aspects. –
8 *Leiden JIL* 1995, pp.203-216

HERTWIG, A. – Eurocontrol's exercise of detention rights in the United Kingdom illegal? –
20 *Air and Space Law* 1995, pp.277-287

MOUSSÉ, J. – The recovery of route charges and the exercise of the right of detention in the United Kingdom. –
20 *Air and Space Law* 1995, pp.137-145

SKILBECK, J. – The US/UK arbitration concerning Heathrow airport user charges. –
44 *ICLQ* 1995, pp.171-179

WITTEN, S.M. – The U.S.-U.K. arbitration concerning Heathrow Airport user charges. –
89 *AJIL* 1995, pp.174-192

The Americas

PINO ICHAZO, R. – Los convenios bilaterales en América. –
La Paz 1990, 206 pp.

Argentina

VIDELA ESCALADA, F. – The Warsaw Convention within Argentine law. –
40 *ZLW* 1991, pp.339-362

DELUCA, H.O. – El derecho de huelga: alcances. Los servicios públicos esenciales. Situación en la República Argentina, España e Italia. República Argentina. –
8 *Revista europea DNMA* 1992, pp.1411-1418

Brazil

DRUMMOND, I. DE FARIA – Aspectos jurídicos e organizacionais da infrastrutura aeronáutica e dos aeródromos brasileiros. –
25 *RBDA* 1987, no. 42, pp.139-144

PACHECO, J. DA SILVA – Da responsabilidade contratual no Código Brasileiro de Aeronáutica. –
25 *RBDA* 1987, no. 42, pp.42-58

PACHECO, J. DA SILVA – Comentários ao Código Brasileiro de Aeronáutica. –
Rio de Janeiro 1990, 817 pp.

BRASIL, S.M. – O atraso no transporte de passageiros de acordo com o Código Brasileiro de Aeronáutica. –
RBDAE, March-April 1991, no. 53, p.44

BORGES FORTES, B.Y.B. – A Convençaõ de Montego Bay de 1982 e seus reflexos no espaço aéreo e mar territorial e o Ato Presidencial que altera a extensaõ do mar territorial brasileiro. –
RBDAE, May-June 1993, no. 63, pp.3-6

BRASIL, S.M. – Tratdos e convenções internacionais no direito constitucional brasileiro. –
RBDAE, July-Dec. 1993, no. 64, pp.14-17

DE CASTRO FARIAS, H. – Tribunal aeronáutico, uma lacuna a ser preenchida. –
RBDAE, July-Dec. 1993, no. 64, pp.7-8

DA FONSECA, R.G. – O regime jurídico dos sistemas computerizados de reservas ('CRS') no Brasil. –
RBDAE, March-April 1993, no. 62, pp.16-23

Canada

BOURGEOIS, M. – Une étude des enquêtes sur les accidents d'aviation en Canada. –
Diss. McGill. Montreal 1981, iii-120 pp.

CHRISTOPHER, J. – Airline deregulation in Canada. –
Library of Parliament, Current issue review 89-2E, 15 pp.

BUNKER, D.H. – The intricacies of Canadian leasing regulations. –
Airfinance J, Sept. 1990, no. 118, pp.84 and 86

CHANDLER, H. – Notes for an address to the McGill conference on EEC transport policy and regulation. –
In: EEC air transport policy and regulation, Deventer 1990, pp.127-131

DEMPSEY, P.S.; THOMS, W.E. and CLAPP, S. – Canadian transport liberalization: planes, trucks & buses rolling across the Great White North. –
19 *Transportation LJ* 1990, pp.113-192

HADROVIC, C. – Airline globalization: a Canadian perspective. –
19 *Transportation LJ* 1990, pp.193-217

PETSIKAS, G. – Competition in the Canadian airline industry: a contradiction in terms? –
15 *AASL* 1990, pp.207-217

ZUZAK, C.A. – Liability for breaches of aviation security obligations: a Canadian perspective. –
Diss. McGill. Montreal 1990

CUPERFAIN, J. – A Canadian central registry for security interests in aircraft: a good idea but will it fly? –
17 *Canadian Business LJ* 1991, pp.380-414

EBOE-OSUJI, C. – Aviation incidents and the earth-based victims: a review of Anglo-Canadian tort law. –
Diss. McGill. Montreal 1991, xxv-203 pp.

OUM, T.; SANBURY, W. and TRETHEWAY, M. – Airline deregulation in Canada. –
In: Airline deregulation. International experiences. London 1991, x-191 pp., at pp.124-187

PETSIKAS, G. – A Canadian perspective on 'open skies' between Canada and the United States. Unprecedented opportunities or the end of a viable Canadian airline industry? –
16 *AASL* 1991, pp.161-178

RICHARD, G. – The Civil Aviation Tribunal of Canada after five years. –
16 *AASL* 1991, pp.179-194

ROSALES, R.K. – Recordation of rights in aircraft and international recognition: a comparison between the American and Canadian situations. –
16 *AASL* 1991, pp.195-241

BOIDMAN, N. – Proposed exemption for U.S. and other foreign aircraft lessors. –
21 *Tax Management Int. J* (Washington DC) 1992, pp.88-91

BRENNER, D.I. – Recent aviation developments in Canada. –
17 *Air and Space Law* 1992, pp.227-230

LANG, D. – Taxation of international aviation: a Canadian perspective. –
40 *Canadian Tax J.* 1992, pp.881-901

MILDE, M. – New Headquarters Agreement between ICAO and Canada. –
17 *AASL* 1992, vol. II, pp.305-322 (text at pp.571-594)

SWIECICKI, E. – Legal aspects of licensing of airline transport pilots: international standards versus Canadian aviation safety regulations. –
Thesis McGill. Montreal 1992, xx-180 pp.

DRISCOLL, D.L. – A comparative analysis of the labor statutes which govern the United States and Canadian airline industries and how the relationship may be affected by a new bilateral air agreement. –
60 *Transportation Practitioners J.* (Washington DC) 1993, pp.119-142

FIORITA, D.M. – The registration of aircraft and the recordation of security interests in aircraft (Canadian practice). –
18 *Oklahoma City Univ. LR*, spring 1993, pp.57-85

LEWIS, A. – Playing fast and loose with the 'regional notes'. –
73 *Business & Commercial Aviation*, Dec. 1993, pp.C12-C15

SWIECICKI, E.M. – Liability of the Canadian government for the negligent enforcement of aviation safety legislation. –
18 *AASL* 1993, pp.275-313

WHITTINGTON, H. – Canada is set to 'commercialize' ANS. –
75 *Business & Commercial Aviation* 1994, no. 5, pp.58-61

LACY, M.W. – Freedom in the air: the 1995 Canada-United States bilateral air transport agreement. –
20 *AASL* 1995, vol. II, pp.139-165

Colombia

SARMIENTO GARCÍA, M.G. – La nueva política de transporte aéreo en Colombia. –
In: El derecho de los negocios internacionales. Libro en homenaje a Enrique LOW MURTRA. Bogotá 1991, Universidad Externada de Colombia

Latin America

GULMAN CHECA, G. – Avance tecnológico e intercambio de derechos de tráfico. –
XIV Jornadas iberoamericanas, Lima 1984, pp.135-154

RIZZ LARRIBE, L.A. – Empresas de servicio. Desarrollo comerical y política aerocomercial. –
XIV Jornadas iberoamericanas, Lima 1984, pp.157-162

ALBANO DE SILVEIRA, E. – Aviaçaõ comercial iberoamericana e africana de expressão portuguesa e espanhola. –
XVII Jornadas iberoamericanas, Rio de Janeiro 1987, pp.9-20

BRESCIANO, J. – Aviación comercial iberoamericana y africana de expresión portuguesa y española. –
XVII Jornadas iberoamericanas, Rio de Janeiro 1987, pp.20-24

CASTEJÓN, B. – La desreglementación en los Estados Unidos. El movimiento hacia la liberalización en Europa. Sus consecuencias en la región iberoamericana en relación con el transporte aéreo. –
XVII Jornadas iberoamericanas, Rio de Janeiro 1987, pp.26-33

COSENTINO, E.T. and CASTELLI, L. – Enfoques sobre la 'deregulación' en la Comunidad Económica Europea y Latina América. –
XVII Jornadas iberoamericanas, Rio de Janeiro 1987, pp.54-59

DONATO, A.M. – La desregulación en el transporte aéreo, un punto de vista latinoamericano. –
25 *RBDAE* 1987, no. 42, pp.59-68. XVII Jornadas iberoamericanas, Rio de Janeiro 1987, pp.60-69

PAPKIN, R.D. – Liberalización de las aerolíneas de los Estados Unidos: la experiencia estadounidense y su posible impacto en el futuro del transporte aéreo latinoamericano. –
XVII Jornadas iberoamericanas, Rio de Janeiro 1987, pp.34-45

VÁSQUEZ ROCHA, E. – La desreglementación en los Estados Unidos. El movimiento hacia la liberalización en Europa. Sus consecuencias en la región iberoamericana en relación con el transporte aéreo. –
XVII Jornadas iberoamericanas, Rio de Janeiro 1987, pp.46-53

ANDRÉU MUSTÉ, N. – La nueva política aérea de la CEE y su relación con Iberoamérica. –
XIX Jornadas iberoamericanas, Madrid 1989, pp.23-28

BAUZÁ ARAÚJO, A. – La nueva política aérea en la Comunidad Económica Europea y su relación con Iberoamérica. –
XIX Jornadas iberoamericanas, Madrid 1989, pp.29-34

GAYNES, J. – Desregulamentação norte-americana: iniciativas na América Latina, resultados, anseios e implicações. –
RBDAE 1989, no. 46, pp.42-45

PINO MUÑOZ, J.H. – La política aérea en América Latina. Perspectivas. –
XIX Jornadas iberoamericanas, Madrid 1989, pp.59-63

TOVAR, J. and ZUMARÁN, C. – Efectos del proceso de liberalización europea en Iberoamérica. –
XIX Jornadas iberoamericanas, Madrid 1989, pp.65-71

CASANOVAS VALDERRAMA, F. – Política aérea revolucionaria en el Pacto Andino de Cartagena. –
8 *Revista europea DNMA* 1992, pp.1237-1244

DONATO, M. – El transporte aéreo. Perspectivas de servicio público. Metamorfosis de uno de los elementos del acervo jurídico-político internacional con especial referencia a Latinoamérica. –
8 *Revista europea DNMA* 1992, pp.1361-1364

FERRADAS PLATAS, J.M. – Política aerocomercial andina. –
8 *Revista europea DNMA* 1992, pp.1303-1316

FREIDENBERG, E. – Significant legal developments in aviation in South America, –
Brussels symposium, April 1992, 11 pp.

FREIDENBERG, E.M. – South American latest developments in the air law and airpolicy fields. –
41 *ZLW* 1992, pp.219-225

FOLCHI, M.O. – Air transport policy in Latin America. –
19 *AASL* 1994, vol. II, pp.311-325

Peru

FERRADAS PLATAS, J.M. – La política aérea en el Perú. –
XIV Jornadas iberoamericanas, Lima 1984, pp.283-296

TAUS REGGI, S.J. – El Perú: política aerocomerical y la quinta libertad. –
Lima 1991, 182 pp.

Surinam

KOOIJMANS, P.H. – State succession and the 1929 Warsaw Convention – A case-study. –
In: Air and space law: De lege ferenda, Essays in honour of Henri A.WASSENBERGH, Dordrecht 1992, at pp.113-133

VAN BAREN, W.H. – Recent aviation case law from the Benelux. 4. Aviation accident reports. –
18 *Air and Space Law* 1992, pp.29-35, at pp.34-35

United States of America

DOBSON, A.P. – The other air battle: the American pursuit of post-war civil aviation rights. –
28 *The Historical J.* 1985, pp.429-439

GIEMULLA, E. and WENZLER, Th. – Produkthaftpflicht in der Luftfhart. Der ausländische Klager vor US-amerikanischen Gerichten. –
35 *Recht der intern. Wirtschaft* 1989, pp.946-951

HONG, S.-K. – A reevaluation of the U.S.-Korea bilateral air services agreement and some suggestions to improve it. –
1 *Korean JAL* 1989, pp.125-146 (in Korean) and pp.145-146 (English summary)

VELLIGAN, T.L. – 1988-1989 airline law update. –
8 *Corporate Counsel R.* (Houston TX) 1989, pp.411-425

BROWN, J.D. – Foreign investment in U.S. airlines: what limits should be placed on foreign ownership of U.S. carriers? –
41 *Syracuse LR* (Syracuse NY) 1990, pp.1269-1291

CARLSON, E.J. – First amendment protection of free speech in public airports. –
55 *JALC* 1990, pp.1075-1115

CHOI, W.-S. – Aviation products liability in tort – with particular reference to aviation case law in the United States. –
35 *Korean JIL* 1990, pp.59-79 (in Korean)

CRESWELL, L.L. – Airport policy in the United States: the need for accountability, planning, and leadership. –
19 *Transportation LJ* 1990, pp.1-111

CURTIS, E.F. – Negative impacts of leveraged buyouts on the domestic airline industry. –
44 *Transportation Quarterly*, Oct. 1990, pp.517-532

DAVISON, C. and HALLOWAY, L.B. – The two faces of Section 105 – Airline shield or airport sword. –
56 *JALC* 1990, pp.93-123

EASTON, R.L. – Airline mergers and acquisitions: the U.S. experience and likely trends. –
2 EALA Conference papersn 1991, pp.107-114

FELDMAN, J.M. – The bilateral shuffle. –
27 *Air Transport World*, Dec. 1990, pp.26-29 and 32

GIEMULLA, E. and WENZLER, Th. – Product liability in the field of aviation – the foreign plaintiff in the U.S.-American court. –
15 *Air Law* 1990, pp.110-121

KRAUSE, Ch.F. – Recent developments in aviation law in the United States. –
62 *NY State Bar J.*, April 1990, pp.14-18

NOMURA, Y. – Jurisdiction and forum non conveniens in airplane crash cases: a U.S.-Japan comparison. (in Japanese) –
156 *Handai Hogaku* 1990, pp.341-385

OTT, J. – Justice Dept. investigates carriers' pricing practices. –
133 *AW&ST*, 16 July 1990, pp.18-20

PETKOFF, G.S. – Recent cases and developments in aviation law. –
56 *JALC* 1990, pp.1-91

PETROSKI, D. – The airlines' response to the DPTA Section 1305 preemption. –
56 *JALC* 1990, pp.125-153

RATLIFF, A.G. – Congress deals aviation a bad hand: time to learn how to play the ace. –
55 *JALC* 1990, pp.1159-1215

ROBERTS, M.J. – Evolving U.S. international aviation policy. –
58 *Transportation Practitioners J* (Washington DC), fall 1990, pp.65-67

STARKIE, D. – Slot trading at United States airports: a report for the Director General for Transport of the Commission of the European Communities. –
London 1990, 34-24 pp.

THOMS, W.E. and DOOLEY, F.J. – Airline labor law. –
Westport CT 1990, 193 pp.

WENZLER, Th. – Art. 28 Abs. 1 Warschauer Abkommen in der Rechtsprechung US-amerikanischer Gerichte. –
13 *Transportrecht* 1990, pp.414-418

ADAMS, T.L. – Federal preemptions in the airline industry: is there room for a common law breach of contract claim? West v. Northwest Airlines 923 F.2d 657 (9th Cir. 1990). –
8 *Cooley LR* (Lansing MI) 1991, pp.679-702

AGNEW, D.P. – US cabotage policy. –
European infrastructure development 1991, London/Hong Kong, pp.14-24

ARMSTRONG, A. – Defending false statement charges relating to the FAA's medical application form. –
57 *JALC* 1991, pp.357-394

CHOI, W.-S. – A study on aviation products liability in torts – with particular reference to aviation case law in the United States. –
3 *Korean JAL* 1991, pp.113-141 (in Korean)

COLLOGAN, D. – The national noise policy. –
69 *Business & Commercial Aviation*, Dec. 1991, p.94

CREEDY, K.B. – Foreign money lures US airlines. –
46 *Interavia Aerospace Review*, Febr. 1991, pp.48-50

DOBSON, A.P. – Peaceful air warfare. The United States, Britain, and the politics of international aviation. –
Oxford 1991, xiii-307 pp.

ELLETT, E.T. – International and U.S. legal and policy impediments to the growth of the airline industry: time for a change in the world order?
5 *Air and Space Lawyer* (ABA) 1991, no. 3, pp.3-11

FALLON JR, R.H. – Enforcing aviation safety regulations: the case for a split-enforcement model of agency adjudication. –
4 *Administrative LJ* (Washington DC) 1991, pp.389-431

FELDMAN, J. – Chapter 11: balancing the scales of justice. –
Airfinance J, May 1991, no. 126, pp.36-39

FELDMAN, J.F. – The foreign-ownership dilemma. –
28 *Air Transport World*, Jan. 1991, pp.19-20 and 22-24

GRAHAM, B.L. – Navigating the mists of metaphor: an examination of the doctrine of piercing the corporate veil. –
56 *JALC* 1991, pp.1135-1183

HARDAWAY, R.M. – Airport regulation, law, and public policy: the management, and growth of infrastructure. –
New York 1991

HARRINGTON, M.J. – A review of state, diversity jurisdiction, and FTCA decisions concerning choice of law rules in the United States. –
5 *Air and Space Lawyer* (ABA) 1991, no. 4, pp.3-11

HIRT, M. – The constitutions of Italy, the Federal Republic of Germany and the United States in relation to Article 22 of the Warsaw Convention. –
Diss. Montreal 1991

JORDAN, A.I. and HOFFMAN, K.R. – Federal preemption of state laws regulating for-hire motor carriers transporting property (including baggage) as part of an intrastate air/truck shipment. –
19 *Transportation LJ* 1991, pp.335-355

LARSEN, P.B. – Air law education (1976-1991). –
56 *JALC* 1991, pp.705-718

MURPHY, P.V. – Changes in the airline industry. –
6 *Air and Space Lawyer* (ABA) 1991, no. 2, pp.3-4

PETSIKAS, G. – A Canadian perspective on 'open skies' between Canada and the United States. Unprecedented opportunities or the end of a viable Canadian airline industry? –
16 *AASL* 1991, pp.161-178

ROSALES, R.K. – Recordation of rights in aircraft and international recognition: a comparison between the American and Canadian situations. –
16 *AASL* 1991, pp.195-241

SINCLAIR, R.A. – Airport dominance and state action antitrust immunity for airport operators. –
96 *Dickinson LR* (Carlisle PA), fall 1991, pp.1-10

VIDAL, E. – Registering aircraft in the US: the legal requirements. –
Legal aspects of aircraft finance, supplement of *Airfinance J*, May 1991, no. 126, pp.12-15

WALLS, J. – Airline mergers, acquisitions and bankruptcies: will the collective bargaining agreement survive? –
56 *JALC* 1991, pp.847-893

YODICE, J.S. – New medical application form. –
34 *AOPA Pilot*, August 1991, pp.117-119

ASSELTA, J.J. – Products liability: new ball games in the United States and Europe. A United States view. –
Brussels symposium, April 1992, 18 pp.

BARNUM, J. – Prospects for a new relationship between the EC and the US. –
4 EALA Conference papers, Berlin 1991, pp.81-84

BLATTNER, L. and ROSENBERG, B. – US aviation and Europe 1992. –
Washington DC 1992, iv-147 pp.

CLEMEN, J.D. and ROSENZWEIG, J.S. – Federal preemption in the area of airline services and tort-shopping. The air carrier's dilemma. –
20 *Transportation LJ* 1992, pp.339-352

COOK, J.T. – The product liability crisis: is it the demise of aviation manufacturers? Two myths from hell. –
6 *Air and Space Lawyer* (ABA) 1992, no. 4, pp.1 and 11

CRAFT JR, R.R. – Survol rapide des récentes décisions américaines relatives aux préjudices indemnisables sous l'empire de la Convention de Varsovie. –
45 *RFDAS* 1992, pp.223-227

DEMPSEY, P.S.; HARDAWAY, R.M. and THOMS, W.E. – Aviation law and regulation. –
Butterworth 1992, 2 vols., loose-leaf

DIERIKX, M.L.J. – Shaping world aviation: Anglo-American civil aviation relations, 1944-1946. –
57 *JALC* 1992, pp.795-840

DUTHEIL DE LA ROCHÈRE, J. – La libéralisation du transport aérien communautaire et les relations avec les pays tiers. L'accord de 'ciel ouvert' Pays-Bas/États-Unis, un contre-exemple? –
38 *AFDI* 1992, pp.983-998

The ECAC/US Memorandum of Understanding: end of MoU could lead to end of IATA. –
9 *The Avmark Aviation Economist*, April 1992, pp.2-4

ENROTH, K.B. – United States v. Geogescu: special aircraft jurisdiction in the United States. –
18 *Brooklyn JIL* 1992, pp.225-249

FELDMAN, J.M. – A trust buster by any other name ... –
29 *Air Transport World*, March 1992, pp.40-42 and 44

GIEBLER, W. – Reclaiming the skies from terrorism: the Aviation Security Improvement Act of 1990. –
16 *Seton Hall Legislative J* (Newark NJ) 1992, pp.757-813

HARAKAS, A.J. – The Montreal Protocols in the United States 17 years later. The road to ratification or final defeat? –
41 *ZLW* 1992, pp.354-359

HOFFMAN, J.M. and HARRIS, Ph.S. – Recent developments in aviation case law. 58 *JALC* 1992, pp.1-101

KUZNICKI, Th. – Terrorismus und luftspezifische Gefahr in Bezug auf eine Haftung des Luftfrachtführers gemäss Artikel 17 des Warschauer Abkommens. USA. –
41 *ZLW* 1992, pp.360-376, at pp.361-364

LANDRY, J.E. – Airline liability: the long overdue updating of the Warsaw regime in the United States. –
17 *AASL* 1992-I, pp.49-65

MIFSUD, P.V. – The fast track to a modern air transport policy. –
Essays in honour of Henri A.Wassenbergh, Dordrecht 1992, pp.63-70

DE MONTLAUR-MARTIN, E. – Récentes mesures prises aux États-Unis et en Grande-Bretagne contre le terrorisme aérien. I. États-Unis. –
45 *RFDAS* 1992, pp.81-83, at pp.82-83

PETSIKAS, G. – 'Open skies' – North America. –
17 *AASL* 1992-I, pp.281-291

PINO JR, R.V. – The product liability crisis and the demise of aviation manufacturers? –
6 *Air and Space Lawyer* (ABA) 1992, no. 3, pp.12-14

PLATT, J.R. – The creation of a Community cabotage area in the European Community and its implications for the US bilateral aviation system. –
17 *Air and Space Law* 1992, pp.183-198. See also: 22 *Transportation LJ* 1994, pp.61-85

POSNER, K. – The status of aviation legislation. –
6 *Air and Space Lawyer* (ABA) 1992, no. 3, pp.6-11

Regulation. Closed minds on open skies. –
10 *The Avmark Aviation Economist*, June 1992, pp.8-10

RICHARDSON, J. – FAA passenger taxes assist airports, annoy airlines. –
56 *Tax Notes* (Arlington VA) 1992, pp.974-976

RIVERA CESTERO, G. – Actuaciones de las líneas aéreas internacionales estatales a través de sus agentes que producen la pérdida de inmunidad del soberano en los Estados Unidos y Puerto Rico. –
8 *Revista europea DNMA* 1992, pp.1355-1359

RIVERA CESTERO, G. – Las agencias de viajes en el derecho norteamericano. –
8 *Revista europea DNMA* 1992, pp.1337-1347

ROBERTS, M.J. – Congressional proposals to enhance airline competition and passenger protection. –
59 *Transportation Practitioners J* (Washington DC) 1992, pp.241-262 and 292-295

SABINO, A.M. – Flying the unfriendly skies: a year of reorganizing airlines, aircraft lessors, and the Bankruptcy Code. –
59 *JALC* 1992, pp.841-903

SOIRET, J. – Choice of forum: have United States courts closed the door? –
6 *Air and Space Lawyer* (ABA) 1992, no. 3, pp.3-5

STERNS, G.C. – The law of products liability in the United States and Europe. –
Brussels symposium, April 1992, 14-38 pp.

LA TORRE, U. – Il risarcimento complementare nel trasporto aereo internazionale di persone: il piano statunitense del 1990. –
Diritto dei Trasporti 1992, pp.71-

TRINDER, R.B. – A perspective on the US approach to international civil aviation in the Pacific. –
In: The highways of air and outer space, 1992, pp.19-32

TSILAS, V. – An analysis of the phase-out provisions of the Airport Noise and Capacity Act of 1990. –
4 *Fordham Environmental Law Report*, fall 1992, pp.83-101

VALBUSA, S. – Handling aeroportuale e regolamenti C.E.E. –
Diritto dei Trasporti 1992, pp.109-

VANDYK, A. – US decried on Warsaw system. –
29 *Air Transport World* 1992, no. 4, pp.92-93

WELLS, M.A. and MAYHAN, D.G. – Federal preemption of strict liability claims in aviation litigation. –
27 *Tort & Insurance LJ* (ABA) 1992, pp.693-708

WHALEN, Th.J. and LYNES, T.J. – Foreign ownership of US registered aircraft: the voting trust. –
17 *Air and Space Law* 1992, pp.153-159

ARLINGTON, D.T. – Liberalization of restrictions on foreign ownership in U.S. air carriers: the United States must take the first step in aviation globalization. –
59 *JALC* 1993, pp.133-192

The bankruptcy virus in the US airline industry: causes and cures. –
Washington DC, George Washington University, April 1993

CORDES, J.H. – Flying the open skies: an analysis and historical perspective of the U.S.-Netherlands bilateral air transport agreement of September 4, 1992. –
6 *The Transnational Lawyer* (Sacramento CA) 1993, pp.301-327

COTUGNO, E. – No rescue in sight for Warsaw plaintiffs from either courts or legislature: Montreal Protocol 3 drowns in committee. –
58 *JALC* 1993, pp.745-793

DRAKE, M.H. – The D.C. Circuit's dubious approval of US long-arm jurisdiction over extraterritorial crimes. United States v. Yunis 924 F.2d 1086 (D.C. Cir. 1991). –
87 *Northwestern Univ. LR* (Chiacgo IL) 1993, pp.697-734

DRISCOLL, D.L. – A comparative analysis of the labor statutes which govern the United States and Canadian airline industries and how the relationship may be affected by a new bilateral air agreement. –
60 *Transportation Practitioners J* (Washington DC) 1993, pp.119-142

GLISSON, L.M. – Market globalization. Analyzing the U.S. domestic airline industry. –
61 *Transportation Practitioners J*, fall 1993, pp.39-50

JACOBSON, M.D. and THOMPSON, M.J. – Financial crisis in the airline industry. United States. –
18 *Air and Space Law* 1993, pp.168-182

LÉGIER, G. – L'application de la Convention de Varsovie par les juridictions américaines: évolution de la jurisprudence. –
46 *RFDAS* 1993, pp.123-170

LEVICK, M.J. – The production of civil aircraft: a compromise of two world giants. –
21 *Transportation LJ* 1993, pp.433-467

LEVINE, M.E. – The U.S. experience with slot allocation. –
28 *ETL* (Belgium) 1993, pp.69-76

LEWIS, A. – Playing fast and loose with the 'regional notes'. –
73 *Business & Commercial Aviation*, Dec. 1993, pp.C12-C15

MACLURE, E.W. – Morales v. Trans World Airlines, Inc.: federal preemption provision clips states' wings on regulation of air fare advertising. –
71 *North Carolina LR* 1993, pp.906-927

MENDES DE LEON, P. and MIRMINA, S. – The international and American law implications of the Bijlmer air disaster. –
6 *Leiden JIL* 1993, pp.111-122

DE MONTLAUR-MARTIN, E. – L'interprétation de l'article 17 de la Convention de Varsovie dans la jurisprudence américaine récente. –
46 *RFDAS* 1993, pp.33-35

The National Commission to Ensure a Strong Competitive Airline Industry. –
40 *Federal Bar News & J* 1993, pp.620-643

NUUTINEN, H. – US-Europe aviation negotiations: Bermuda 3 – or the end of bilateralism? 10 *The Avmark Aviation Economist*, May 1993, pp.5-7

PARKE, R.B. – Realities of the new Disability Law. –
73 *Business & Commercial Aviation*, Aug. 1993, pp.74-75 and 77

RECKEWERTH, S. – Zusammenarbeit der Luftverkehrsgesellschaften nach europäischem und US-amerikanischem Recht. –
Diss. Göttingen. Studien zum int. Wirtschaftsrecht und Atomenergierecht Bd. 85. Köln 1993, 437 pp.

SCHUBERT, F. – La responsabilité des services de la circulation aérienne. États-Unis. –
ASDA Bulletin 1993-2, no. 115, pp.5-34, at pp.22-23 and 29-30

STARRY, S.J. – Federal preemption in commercial aviation: tort litigation under 49 U.S.C. §1305. –
58 *JALC* 1993, pp.657-701

STROUD, J.C. – Recent developments in aviation case law. –
59 *JALC* 1993, pp.1-75

TRENT, J. – Cabotage rights: the minimal impact of opening up cabotage. –
10 *The Avmark Aviation Economist*, May 1993, pp.7-10

WARNER, S.M. – Liberalize open skies: foreign investment and cabotage restrictions keep noncitizens in second class. –
43 *American Univ. LR* (Washington DC) 1993, pp.277-323

YODICE, J.S. – Product liability on trial. –
36 *The AOPA Pilot*, May 1993, pp.123-124

ABEYRATNE, R.I.R. – The evolution from FANS to CNS/ATM and products liability of technology providers in the United States. –
43 *ZLW* 1994, pp.156-186

ANDERSEN, D.R. – Recent cases and developments in aviation law. –
60 *JALC* 1994, pp.3-178

Aviation noise policy and regulation. –
46 *Administrative LR* (Chicago IL) 1994, pp.413-427

BASEDOW, J. – Airline deregulation in the European Community – Its background, its flaws, its consequences for EC-US relations. –
In: German national reports in civil law matters for the XIVth Congress of Comparative Law in Athens, 1994; pp.41-66. 13 *J of Law and Commerce* (Pittsburgh PA) 1994, pp.247-277

BOCK, A.K. – How to restore the airline industry to its full upright position: an analysis of the National Commission to Ensure a Strong, Competitive Airline Industry report. –
59 *JALC* 1994, pp.663-707

BOSTON, W.C. – Registration of aircraft and recording of security instruments under federal law. –
48 *Consumer Finance Law Quarterly Report* (Oklahoma City) 1994, pp.466-475

BROWN III, J.C. – Problems arising from the intersection of traditional maritime law and aviation death and personal injury liability. –
68 *Tulane LR* (New Orleans LA) 1994, pp.577-594

CONWAY, J.A. – The Americans with Disabilities Act: new challenges in airline hiring practices. –
59 *JALC* 1994, pp.945-982

DAVIDSON, G.E. – United States' use of economic sanctions, treaty bending, and treaty breaking in international aviation. –
59 *JALC* 1994, pp.291-356

GANGNES, H.B. and MCKENZIE, C.P. – Does the Act on the High Seas Act apply to interisland Hawaii flights? –
6 *Univ. of San Francisco Maritime LJ* 1994, pp.533-545

GLISSON, L.M. and DI LORENZO-AISS, J. – Strategic marketing alliances. Analyzing the U.S. domestic airline industry. –
61 *Transportation Practitioners J* 1994, pp.173-186

GLISSON, L.M. and JONES, M.K. – Analyzing the U.S. domestic airline industry. A model for airline mergers. –
61 *Transportation Practitioners J* 1994, pp.307-319

GRANT, Th.D. – Foreign takeovers of United States airlines: free trade process, problems, and progress. –
31 *Harvard J on Legislation*, winter 1994, pp.63-151

GRAUMANN, H. – Die Luftverkehrsbeziehungen Deutschland/USA nach dem Stand vom September/Oktober 1993: ein kurzer Überblick. –
43 *ZLW* 1994, pp.3-10

GRITTA, D.; LIPPMAN, E. and CHOW, G. – Lease capitalization and the effect on the debt ratios of the major US airlines. –
22 *Transportation LJ* 1994, pp.1-14

DE GROOT, J.E. – Code-sharing. United States' policies and the lessons for Europe. –
19 *Air and Space Law* 1994, pp.62-74

GROSS, R.J. – Special considerations in military flying club litigation. –
59 *JALC* 1994, pp.561-586

HAANAPPEL, P.P.C. – Les activités de l'IATA (hiver 1994). 3. La coordination tarifaire, l'immunité 'antitrust' aux États-Unis et les exemptions de groupe dans l'Union européenne. –
47 *RFDAS* 1994, pp.139-142, at pp.140-142

HALLIDAY, S.D. – Tax issues arising from the use of non-commercial aircraft. –
46 *Tax Executive* (Washington DC) 1994, pp.190-197

HAMILTON, J.S. – Allocation of air space as a scarce national resource. –
22 *Transportation LJ* 1994, pp.251-290

HARPER, G.R. – Cambios en la ley estadounidense: inversión extranjera en líneas aéreas de dominio extranjero. –
Aviación comercial, turismo, etc., Buenos Aires 1994, pp.215-217

HEDLUND, D.C. – Toward open skies: liberalizing trade in international airline services. –
3 *Minnesota J of Global Trade* (Minneapolis MN) 1994, pp.259-299

HOFF-PATRINOS, K. – The last chapter. –
Airfinance J, Dec. 1994, no. 168, pp.34-35

HUNT, A. – Assault on the airline industry: private antitrust litigation and the problem of settlement. –
59 *JALC* 1994, pp.983-1021

JENKINS JR, J.J. – The Airport Noise and Capacity Act of 1990: has Congress finally solved the aircraft noise problem? –
59 *JALC* 1994, pp.1023-1055

KASS, H.E. – Cabotage and control: bringing 1938 U.S. aviation policy into the jet age. –
26 *Case Western Reserve JIL* (Cleveland Ohio) 1994, pp.143-181

LIN, A. – Jurisdictional splashdown: should aviation torts find solace in admiralty? –
60 *JALC* 1994, pp.409-452

MILLER, J.L. – Search and seizure of air passengers and pilots: the Fourth Amendment takes flight. –
22 *Transportation LJ* (Denver CO) 1994, pp.199-223

MINTER, V.L. – Certification of unfit pilots: is the United States flying blind?
59 *JALC* 1994, pp.763-811

DE MONTLAUR-MARTIN, E. – États-Unis. –
47 *RFDAS* 1994, pp.44-48

MOORE, M.F. – Hit and run strikes. Protected activity or suicidal actions under the Railway Labor Act? –
59 *JALC* 1994, pp.867-903

MURIEL, A. and CLARK, D. – Security assignments and the lessee. –
Airfinance J, March 1994, no. 160, pp.40-41

PAPKIN, R.D. – El tratamiento de la Convención de Chicago en los tribunales de Estados Unidos. –
RBDAE, May-Sept. 1994, no. 66, pp.26-30. XVIII Jornadas latinoamericanas, Buenos Aires 1994, pp.47-52

PETERS, R.J. – Northwest Airlines v. County of Kent, Michigan: more than you ever wanted to know about airport rate setting. –
22 *Transportation LJ* 1994, pp.291-307

PLATT, J. – European Community cabotage. –
22 *Transportation LJ* 1994, pp.61-85. See also: 17 *Air and Space Law* 1992, pp.183-198

RAS, L.F. – Warsaw's wingspan over state laws: towards a streamlined system of recovery. –
59 *JALC* 1994, pp.587-615

ROKITA, Th.E. – Why U.S.-enforced flight suspension due to deficient foreign airport security should be a no-go. –
5 *Indiana Int. & Comp. LR* 1994, pp.205-236

SCHLESS, A.L. – Open skies: loosening the protectionist grip on international civil aviation. –
8 *Emory ILR* (Atlanta GA) 1994, pp.435-471

SHELTON, H. – US international aviation policy: the last of Yankee imperialism? –
11 *The Avmark Aviation Economist*, Nov. 1994, pp.2-5

STEPPICK, D.C. – Military mess: CERCLA liability and the Base Closure and Realignment Act. –
59 *JALC* 1994, pp.449-491

United States-United Kingdom arbitration. Heathrow Airport user charges. –
88 *AJIL* 1994, pp.738-744

VANWORMER, J.A. – Federal preemption of aircraft design certification standards after Cleveland v. Piper Aircraft Corp.: can general aviation manufacturers recover? –
19 *J of Corporation Law* (Iowa City) 1994, pp.665-679

VITALE, R. – US ownership rules hang in the air on the issue of control. –
Airfinance J, Febr. 1994, no. 159, pp.38-40

WHALEN, Th. – US commission breathes new life into liability debate. –
Airfinance J, Jan. 1994, no. 158, pp.41 and 43

WITTE, R.J. – ... or would you rather have what's behind door number two? Uniform choice of law proposals: big deal of the day or just another zonk? –
59 *JALC* 1994, pp.617-659

YODICE, J. – Current issues in aviation involving airports. –
19 *Air and Space Law* 1994, pp.89-92

ALIMONTI, F.P. – Death by misinformation? Governmental liability for faulty FAA weather information. –
60 *JALC* 1995, pp.961-996

BECHKY, P.S. – Mismanagement and misinterpretation: U.S. judicial implementation of the Warsaw Convention in air disaster litigation. –
60 *JALC* 1995, pp.455-531

BLACKER, J. – 'Fly to London for $298: The battle between federal and state regulation of airfare advertising heats up. –
61 *JALC* 1995, pp.205-242

BLISS, F.A. – Rethinking restrictions on cabotage: moving to free trade in passenger aviation. –
33 *Duquesne LR* (Pittsburgh PA) 1995, pp.283-307

DEMPSEY, P.S. – Airlines in turbulence: strategies for survival. –
23 *Transportation LJ* 1995, pp.15-98

FUKUI, N. – Responsibility of airlines. –
In: The use of airspace and outer space, The Hague 1995, pp.161-173

VAN HAERSOLTE-VAN HOF, J.J. – US/UK arbitration concerning Heathrow Airport user charges. Some procedural aspects. –
8 *Leiden JIL* 1995, pp.203-216

IMES, S. – Airline passenger facility charges: what do they mean for an ailing industry? –
60 *JALC* 1995, pp.1039-1089

KENNEY, S.C. – Recent developments in aviation law. –
61 *JALC* 1995, pp.3-161

LACY, M.W. – Freedom in the air: the Canada-United States bilateral air transport agreement. –
20 *AASL* 1995, vol. II, pp.139-165

MCALLISTER, T.S. – A 'tail' of liability reform: the General Aviation Revitalization Act of 1994 and the general aviation industry in the United States. –
20 *Transportation LJ* 1995, pp.301-322

MCNatt JR, C.C. and ENGLAND, S.L. – The push for statutes of repose in general aviation. –
20 *Transportation LJ* 1995, pp.323-343

POWELL, K.F. – Southwest Airlines v. high-speed rail: more powerful than a locomotive? 60 *JALC* 1995, pp.1091-1138

SKILBECK, J. – The US/UK arbitration concerning Heathrow airport user charges. –
44 *ICLQ* 1995, pp.171-179

VALETTI, M.A. – Preemption of state law tort claims in the context of aircraft manufacturers. –
60 *JALC* 1995, pp.699-746

WEBER, L. – Modern trends in the antitrust/competition law governing the aviation industry. –
20 *Air and Space Law* 1995, pp.101-109

WITTEN, S.M. – The U.S.-U.K. arbitration concerning Heathrow Airport user charges. –
89 *AJIL* 1995, pp.174-192

United States of America. Deregulation

CASTEJÓN, B. – La desreglementación en los Estados Unidos. El movimiento hacia la liberalización en Europa. Sus consecuencias en la región iberoamericana en relación con el transporte aéreo. –
XVII Jornadas iberoamericanas, Rio de Janeiro 1987, pp.26-33

PAPKIN, R.D. – Liberalización de las aerolíneas de los Estados Unidos: la experiencia estadounidense y su posible impacto en el futuro del transporte aéreo latinoamericano. –
XVII Jornadas iberoamericanas, Rio de Janeiro 1987, pp.35;45

VÁSQUEZ ROCHA, E. – La desreglementación en los Estados Unidos. El movimiento hacia la liberalización en Europa. Sus consecuencias en la región iberoamericana en relación con el transporte aéreo. –
XVII Jornadas iberoamericanas, Rio de Janeiro 1987, pp.46-53

Deregulation and airline competition. –
OECD, Paris 1988, 169 pp.

KATZ, M.A. – The American experience under the Airline Deregulation Act of 1978 – an airline perspective. –
6 *Hofstra Labor LJ* (Hempstead NY) 1988, pp.87-100

La libéralisation du transport aérien dans la CEE: le point de vue des pays voisins. – Air transport liberalization in the EEC: the viewpoint of neighbouring countries.

PAVAUX, J.	- The lessons of airline deregulation in the United States, pp.5-21
SCOCOZZA, M.	- The U.S. experience with airline deregulation, pp.23-33
AARONSON, R.J.	- US airline deregulation: effects on airports, pp.35-42
COSENTINO, E.T.	- Relations between Latin American countries and the U.S., pp.43-54

ITA Études & documents/Studies & reports 88/4, vol. 11, viii-256 pp.
Symposium proceedings Marrakech, 13-14 October 1988

DEMPSEY, P.S. – The social and economic consequences of deregulation: the transportation industry under transition. –
NY/London 1989, xvi-277 pp.

GAMACHE, C.R. – Air service to small communities since deregulation. –
17 *Transportation LJ* (Denver CO) 1989, pp.345-359

GAYNES, J. – Desregulamentação norte-americana: iniciativas na América Latina, resultados, anseios e implicações. –
RBDAE 1989, no. 46, pp.42-45

LEVINE, M.E. – US deregulation: results and strategies. –
Symposium proceedings Lahore, 11-12 December 1989
ITA Études & documents/Studies & reports 90/2, vol. 19, iv-104 pp., at pp.21-30

ALLEN, S.A.; CUNNINGHAM, L.F. and WOOD, W.R. – Airline industry deregulation and changes in systematic risk. –
17 *Transportation LJ* 1990, pp.49-66

DEMPSEY, P.S. – Flying blind: the failure of airline deregulation. –
Washington DC 1990, Economic Policy Institute, 89 pp.

DEMPSEY, P.S. – Airline deregulation and laissez-faire mythology: economic theory in turbulence. –
56 *JALC* 1990, pp.305-412

MAJONE, G., ed. – Deregulation or re-regulation? Regulatory reform in Europe and the United States.

SOETZER, M.-W.	Efficiency and prices in the European air transport market, pp.124-138
BREYER, S.	Regulation and deregulation in the United States: airlines, telecommunications and antitrust, pp.7-58

London/New York 1990, 262 pp.

DONN, C.B. and MARETT, P.C. – Deregulation and the future of transportation trade unionism in the United States. –
41 *Labor LJ* (Chicago IL) 1990, pp.492-497

EBKE, W.F. and WITTMANN, M. – Wettbewerb im Luftlinienverkehr: Erfahrungen mit der Deregulierung in den USA. –
36 *Recht der intern. Wirtschaft* 1990, pp.962-968

GIL, A. – Air transport deregulation and its implications for flight attendants.
129 *Int. Labour Review* 1990, pp.317-331

RULE, C.F. – Deregulation of US airlines and the continuing role of the antitrust laws. –
In: EEC air transport policy and regulation, Deventer 1990, at pp.99-126

SAMUELS, G.E. – Airline deregulation: its effects and the competitive environment. –
17 *Int. J of Transport Economics*, June 1990, pp.131-146

VAN WEZEL STONE, K. – Labor relations of the airlines: the Railway Labor Act in the era of deregulation. –
42 *Stanford LR* 1990, pp.1485-1547

WILSON, J.B. – The lessons of airline deregulation and the challenge of foreign ownership of U.S. air carriers. –
24 *George Washington JIL and Economics* 1990, pp.103-147

BEYEN, R.K. and HERBERT, J. – Deregulierung des amerikanischen und EG-europäischen Luftverkehrs: theoretische Grundlagen und Analyse der verkehrspolitischen Umsetzung. –
Giessener Studien zur Transportwirtschaft und Kommunikation, 5. Hamburg 1991, xlvi-146 pp.

BRIGGS, M. – Deregulation of the aviation and travel industry. –
13 *Comparative Law Yb of Int. Business* (Netherlands) 1991, pp.331-345

BUTTON, K., ed. – Airline deregulation: international experiences. –
London 1991, x-191 pp.

HEUER, J.S. and VOGEL, M.H. – Airlines in the wake of deregulation: bankruptcy as an alternative to economic regulation. –
19 *Transportation LJ* 1991, pp.247-286

LEVINE, M.E. – Airline deregulation: a perspective. –
60 *Antitrust LJ* (Chicago IL) 1991, pp.687-694

PICKRELL, D. – The regulation and deregulation of US airlines. –
In: Airline deregulation: international experiences. London 1991, at pp.5-47

Transportation Research Board. National Research Council – Winds of change: domestic air transport since deregulation. –
Special report 230. Washington DC 1991, xiv-399 pp.

BRUNEAU, J.M. – Concentration within the U.S. airline industry: a 'natural phenomenon' or an 'ordinary' monopoly/oligopoly resulting from the behaviour of competitiors? –
17 *AASL* 1992, vol. II, pp.123-152

BUTTON, K.J. and SWANN, D. – Transatlantic lessons in aviation deregulation: E.E.C. and U.S. experiences. –
37 *Antitrust Bulletin* (NY) 1992, pp.207-

DEMPSEY, P.S. – Airline deregulation in the United States: competition, concentration, and market Darwinism. –
17 *AASL* 1992, vol. II, pp.199-243

DEMPSEY, P.S. – The U.S. airline industry. Flying from deregulation to concentration. –
Brussels symposium, April 1992, 58 pp.

GESELL, L.E. and FARRIS, M.T. – Airline deregulation: an evaluation of goals and objectives. –
21 *Transportation LJ* 1992, pp.105-127

MILLER, B.F. – The airline industry: labor relations in the era of deregulation, mergers, bankruptcies, and layoffs. –
43 *Labor LJ* (Chicago IL) 1992, pp.388-394

MONK, D.G. – The lessons of airline regulation and deregulation: will we make the same mistakes in space? –
57 *JALC* 1992, pp.715-753

RAKOWSKI, J.P. and BEJOUR, D. – Structural change and the nature of competition in the deregulated U.S. airline industry. –
59 *Transportation Practitioners J* (Washington DC) 1992, pp.241-262

CUDAHY, R.D. – The coming demise of deregulation. –
10 *Yale J on Regulation*, winter 1993, pp.1-15

SCHIESSL, M. and WEHLAU, A. – Die Auswirkungen von Flugzeugleasing und Übernahmeangeboten auf Fluglinien in deregulierten Märkten. –
39 *Recht der internationalen Wirtschaft* 1993, pp.709-716

GILES, L. – Interpreting the Airline Deregulation Act of 1978: federal preemption over state deceptive advertising laws. –
22 *Transportation LJ* 1994, pp.87-103

REITZ, J.C. – Legal and administrative problems of airline deregulation. –
US National reports to the XIVth Congress of the Int. Academy of Comparative Law, supplement to 42 *American J of Comparative Law* 1994, pp.419-451

SCHODER, L. – Flying the unfriendly skies: the effect of airline deregulation on labor relations. –
22 *Transportation LJ* 1994, pp.105-132

Uruguay

GAGGERO, E.D.; ALGORTA, O. and MILLER, A. – Comentarios al proyecto de ley-tipo de transporte multimodal de mercancías. –
15 *Revista del CIDA-E* 1991, pp.45-58

Venezuela

GONZALEZ DE MANSILLA, A. – Régimen jurídico laboral del personal de vuelo en Venezuela. –
8 *Revista europea DNMA* 1992, pp.1185-1209

ELEIZALDE PEÑA, J. – Algunos aspectos de la situación de las líneas aéreas en Venezuela. XXIV Jornadas iberoamericanas, Salamanca 1994, pp.417-427

Africa

L'Afrique face à la libéralisation réglementaire du transport aérien. Africa and the liberalization of the air transport regulatory system. –
ITA Études & documents/Studies & reports 90/3, vol. 20, v-110 pp.

KAUNDA, G. – Legal aspects of African airline deregulation. –
17 *AASL* 1992, vol. I, pp.263-270

HENAKU, B.D.K. – Regionalism in international air transport regulation. –
Leiden (Neth.) 1993, xix-187 pp.

MAGDELÉNAT, J.-L. – Une nouvelle organisation régionale du transport aérien en Afrique australe: SARATA. –
47 *RFDAS* 1994, pp.265-270

POONOOSAMY, V. – Challenges facing African countries in the field of civil aviation and the impact of European aeropolitical developments on African countries. –
29 *ETL* 1994, pp.245-256

GARABGA, T. – Air finance for Africa, legal issues. The airline perspective. –
20 *Air and Space Law* 1995, pp.18-21

MAKONNEN, A. – Inter-airline cooperation in Africa. –
20 *Air and Space Law* 1995, pp.92-96

Israel

KUZNICKI, Th. – Terrorismus und luftspezifische Gefahr in Bezug auf eine Haftung des Luftfrachtführers gemäss Artikel 17 des Warschauer Abkommens. Israel. –
41 *ZLW* 1992, pp.360-376, at pp.369-370

LESHEM, M. – Israel: recent aviation law developments. –
17 *Air and Space Law* 1992, pp.178-182

Lebanon

DAVIDSON, G.E. – United States' use of economic sanctions, treaty bending, and treaty breaking in international aviation. Lebanon. –
59 *JALC* 1994, pp.291-356, at pp.312-316 and 334-337

Libya

EL-MIILLATI, A. – Aviation law in Lybia. –
Diss. McGill. Montreal 1988

DAVIDSON, G.E. – United States' use of economic sanctions, treaty bending, and treaty breaking in international aviation. Libya. –
59 *JALC* 1994, pp.291-356, at pp.317-319 and 332-334

Nigeria

UWECHIA, U. – Aviation insurance: a case for compulsory air insurance law. –
16 *Air Law* 1991, pp.284-286

South Africa

SMIT, J.; PRINS, V. and VICTOR, W.C. – The new international aviation policy of South Africa. –
18 *Air and Space Law* 1993, pp.85-95

DAVIDSON, G.E. – United States' use of economic sanctions, treaty bending, and treaty breaking in international aviation. South Africa. –
59 *JALC* 1994, pp.291-356, at pp.319-330 and 348-353

Syria

DAVIDSON, G.E. – United States' use of economic sanctions, treaty bending, and treaty breaking in international aviation. Syria. –
59 *JALC* 1994, pp.291-356, at pp.316-317 and 331-332

Asia

BUNYA-ANANTA, Ch. – The commercial and regulatory aspects of traffic between Asia and Europe, and Asia and North America. –
In: The highways of air and outer space, Dordrecht 1992, pp.11-17

CHENG, Ch.-J. – Asian deregulation policy: which example to follow? –
In: The highways of air and outer space, Dordrecht 1992, pp.33-46

CHENG, Ch.-J. – The changing features of aviation policy in Asian countries. –
Essays in honour of Henri A. Wassenbergh, Dordrecht 1992, pp.3-9

SOEPARNO, M. – Prospects for cooperation in Asia., –
In: The highways of air and outer space, Dordrecht 1992, pp.329-335

Asia Pacific

HARBISON, P. – Aviation multilateralism in the Asia Pacific region: regulatory and industry pressures for change. –
19 *Air and Space Law* 1994, pp.138-145

SAMUEL, M.; FINDLAY, Chr. and FORSYTH, P. – International aviation problems and responses: an Asian Pacific perspective. –
19 *Air and Space Law* 1994, pp.167-173

China (PR)

JIANDUAN, W. – The current system relating to the compensation for bodily injury or death of passengers in domestic air transport in China. –
15 *Air Law* 1990, pp.87-92

JIANDUAN, W. – Some thoughts on compensation for passengers in China in a recent air crash. –
16 *Air Law* 1991, pp.76-81

LIU, Y. – Legal issues on aircraft finance in China. –
16 *Air Law* 1991, pp.2-8

BARRETT, J. and PILKINGTON, M. – CAAC Guangzhou hi-jacking – Insurance issues. –
17 *Air and Space Law* 1992, pp.133-136

PARK, O-H. – Research on the civil aviation industry of China and the design for Korea-China aviation cooperation. –
5 *Korean JAL* 1993, pp.321-383 (in Korean) and p.384 (English summary)

GAU, M.S. – The future Taiwan-Mainland China air links and the cabotage concept under current international air law. –
19 *Air and Space Law* 1994, pp.317-325

CHENG, C.-J. – Recent developments in the aviation industry of the People's Republic of China. –
20 *Air and Space Law* 1995, pp.68-70

JIANDUAN, W. – Investment in China civil air transportation. Some legal aspects. –
20 *Air and Space Law* 1995, pp.201-205

PENGNIAN, He – The prospect of cooperation between Chinese and foreign airlines. –
20 *Air and Space Law* 1995, pp.318-321

Hong Kong

ABEYRATNE, R.I.R. – Hong Kong and air traffic rights in 1992 – some legal issues. –
15 *Air Law* 1990, pp.64-78

LEWIS, D. – Dispute resolution in the new Hong Kong International Airport core programme projects. –
10 *Int. Construction LR* (NY) 1993, pp.76-87; 11 *ICLR* 1994, pp.25-45; 12 *ICLR* 1995, pp.131-136

India

SARAF, D.N. – Public utility services with special reference to air services and the consumer. –
31 *J of the Indian Law Institute* 1989, pp.136-153

NAYAR, B.R. – The State and international aviation in India. Performance and policy on the eve of aviation globalization. –
New Delhi 1994, ix-349 pp.

Iraq

WASSENBERGH, H.A. – Iraq/Kuwait and international civil aviation relations.
ITA Magazine, Sept./Oct. 1990, no. 63, pp.8-15

MILDE, M. – Aeronautical consequences of the Iraqi invasion of Kuwait. –
16 *Air Law* 1991, pp.63-75

Japan

SEKIGAWA, E. – Unification of the EC market and Japan. –
Symposium proceedings Lahore, 11-12 December 1989.
ITA Études & documents/Studies & reports 90/2, vol. 19, pp.101-104

NOMURA, Y. – Jurisdiction and forum non conveniens in airplane crash cases: a U.S.-Japan comparison. (in Japanese) –
156 *Handai Hogaku* 1990, pp.341-385

MARGADANT S., G.F. – La fórmula japonesa para la indemnización de víctimas de accidentes aéreos. –
Estudios jurídicos en memoria de Alfonso Noriega Cantú, Ciudad de México 1991, pp.147-154

YASUTOMI, K. – Political offenses and extradition with the Japanese law for the extradition of fugitives from justice. –
34 *Japanese Annual for IL* 1991, pp.69-81

HAYASHIDA, K. – Jurisdiction and applicable law in aviation cases in Japan. –
Brussels symposium, April 1992, 13 pp.

HAYASHIDA, K. – Jurisdiction in aviation cases in Japan. –
42 *ZLW* 1993, pp.250-257

MERCER, A.G. – The Montreal Protocols and the Japanese initiative: can the Warsaw system survive? –
19 *Air and Space Law* 1994, pp.301-317

HAYASHIDA, K. – Jurisdiction and applicable law in aviation cases in Japan. –
In: The use of airspace and outer space, The Hague 1995, pp.297-307

OKABE, S. – Aviation personal injury claim settlement practice in Japan. –
In: The use of airspace and outer space, The Hague 1995, pp.319-328

SAKAMOTO, T. – Legal and administrative problems of airline deregulation. The tardy progress in Japan. –
In: Japanese reports for the XIVth Int. Congress of Comparative Law, Athens 1994; Tokyo 1995, pp.179-186

SEKIGUCHI, M. – Why Japan was compelled to opt for unlimited liability. –
20 *AASL* 1995, vol. II, pp.337-355

Korea

HONG, S.-K. – A reevaluation of the U.S.-Korea bilateral air services agreement and some suggestions to improve it. –
1 *Korean JAL* 1989, pp.125-145 (in Korean) and pp.145-146 (English summary)

CHOI, W.S. – Some aspects of the new Korean Aviation Law. –
15 *Air Law* 1990, pp.2-16

KIM, H.-R. – Das Planungsverfahren umweltrelevanter Grossvorhaben in der Bundesrepublik Deutschland und der Republik Korea am Beispiel der Flughafenplanung. –
Diss. Speyer. Speyer 1990, 349 pp.

LEE, K.-B. – A study on the problem of domestic legislation regarding air transportation. 3 *Korean JAL* 1991, pp.51-111 (in Korean)

KIM, J.S. – Bilateralism v. multilateralism in the international aviation order: historical & analytical aspects, and Korean responses. –
4 *Korean JAL* 1992, pp.139-153 (in Korean)

LEE, T.H. – Legal and insurance developments in aviation in Korea. –
4 *Korean JAL* 1992, pp.53-63

PARK, O-H. – Research on the civil aviation industry of China and the design for Korea-China aviation cooperation. –
5 *Korean JAL* 1993, pp.321-383 (in Korean) and p.384 (English summary)

HONG, S.-K. – A study of the Korean Aviation and Tourism Policy in relation to the EC and NAFTA integration. –
7 *Korean JAL* 1995, pp.17-52 (in Korean) and p.53 (English summary)

HUNTER, D.W. – Establishing regional airport authorities in Korea. –
7 *Korean JAL* 1995, pp.55-62

Kuwait

WASSENBERGH, H.A. – Iraq/Kuwait and international civil aviation relations. –
ITA Magazine, Sept./Oct. 1990, no. 63, pp.8-15

MILDE, M. – Aeronautical consequences of the Iraqi invasion of Kuwait. –
16 *Air Law* 1991, pp.63-75

Mauritius

KNEIFEL, J.L. – Bilateral aviation agreements of Mauritius and a comparison between the Mauritian Civil Aviation Act of 1974 and the Civil Aviation

Regulations of the Federal Republic of Germany. –
Nördlingen 1989, 289 pp.

Taiwan

TZOU, Ch.-K. and CHENG, C.-J. – New types of agreements in international air transport. –
In: The highways of air and outer space, Dordrecht 1992, pp.299-310

GAU, M.S. – The future Taiwan-Mainland China air links and the cabotage concept under current international air law. –
19 *Air and Space Law* 1994, 317-325

Australia

RYAN, K. – Deregulation in Australia. –
Australian Aviation, March 1989, pp.94-98; May 1989, pp.22-24 and 29-30

MCEVOY, K. and OWENS, R. – The flight of Icarus: legal aspects of the pilots' dispute. –
3 *Australian J of Labour Law*, August 1990, pp.87-129

O'ROURKE, S. and MERRYWEATHER, P. – Tailwinds. Australian aircraft financing takes a new direction. –
Legal aspects of aircraft finance, supplement to *Airfinance J*, Febr. 1990, no. 111, pp.14-17

CHIPKIN, S. – Cross-border U.S. FSC aircraft deals – an Australian perspective.
Legal aspects of aircraft finance, supplement to *Airfinance J*, May 1991, no. 126, pp.8-11

PICKRELL, D. – The regulation and deregulation of Australia's domestic airline industry. –
In: Airline deregulation. International experiences. London 1991, at pp.48-84

KIRBY, M. – Civil aviation liabilities: Australian developments in a global context. –
17 *AASL* 1992, vol. II, pp.255-281

ABEYRATNE, R.I.R. – Sydney's third runway. A global runway. –
10 *Environmental and Planning LJ* 1993, pp.355-364

DE MAROLLES, O. and LENOIR, A. – La déréglementation du transport aérien en Australie. The deregulation of air transport in Australia. –
Paris, Études & documents/Studies & reports 93/2, vol. 30, 110 pp.

SINGH, P. – Some significant developments in Australia's international aviation.
–
18 *Air and Space Law* 1993, pp.71-75

CORONES, S. – Structural and conduct considerations in the airline industry: recent Trade Practices Commission authorisations. –
22 *Australian Business LR* 1994, pp.148-151

MCGILL, D. – Building works intruding into air space. –
24 *Queensland Law Society J* 1994, pp.159-163

PYMAN, T.A. – Reflections on the rationale, legality and continuity of Australian 'two-airline' interstate domestic air services. –
20 *Air and Space Law* 1995, pp.146-163

PYNE, T. – An historical overview and recent developments in products liability law in Australia. –
44 *ZLW* 1995, pp.413-443

VENNELL, M.A. McGregor – Acts of interference with civil aviation in Australia and New Zealand. –
20 *Air and Space Law* 1995, pp.208-210

New Zealand

VENNELL, M.A. McGregor – Acts of interference with civil aviation in Australia and New Zealand. –
20 *Air and Space Law* 1995, pp.208-210

17. Case law

STIVEN, J.F. – Recent cases and developments in aviation law.
I Jurisdiction, pp.1-9
II Product liability, pp.9-29
III Federal Tort Claims Act, pp.29-39
IV Contribution and indemnity, pp.39-41
V Airports, pp.41-58
VI Warsaw Convention, pp.58-83
VII Limitations of actions, pp.83-85
VIII Insurance coverage, pp.85-101
IX FAA enforcement/Local regulations/Administrative law, pp.101-107
X Negligence, pp.107-115
XI Antitrust, pp.115-118
XII Miscellaneous, pp.118-121
55 *JALC* 1989

CARTER JR, J.D.; BECKWORTH, J.B.; HOGAN, J.B.; SULLIVAN, J.F.; FINCH, N.D. and SIEGEL, M. – Aviation and space law: annual survey.
I Jurisdiction, pp.209-215
II Warsaw Convention, pp.215-219
III Governmental contractor defense, pp.219-223
V Damages, pp.223-225

VI Evidence and practical developments, pp.225-227
25 *Tort & Insurance LJ* (ABA) 1990, pp.209-227

GIEMULLA, E. and SCHMID, R. – Ausgewählte internationale Rechtsprechung zum Warschauer Abkommen in den Jahren 1987-1989. –
39 *ZLW* 1990, pp.165-187

GRIGOLI, M. – L'aeromobile nella giurisprudenza. –
14 *DPAC* 1990, pp.154-198

PETKOFF, G.S. – Recent cases and developments in aviation law.
I Jurisdiction, pp.2-37
II Products liability, pp.37-49
III Foreign Sovereign Immunities Act, pp.49-69
IV Warsaw Convention, pp.69-91
56 *JALC* 1990, pp.1-91

PETKOFF, G.S. – Recent cases and developments in aviation law.
V Federal Tort Claims Act, pp.492-509
VI Indemnification, pp.509-510
VII Negligence, pp.511-515
VIII Evidence, pp.516-522
IX Insurance, pp.522-526
X Airports, pp.526-530
XI FAA regulations, pp.530-542
XII Passenger actions against air carriers, pp.542-546
XIII Contractual claims, pp.546-549
XIV Handicapped passengers, pp.550-554
XV Miscellaneous, pp.554-556
56 *JALC* 1990, pp.491-556

CARTER JR, W.D.; INCERTO, M.S.; HOGAN, J.B.; SULLIVAN, J.F.; COFFMAN, S. and NICHOLS, M. – Aviation and space law: annual survey.
I Jurisdiction, pp.177-180
II Warsaw Convention, pp.181-184
III Government contractor defense, pp.184-187
IV Governmental immunity, pp.187-191
V Damages, pp.191-193
VI Evidence and practical developments, pp.193-195
26 *Tort & Insurance LJ* (ABA) 1991, pp.177-195

CRAFT JR, R.R. – Aviation liability law developments in 1990.
I General legal issues, pp.3-50
II Liability of air carriers in Warsaw Convention carriage, pp.50-68
III Liability of operators of aircraft in non-Warsaw carriage, pp.68-93
IV Liability of manufacturers and suppliers, pp.93-124
V Liability of the United States: the Federal Tort Claims Act, pp.125-139
VI Liability of foreign States: the Foreign Sovereign Immunities Act, pp.140-151

VII Liability of airports, pp.151-154
VIII Liability of insurers, pp.154-164
IX Miscellaneous, pp.164-172
57 *JALC* 1991, pp.1-172

CRAFT JR, R.R. – Survol rapide des récentes décisions américaines relatives aux préjudices indemnisables sous l'empire de la Convention de Varsovie. – 45 *RFDAS* 1992, pp.223-227

HOFFMAN, J.M. and HARRIS, Ph.S. – Recent developemnts in aviation case law.
I Jurisdiction, pp.3-18
II Products liability, pp.18-31
III Federal Tort Claims Act (FTCA), pp.31-38
IV Preemption, pp.38-41
V Practice and procedure, pp.41-47
VI Airports, pp.47-57
VII Warsaw Convention and air carrier liability, pp.57-66
VIII Limitation of actions, pp.66-68
IX Damages, pp.68-75
X Insurance coverage, pp.75-83
XI FAA enforcement/Local regulations, pp.83-89
XII Strict liability, pp.89-92
XIII Negligence, pp.92-97
XIV Debtor-creditor, pp.97-100
XV Frequent flyer programs, pp.100-101
58 *JALC* 1992, pp.1-101

KOLCZYNSKI, P.J.; SEHR, M.J.; GILMORE, P.; MARCUS, A.; MADOLE, J.; PARKS, R.L. and TESANOVICH, M.D. – Aviation and space law: annual survey.
I Aviation product liability, pp.156-158
II Aviation insurance, pp.158-161
III Governmental liability, pp.161-165
IV Jurisdiction and Warsaw Convention center, pp.165-168
V Noteworthy damage and liability decisions, pp.168-170
VI Discovery, evidence, and practice developments, pp.170-172
27 *Tort & Insurance LJ* 1992, pp.156-172

VAN BAREN, W.H. – Recent aviation case law from the Benelux.
1 Warsaw Convention, pp.29-33
2 Non-Warsaw carriage, pp.33-34
3 The 1933 Rome Convention on precautionary arrest, p.34
4 Aviation accident reports, pp.34-35
18 *Air and Space Law* 1993, pp.29-35

CHOI, J.-S. and KANG, S.-H. – Recent developments in aviation case law. – 5 *Korean JAL* 1993, pp.119-167 (in Korean) and pp.168-169 (English summary)

CHUN, S.-H. – A case study of German air law. –
5 *Korean JAL* 1993, pp.385-430 (in Korean)

GIEMULLA, E. and SCHMID, R. – Ausgewählte internationale Rechtsprechung zum Warschauer Abkommen in den Jahren 1991-1993. –
42 *ZLW* 1993, pp.386-400

HOLLOWELL, D. – 1991-92 survey of international law in the Second Circuit. I. Warsaw Convention. –
19 *Syracuse JILC* 1993, pp.98-163, at pp.98-106

LÉGIER, G. – L'application de la Convention de Varsovie par les juridictions américaines: évolution de la jurisprudence. –
46 *RFDAS* 1993, pp.123-170

DE MONTLAUR-MARTIN, E. – L'interprétation de l'article 17 de la Convention de Varsovie dans la jurisprudence américaine récente. –
46 *RFDAS* 1993, pp.33-35

STROUD, J.C. – Recent developments in aviation case law.
I Foreign Sovereign Immunities Act, pp.2-8
II Warsaw Convention, pp.8-27
III Federal Tort Claims Act, pp.27-36
IV Insurance, pp.36-46
V Products liability, pp.46-53
VI Federal Aviation Act, pp.53-58
VII Federal Aviation Administration, pp.59-60
VIII Airports, pp.60-64
IX Commercial, pp.64-68
X Miscellaneous, pp.69-75
59 *JALC* 1993, pp.1-75

ANDERSEN, D.R. – Recent cases and developments in aviation law.
I Jurisdiction, pp.5-14
II Preemption, pp.14-51
III Warsaw Convention and air carrier liability, pp.51-80
IV Products liability, pp.80-106
V Federal Tort Claims Act (FTCA), pp.106-120
VI Airports, pp.120-123
VII Practice and procedure, pp.123-143
VIII Damages, pp.143-150
IX Insurance coverage, pp.150-165
X FAA enforcement/Local regulation, pp.165-177
XI Debtor-creditor, pp.177-178
60 *JALC* 1994, pp.5-178

BLAKELY, W.D.; DOEBL, R.A.K. and JOHNSTON, D.C. – Developments in aviation law. –
29 *Tort & Insurance LJ* (ABA) 1994, pp.189-206

Giemulla, E. and Schmid, R. – Ausgewählte internationale Rechtsprechung zum Warschauer Abkommen in den Jahren 1993-1994. –
43 *ZLW* 1994, pp.388-394

Munro, M.P. – Subject matter jurisdiction in Warsaw Convention cases after Malik v. Butta. –
7 *NY Intern. LR* 1994, pp.171-188

Papkin, R.D. – El tratamiento de la Convención de Chicago en los tribunales de Estados Unidos. –
RBDAE, May-Sept. 1994, no. 66, pp.26-30. XVIII Jornadas latinoamericanas, Buenos Aires 1994, pp.47-52

Schmid, R. – Rechtsprobleme bei der Luftbeförderung im Rahmen von Flugpauschalreisen. –
38 *NJW* 1994, pp.2451-2456

Burckhardt, Th. – Aus der deutschen Rechtsprechung zum Warschauer Abkommen. –
ASDA Bulletin 1995-1, no. 118, pp.4-27

Kenney, S.C. – Recent developments in aviation law. –
II. Jurisdiction, pp.6-11
III. Air carrier liability and defenses, pp.11-80
IV. Sellers' and manufacturers' liability and defenses, pp.80-89
V. United States Government tort liability and defenses, pp.89-99
VI. Airports and fixed base operators, pp.99-118
VII. Practice and procedure, pp.118-138
VIII. Punitive damages, pp.138-139
IX. Insurance coverage, pp.139-142
X. FAA enforcement/local regulation, pp.142-155
XI. Debtor-creditor, pp.155-157
XII. Penal actions against pilots and passengers, pp.157-161
61 *JALC* 1995, pp.3-161

Savitt, L.J. and Colleran, M.J. – Recent developments in aviation and space law. –
I Aviation products liability, pp.249-254
II Evidence, pp.254-256
III Preemption, pp.256-258
IV Warsaw Convention, pp.258-260
V Miscellaneous, pp.260-261
30 *Tort & Insurance LJ* (ABA) 1995, pp.249-261

Chapter II. Organizations in the field of civil aviation

28. The International Civil Aviation Organization

a. General

SOCHOR, E. – Conflicts in international civil aviation: safeguarding the air routes. –
8 *Conflict* 1988, pp.271-284. Also in: Peace by pieces, edited by R.N.Wells Jr, London 1991, pp.136-160

MILDE, M. – Organisation de l'Aviation Civile Internationale (OACI). International Civil Aviation Organization (ICAO). –
15 *AASL* 1990, pp.454-459

SOCHOR, E. – The politics of international aviation. –
London 1990, 288 pp.

ZEIDLER, F. – Der Austritt und Ausschluss von Mitgliedern aus den Sonderorganisationen der Vereinten Nationen. Der Austritt aus der ICAO, pp.59-61. Der Ausschluss aus der ICAO, pp.192-201. –
Diss. Heidelberg. Frankfurt am Main 1990, x-318 pp.

FALLER, E. – ICAO – Internationale Zivilluftfahrtorganisation. –
In: Handbuch Vereinte Nationen, eds. R.Wolfrum and Chr.Philipp, München 1991, 2nd ed., pp.297-304

MOORMAN, R.W. – What's wrong with ICAO? –
28 *Air Transport World*, Jan. 1991, pp.80-81

SCHAAF, R.W. – International Civil Aviation Organization (ICAO): legal activities and documentation. –
19 *Int. J of Legal Information* (Washington DC) 1991, pp.248-251

UCHIGASAKI, Y. – ICAO jiken saikō. –
98 *Hōgaku Shimpō* (Japan) 1991, no. 3/4, pp.121-154

CHOI, W.S. – The International Civil Aviation Organization and recent developments of air law in a changing environment. –
4 *Korean JAL* 1992, pp.7-32 (in Korean) and pp.33-35 (English summary)

VAN DAM, R.D. – Air liability: ICAO policy. –
17 *AASL* 1992, vol. I, pp.85-95

VAN DAM, R. – OACI/ICAO. –
17 *AASL* 1992, vol. II, pp.482-499

VAN DAM, R.D. – Regulating international civil aviation: an ICAO perspective. –
In: Essays in honour of Henri A. Wassenbergh, Dordrecht 1992, pp.11-25

DRESNER, M. and TRETHEWAY, M.W. – ICAO and the economic regulation of international air transport. –
17 *AASL* 1992, vol. II, pp.195-216

FALLER, E. – Aviation security: the role of ICAO in safeguarding international civil aviation against acts of unlawful interference. –
17 *AASL* 1992, vol. I, pp.369-381

ICAO. World-wide air transport colloquium, Montreal, 6-10 April 1992. Proceedings. Exploring the future of international air transport regulation. –
ICAO, Montreal 1992

KRÄMER, P.M. – International Civil Aviation Organization. World-wide air transport colloquium: Exploring the future of international air transport regulation. Montreal, 6-10 April 1992. –
41 *ZLW* 1992, pp.275-283

MILDE, M. – Air law and the challenges of the 21st century. –
4 *Korean JAL* 1992, pp.156-165

MILDE, M. – New Headquarters Agreement between ICAO and Canada. –
17 *AASL* 1992, vol. II, pp.305-322 (text of Agreement on pp.571-594)

VAN DAM, R. – ICAO/OACI. –
18 *AASL* 1993, vol. I, pp.408-429

HENAKU, B.D.K. – ICAO: Fourth Air Transport Conference. An examination of the underlying objectives. –
43 *ZLW* 1994, pp.247-256

ICAO.

CLARK, L.S.	IATA and ICAO: the first fifty years, pp.125-134
DONATO, M.	ICAO's golden anniversary: The necessity of golden rules for the international air transport industry, pp.221-238
DUCREST, J.	L'Union Européenne, futur membre de l'OACI?, pp.239-281
TOMPKINS JR, G.N. and HARAKAS, A.J.	ICAO and aviation accident investigation – lessons to be learned from the Korean Air Lines 007 investigation, pp.375-398
HONG, S.-K. and SHIN, H.-K.	The need to improve the role of ICAO in relation to the legal other aspects of ICAO CNS/ATM system implementation for the 21st century, pp.397-427

KAKKAR, G.M. The registration and publication of aeronautical agreements and arrangements with the ICAO, pp.451-464

VAN DAM, R. ICAO/OACI, pp.652-673

19 *AASL* 1994, vol. II

LAMBERT, Y. – Eurocontrol et l'OACI. –
19 *AASL* 1994, vol. I, pp.349-369

MAPELLI, E. – 50 años de la Organización de la Aviación Civil Internacional (OACI). –
6 *Airline*, diciembre 1994, no. 72, pp.53-58

MATTE, N. MATEESCO – The Chicago Convention – Where from and where to, ICAO? –
29 *ETL* 1994, pp.535-552

MATTE, N. MATEESCO – La Convention de Chicago – Quo vadis, OACI? –
47 *RFDAS* 1994, pp.245-263

ABEYRATNE, R.I.R. – The ICAO World-Wide Air Transport Conference. A commentary. 24 *ETL* 1995, pp.131-147

HAILBRONNER, K. – International Civil Aviation Organization. –
In: Encyclopedia of Public International Law, Amsterdam 1995, vol. II, pp.1070-1074

KIRGIS JR, F.L. – Aviation. –
In: United Nations legal order, edited by O.Schachter and Chr.C.Joyner, Cambridge 1995, vol. II, pp.825-857

KRÄMER, P.M. – Chicago Convention. 50th Anniversary Conference. –
44 *ZLW* 1995, pp.57-60

POONOOSAMY, V. – The ICAO world-wide air transport conference. 23 November-6 December 1994. –
30 *ETL* 1995, pp.115-130

WASSENBERGH, H.A. and MENDES DE LEON, P. – Impressions from the fourth ICAO World-wide Air Transport Conference, Montreal, 23 November-6 December 1994. –
20 *Air and Space Law* 1995, pp.22-31

b. The Assembly

MILDE, M. – ICAO – 27th session of the Assembly. –
15 *Air Law* 1990, pp.54-56

c. The Council

SOCHOR, E. – Le processus décisionnel au sein de l'OACI: qui gouverne dans le conseil directeur? –
20 *1;40*
Études internationales (Laval, Québec) 1989, pp.837-851

ABEYRATNE, R.I.R. – Law making and decision making powers of the ICAO Council – a critical analysis. –
41 *ZLW* 1992, pp.387-394

f. Air Navigation Commission

COSTANTINI, C. – La Commission de Navigation Aérienne de l'OACI. –
44 *RFDAS* 1990, pp.155-167

g. The Legal Committee

MILDE, M. – 27th session of the ICAO Legal Committee. –
15 *Air Law* 1990, pp.162-166

VAN DAM, R.D. – ICAO. I. Legal aspects 10th Air Navigation Conference. II. Date and agenda Legal Committee. –
17 *Air and Space Law* 1992, pp.125-126

VAN DAM, R.D. – 28th session of the Legal Committee. –
17 *Air and Space Law* 1992, pp.224-226

VAN DAM, R. – ICAO/OACI. Legal Committee. –
19 *AASL* 1994, vol. II, pp.654-667

VAN DAM, R. – Legal Committee – 29th session. –
19 *Air and Space Law* 1994, pp.235-237

29.a. European Civil Aviation Conference (ECAC)

HUDSON, E. – Current status of work within ECAC. –
Symposium proceedings Lahore, 11-12 December 1989. ITA Études & documents/Studies & reports 90/2, vol. 19, pp.15-19

TENENBAUM, D. – European liberalization: an ECAC perspective. La libéralisation européenne: le point de vue de la CEAC. –
Symposium proceedings Dubrovnik, 9-10 November 1989. ITA Études & documents/Studies & reports 89/5, vol. 17, pp.15-18

DALLO, E. – The triennial meeting in Strasbourg. –
ITA Magazine, July/August 1991, no. 67, pp.26-27

The ECAC/US Memorandum of Understanding: end of MoU could lead to end of IATA. –
9 *The Avmark Aviation Economist*, April 1992, pp.2-4

MOSS, D. – The ECAC outlook. –
IATA Review, Oct./Nov. 1992, pp.5-7

HAANAPPEL, P. – European regulatory framework in transition. –
IATA Review, March/April 1994, pp.9-11

WEBER, L. – European Civil Aviation Conference. –
In: Encyclopedia of Public Int. Law, Amsterdam 1995, vol. II, pp.137-139

29.b. Latinamerican Civil Aviation Commission (CLAC)

PALACÍN FERNÁNDEZ, J. – La OACI y la CLAC en el desarrollo del transporte aéreo en la región. –
Lima 1994, 562 pp.

29.c. African Civil Aviation Commission (AFCAC)

HENAKU, B.D.K. – Regionalism in international air transport regulation. –
Leiden 1993, xix-187 pp.

29.e. Regional organizations

CHIAVARELLI, E. – Evolución de la función internacional de la OACI ante el reto de las politícas regionales del transporte aéreo. –
RBDAE, May-Sept. 1994, no. 66, pp.33-34

30. International Air Transport Association (IATA)

FELDMAN, J.M. – If it didn't exist someone would have to invent it. –
26 *Air Transport World*, Oct, 1988, pp.48-52

VAN DALEN, A.J.T. – International Air Transport Association. –
In: Management van internationale organisaties, Alphen aan den Rijn 1990, pp.122-133

The ECAC/US Memorandum of Understanding: end of MoU could lead to end of IATA. –
9 *The Avmark Aviation Economist*, April 1992, pp.2-4

BRINDLEY, J. – Airlines and insurance. –
IATA Review, Febr./March 1993, pp.16-17

RECKEWERTH, S. – Zusammenarbeit der Luftverkehrsgesellschaften nach europäischem und US-amerikanischem Recht. –
Diss. Göttingen. Studien zum internationalen Wirtschaftsrecht und Atomenergierecht Bd. 85. Köln 1993, 437 pp.

WEBER, L. – IATA. –
18 *AASL* 1993, vol. I, pp.430-439

CARLUCCI, F. – La cooperazione nel settore dell'aviazione civile: l'International Air Transport Association. –
Trasporti 1994, no. 64, pp.137-153

CLARK, L.S. – IATA and ICAO: the first fifty years. –
19 *AASL* 1994, vol. II, pp.125-134

HAANAPPEL, P.P.C. – Les activités de l'IATA (hiver 1994). –
47 *RFDAS* 1994, pp.139-142

HAANAPPEL, P.P.C. – Les activités de l'IATA: son cinquantenaire. –
47 *RFDAS* 1994, pp.404-406

HAECK, L. – L'Association du Transport aérien international. –
19 *AASL* 1994, vol. II, pp.363-373

WEBER, L. – IATA. –
19 *AASL* 1994, vol. II, pp.674-683

DUERI D., E.M. – La conferencia de IATA sobre responsabilidad civil de las aerolíneas. Washington DC, junio 19-23, 1995. –
5 *AITAL Boletín*, mayo-junio 1995, no. 24, pp.14-19

HAANAPPEL, P.P.C. – IATA tariff co-ordination and competition law. –
20 *Air and Space Law* 1995, pp.82-86

HAILBRONNER, K. – International Air Transport Association. –
In: Encyclopedia of Public International Law, Amsterdam 1995, vol. II, pp.1047-1050

MORALES LEBRERO, J.R. – La conferencia sobre la responsabilidad civil de las compañías aéreas. Washington DC, 19-27 de junio de 1995. –
5 *AITAL Boletín*, julio-agosto 1995, no. 25, pp.22-29

WEBER, L. – Legal activities of the International Air Transport Association (IATA) 1993-1994. –
20 *Air and Space Law* 1995, pp.32-34

31. IFALPA

VAN WIJK, A. – IFALPA Legal Committee meeting, Montreal, Canada, 6-7 September 1989. –
15 *Air Law* 1990, pp.157-161

VAN WIJK, A. – International Federation of Airline Pilots' Associations (IFALPA). 45ième Conférence annuelle, Washington DC, USA, 5-10 avril 1990. Report of the forty-fifth Conference, Washington DC, USA, 5-10 April 1990. –
15 *AASL* 1990, pp.468-477

VAN WIJK, A. – International Federation of Airline Pilots' Associations (IFALPA). –
16 *AASL* 1991, pp.436-444

VAN WIJK, A. – IFALPA Legal Committee meeting, Amstelveen, the Netherlands, 5-6 September 1990. –
16 *Air Law* 1991, pp.34-35

GEUT, H. – IFALPA, Legal Committee meeting. San Diego, 30-31 October 1991. –
17 *Air and Space Law* 1992, pp.166-169

GEUT, H. – IFALPA, Legal Committee meeting, Cape Town, South Africa, 19-20 October 1992. –
18 *Air and Space Law* 1993, pp.96-98

32. The ICC

Politique extérieure de la Communauté Européenne relative aux transports par air: vues de la CCI. –
45 *RFDAS* 1992, pp.203-207

33. Other international organizations

a. The ILA

RINALDI BACCELLI, G. – ILA. Conference 1992. Committee on the legal aspects of air traffic control. –
DPAC 1993, no. 1, pp.79-85

c. University air law institutes

BITTLINGER, H. – 40 Jahre Institut für Luft- und Weltraumrecht. 40 Jahre ZLW. –
40 *ZLW* 1991, pp.235-236

MORISETTE, Y.-M. – 40 Years of teaching and research at the IASL. –
17 *AASL* 1992, vol. I, pp.1-6

BITTLINGER, H. and BENKÖ, M. – Geschichte des Instituts für Luft- und Weltraumrecht der Universität zu Köln. –
Köln 1995, 2nd ed., 66 pp.

BITTLINGER, H. and BENKÖ, M. – History of the Institute of Air and Space Law of the University of Cologne. –
Köln 1995, 2nd ed., 71 pp.

d. Air law associations

GONZÁLEZ DE MANSILLA, A. – La doctrina elaborada por el Instituto iberoamericano de derecho aeronaútico y del espacio y de la aviación comercial y su incidencia en las legislaciones nacionales iberoamericanas e internacionales. –
XIX Jornadas iberoamericanas, Madrid 1989, pp.157-174

MAPELLI, E. – Rosario lírico histórico de las Jornadas iberoamericanas de derecho aeronáutico y del espacio y de la aviación comercial. –
XIX Jornadas iberoamericanas, Madrid 1989, pp.189-195

KRÄMER, P.M. – Deutsche Gesellschaft für Luft- und Raumfahrt (DGLR) und Deutsche Vereinigung für Internationales Recht (DVIR). Gemeinsame Sitzung der Ausschüsse für Luft- und Weltraumrecht, Köln, 8. Mai 1990. –
39 *ZLW* 1990, pp.284-290

KRÄMER, P.M. – Deutsche Gesellschaft für Luft- und Raumfahrt (DGLR) und Deutsche Vereinigung für Internationales Recht (DVIR). Gemeinsame Sitzung der Ausschüsse für Luft- und Weltraumrecht. Köln, 30. April 1991. –
40 *ZLW* 1991, pp.284-287

KRÄMER, P.M. – Deutsche Gesellschaft für Luft- und Raumfahrt (DGLR) und Deutsche Vereinigung für Internationales Recht (DVIR). Gemeinsame Sitzung der Ausschüsse für Luft- und Weltraumrecht. Köln, 19. Mai 1992. –
41 *ZLW* 1992, pp.283-287

La Asociación Latino Americana de Derecho Aeronáutico y Espacial. Resultados y perspectivas en sus primeros treinta y cuatro años. –
Buenos Aires 1994, 96 pp.

Instituto Iberoamericano de Derecho Aeronáutico y del Espacio y de la Aviación Comercial. XXX aniversario. –
[Madrid] 1994, 165 pp.

34. Airports Council International

DUNHGAM, O. – AACI – the voice of the airports. –
IATA Review, June/July 1992, pp.5-8

35. International Union of Aviation Insurers (IUAI)

HEFTI, H. – Jahrestagung der 'International Union of Aviation Insurers'. –
ASDA Bulletin 1990-2, no. 109, pp.31-33

HEFTI, H. – Jahrestagung der 'International Union of Aviation Insurers'. –
ASDA Bulletin 1991-2, no. 111, pp.59-62

HEFTI, H. – Jahrestagung der 'International Union of Aviation Insurers'. –
ASDA Bulletin 1993-1, no. 114, pp.45-47

International Union of Aviation Insurers. Annual General Meeting, Kyoto 1992.
18 *Air and Space Law* 1993, pp.36-37

Jahrestagung der 'International Union of Aviation Insurers'. –
ASDA Bulletin 1993-2, no. 115, pp.39-41

Chapter III.

The administration of national and international aviation

41. Sovereignty in the air

b. Sovereignty in the air

CHOI, W.-S. – A legal study of the boundary between airspace and outer space. –
2 *Korean JAL* 1990, pp.31-63 (in Korean) and pp.64-67 (English summary)

NAVEAU, J. – Droit de l'air et nationalisme historique. –
15 *AASL* 1990, pp.183-189

FARIAS, H. DE CASTRO – Limitações no conceito de soberania sobre o espaço aéreo acima do território dos Estados. –
RBDAE, March-April 1991, no. 53, pp.38-40

MAPELLI, E. – La dificil delimitación del espacio aéreo y el espacio ultraterrestre. –
Cuadernos de Derecho Público (Mérida, Ven.) 1991, no. 10, pp.43-55

PARK, K.-G. – La protection de la souveraineté aérienne. –
Publication de la *RGDIP*, nouvelle série no. 44. Paris 1991, 403 pp.

ABEYRATNE, R.I.R. – The philosophy of air law. –
37 *The American J of Jurisprudence* (Notre Dame IN) 1992, pp.135-144

HAANAPPEL, P. – The transformation of sovereignty in the air. –
20 *Air and Space Law* 1995, pp.311-317

KOTAITE, A. – Is there a lessening of State sovereignty or a real will to cooperate globally? –
20 *Air and Space Law* 1995, pp.288-293

d. Entrance of foreign aircraft in peace-time

MULLANY, N.J. – The legal implications of the Soviet Union's assertions concerning the downing of KAL flight 007. –
19 *Univ. of Western Australia LR* 1989, pp.419-435

KIDO, M. – Ryoku-shinpan no kokusai-ho. [International law of aerial intrusions]. –
Tokyo 1990, vii-400 pp.

PERUCCHI, H.A. – Interceptación de aeronaves civiles. –
Buenos Aires 1990, 353 pp.

BENTZIEN, J.F. – Luftzwischenfälle und kein Ende? –
39 *ZLW* 1990, pp.345-359 and 40 *ZLW* 1991, pp.144-162 and 366-385

HORN, L. – Die Anwendung militärischer Gewalt auf zivile Passagierflugzeuge im Friedensvölkerrecht und ihre Rechtsfolgen. –
Frankfurt 1992, 270 pp.

FROSTELL, C. – Completion of the KE 007 investigation made possible by spirit of cooperation. –
48 *ICAO J*, Nov. 1993, pp.14-18

MILDE, M. – KE 007 – 'Final truth' and consequences. –
42 *ZLW* 1993, pp.357-368

MOYANO BONILLA, C. – El Protocolo de Montreal de 1984 y la violación del espacio aéreo por aeronaves civiles. –
26 *Boletín Mexicano de Derecho Comparado* 1993, pp.155-184

MUKAI, M. – The use of force against civil aircraft: the legal aspects of joint international action. –
19 *AASL* 1994, vol. II, pp.567-587

e. Passage of space vehicles

SCHWARTZ, I. – Durchflug von Weltraumgegenständen durch nationale Lufträume. –
Diss. Köln. Köln 1989, 137 pp.

42. Sovereignty in the air above

c. international canals

GUILLAUME, G. – Détroits internationaux et droit aérien. –
15 *AASL* 1990, pp.75-94

d. the high seas

DE MESTRAL, A. – International civil aviation: law of the sea issues. –
Implementation of the Law of the Sea Convention, Law of the Sea Institute 1989, pp.250-257

HAILBRONNER, K. – Airspace over maritime areas. –
In: Encyclopedia of Public International Law, Amsterdam 1992, vol. I, pp.90-94

BORGES FORTES, B.Y.B. – A Convenção de Montego Bay de 1982 e seus reflexos no espaço aéreo e mar territorial e o Ato Presidencial que altera a extensão do mar territorial brasileiro. –
RBDAE, June-May 1993, no. 63, pp.3-6

GRIEF, N. – Public international law in the airspace over the high seas. –
Utrecht Studies in Air and Space Law, vol. 14. Dordrecht etc. 1994, xxvii-305 pp.

e. the polar regions

ORREGO VICUÑA, F. – Air traffic in Antarctica – the need for a legal regime. –
Antarctic challenge III, Berlin 1988, pp.397-423

PUCEIRO RIPOLL, R. – Air traffic in Antarctica. –
Antarctic challenge III, Berlin 1988, pp.424-444

f. oilrigs – offshore

GOUGH, M.P. – Aerial jurisdiction over safety zones surrounding maritime installations. –
Univ. of Cape Town, Institute of Marine Law, vol. 11. Cape Town 1989, 95 pp.

43. Special zones

a. Prohibited areas

MCILMAIL, T.P. – No-fly zones: the imposition and enforcement of air exclusion regimes over Bosnia and Iraq. –
17 *Loyola of LA Int. & Comp. LJ* 1994, pp.35-83

c. FIR's

CORREIA E SILVA, B. – Some legal aspects of flight information regions. –
Diss. McGill. Montreal 1990

44. National authorities

b. The FAA

ALLEN, G.W. – The FAA's designee program: a system under pressure. –
5 *Air and Space Lawyer* (ABA) 1990, no. 2, pp.3-5

PETKOFF, G.S. – Recent cases and developments in aviation law. XI. FAA regulations. –
56 *JALC* 1990, pp.491-556, at pp.530-542

YODICE, J.S. – An outline of FAA enforcement procedures. –
33 *AOPA Pilot*, Dec. 1990, pp.103-104

CASSADY, J.H. – Aviation safety regulation and enforcement: a survey of recent decisions. –
6 *Air and Space Lawyer* (ABA) 1991, no. 2, pp.12-13

FALLON JR, R.H. – Enforcing aviation safety regulations: the case for a split-enforcement model of agency adjudication. –
4 *Administrative LJ* (Washington DC) 1991, pp.389-431

HANCHETT, K.M. – The role of the Federal Aviation Administration in the control of aviation drug-trafficking. –
56 *JALC* 1991, pp.999-1025

JONES, R.H. – Reconsidering the FAA's dual role. –
33 *The J of ATC* 1991, no. 2, pp.19-21

PANGIA, M.J. – The Civil Penalty Assessment Demonstration Program – a demonstration of conflict. –
6 *ASL* (ABA) 1991, no. 2, pp.113-14

BERMANN, G.A. – The regulatory cooperation with counterpart agencies abroad: the FAA's aircraft certification experience. –
24 *Law and Policy in Int. Business* (Washington DC) 1993, pp.669-781

STROUD, J.C. – Recent developments in aviation case law. VII. Federal Aviation Administration. –
59 *JALC* 1993, pp.1-75, at pp.59-60

ANDERSEN, D.R. – Recent cases and developments in aviation law. X. FAA enforcement/local regulation. –
60 *JALC* 1994, pp.3-178, at pp.165-177

BRACKBILL, A.L. – And what if it catches on fire?: the FAA's ineffectual stance on post-crash fire prevention in airline accidents. –
60 *JALC* 1994, pp.369-407

HARRIS, R. – Liability of government agencies for negligent non-enforcement of Air Navigation Orders. –
43 *ZLW* 1994, pp.199-202

ALIMONTI, F.P. – Death by misinformation? Governmental liability for faulty FAA weather information. –
60 *JALC* 1995, pp.961-996

KENNEY, S.C. – Recent developments in aviation law. X. FAA enforcement/local regulation. –
61 *JALC* 1995, pp.142-155

PARKE, R.B. – FAA/JAA harmonization still off-key. –
77 *Business & Commercial Aviation*, July 1995, pp.60-64

c. The JAA

PILLING, M. – More power for Europe's safety body. –
46 *Interavia Aerospace Review*, Sept. 1991, pp.19-20

ARRIGONI, N. – Joint Aviation Authorities. –
17 *Air and Space Law* 1992, pp.130-132

BERMANN, G.A. – Regulatory cooperation with counterpart agencies abroad: the FAA's aircraft certification experience. –
24 *Law and Policy in Int. Business* (Washington DC) 1993, pp.669-781

FOGLIANI, E. – Il controllo della R.a.i. sulla costruzione di aeromobile e cooperazione internazionale. –
Diritto dei Trasporti 1993, pp.505-

TAVERNA, M. – JAA tackles operations. –
48 *Interavia Aerospace Review*, Jan. 1993, pp.36-38

JÄGER, K. – Ueberblick über die Joint Aviation Authorities (JAA). –
ASDA Bulletin 1995-2, no. 119, pp.48-57

LEARMOUNT, D. – Licence to change. –
148 *Flight International*, 26 July-1 August 1995, pp.25-27

PARKE, R.B. – FAA/JAA harmonization still off-key. –
77 *Business & Commercial Aviation*, July 1995, pp.60-64

d. Customs

STROUD, J.C. – Recent developments in aviation case law. III. Federal Tort Claims Act. C. Customs agents. –
59 *JALC* 1993, pp.1-75, at pp.34-36

45. Licensing of aviation companies

a. General

MALMBERG, L.-G. – Rätt till luftfart. –
Diss. Lund. Acta Societatis Juridicae Lundensis Nr 108. Lund 1990, 494 pp.

BALFOUR, J. – Licensing. –
In: The new legal framework for aviation in the European Community. ICC, Paris 1993, 273 pp., at pp.39-51

EBDON, R.J.C. – Market access. –
In: The new legal framework for aviation in the European Communities. ICC, Paris 1993, 273 pp., at pp.31-37

SLOT, P.J. – Harmonised licensing agreements. –
5 EALA Conference papers 1993, pp.21-36

STEINBERG, R. and BIDINGER, R. – Kapazitätsbeschränkungen in der luftrechtlichen Genehmigung und Planfeststellung? –
Umwelt- und Planungsrecht 1993, pp.281-285

TOSI, J.-P. -Le droit d'établissement est-il effectif en matière de transport aérien? –
Mélanges offerts à André Colomer, Paris 1993, pp.503-516

MÜHLKE, H.-H. – Die Genehmigung deutscher Luftfahrtunternehmen unter Anwendung der entsprechenden Verordnung (EWG) 2407/92. –
44 *ZLW* 1995, pp.147-167

c. Common carrier

ZINCKE DOS REIS, A. – Transporte aéreo. Perspectivas de serviço público. –
XXI Jornadas iberoamericanas, Lisboa 1991, pp.87-100

El transporte aéreo: perspectivas del servicio público

DONATO, M.	El transporte aéreo. Perspectivas de servicio público. Metamorfosis de uno de los elementos del acervo jurídico-político internacional con especial referencia a Latinoamérica, pp.1361-1364
INDRIGO, A.M. and RODRÍGUEZ SENESE, J.R.	El transporte aéreo. Perspectivas de servicio público, pp.1365-1368
MORALES RODRÍGUEZ, J.R.	Transporte aéreo y servicio público, pp.1379-1391
LOUSTAU FERRÁN, F.	El transporte aéreo servicio público y el pasajero, pp.1393-1399
LUJÁN RICCHIUTI, D.	El transporte aéreo. Perspectivas de servicio público, pp.1401-1409
DELUCA, H.O.	El derecho de huelga: alcances. Los servicios esenciales. Situación en la República Argentina, España e Italia, pp.1411-1418

8 *Revista europea DNMA* 1992

46. Freedoms of the air

a. General

PINO ICHAZO, R. – Las libertades del aire. –
La Paz 1988, 259 pp.

JAKUBOVICZ, I. – As libertades do ar. –
RBDAE 1990, no. 51, pp.6-10

KLUČKA, J. – Letecké administratívne a pasažierske spojenia – 'nové slobody vzduchu'? –
73 *Právny Obzor* 1990, pp.719-722

PACHECO, J. DA SILVA – As tendências do transporte aéreo no mundo atual. –
RBDAE 1990, no. 50, pp.6-12

HONG, S.-K. – Freedoms of the air and air cabotage: their legal concept and problems of expanded applications. (in Korean) –
4 *Korean JAL* 1992, pp.37-48

LACHS, M. – Freedoms of the air – The way to outer space. –
In: Essays in honour of Henri A. Wassenbergh, Dordrecht 1992, pp.241-245

YANG, D.J.J. – The new dimension of the fifth freedom – The conflict of interest between Asian and American airlines. –
20 *Air and Space Law* 1995, pp.322-327

47. Scheduled v. non-scheduled air transport

a. General

STADLMEIER, S. – Convergence of scheduled and non-scheduled air services. –
45 *Austrian J of Public and Int. law* 1993, pp.159-193

c. Non-scheduled air transport

LASSANDRO, A. – A European leisure air transport policy for the 1990s. –
ITA Magazine, Jan./Febr. 1990, no. 59, pp.9-11

THAKER, J.S. – The regulation of non-scheduled air services under bilateral air transport agreements. –
Diss. McGill. Montreal 1991

ROSENBAUM, A. – Unscheduled moves. –
29 *Air Transport World*, March 1992, pp.30-32

48. Traffic rights

a. General. GATS

PACHECO, J. DA SILVA – A economia do transporte aéreo e o direito aeronáutico. –
RBDAE 1989, no. 46, pp.31-41

Barbin, M. – Le GATT et le transport aérien. –
44 *RFDAS* 1990, pp.33-37

Creedy, K.B. – Should air transport be in or out GATT? –
45 *Interavia Aerospace Review*, Sept. 1990, pp.716-718

Inter-governmental relations in air transport between EEC and non-EEC countries

Haanappel, P.P.C.	Changes in bilateral air transport agreements between EEC member States and countries outside Europe, pp.135-143
Gherson, R.	Practical implications of '1992' for the renegotiation of bilateral air services agreements with the European Community, pp.145-157
Sundberg, J.W.F.	Inter-governmental relations in air transport between EEC and non-EEC countries – general aspects, pp.159-175
Guldimann, W.	Changing relations between the European Community and international civil aviation organizations, pp.177-187

In: EEC air transport policy and regulation, Deventer 1990

Knibb, D.G. – Opening the skies. –
80 *Air Cargo World*, Nov. 1990, pp.11-14

Lipman, G. – Is GATT just another four-letter word? –
4 *Aerospace World*, Sept. 1990, pp.97-98

Machado, W.C. de Campos – Rodada Uruguai do GATT. –
RBDAE 1990, no. 51, pp.15-21

Nuutinen, H. – GATT: multilateral approach to liberalisation. –
7 *The Avmark Aviation Economist*, August 1990, pp.4-6

Mendes de Leon, P.M.J. – De lege ferenda: explanation and application to public international air law. –
In: Essays in honour of Henri A. Wassenbergh, Dordrecht 1992, pp.53-61

Mifsud, P.V. – The fast track to a modern air transport policy. –
In: Essays in honour of Henri A. Wassenbergh, Dordrecht 1992, pp.63-70

Panelists differ on application of trade concepts to air services. –
47 *ICAO J*, June 1992, pp.12-13

Stockfish, B. – Opening closed skies: the prospects for further liberalization of trade in international air transport services. –
57 *JALC* 1992, pp.599-652

WASSENBERGH, H. – The globalization of international air transport. –
In: The highways of air and outer space, Dordrecht 1992, pp.337-349

WASSENBERGH, H.A. – International air transport: regulatory approaches in the nineties. –
17 *Air and Space Law* 1992, pp.68-77

ABEYRATNE, R.I.R. – The air traffic rights debate – a legal study. –
18 *AASL* 1993, vol. I, pp.3-44

GULDIMANN, W. – A flexible multilateral on traffic rights? –
18 *AASL* 1993, vol. I, pp.125-132

HENAKU, B.D.K. – Regionalism in international air transport regulation. –
Leiden 1993, xix-187 pp.

NAVEAU, J. – Airport slots and traffic rights. –
28 *ETL* 1993, pp.61-68

MICHALSKI, W.; ANDRIEU, M.; STEVENS	New policy approaches to international air transport: main issues and summary, pp.7-19
CONDOM, P.	Airline industry performance: past, present and future, pp.21-44
DOGANIS, R.	The bilateral regime for air transport: current position and future prospects, pp.45-73
LEVINE, M.E.	Scope and limits of multilateral approaches to international air transport, pp.75-89

In: International air transport: the challenges ahead; OECD, Paris 1993, 94 pp.

WARNER, S.M. – Liberalize open skies: foreign investment and cabotage restrictions keep noncitizens in second class. –
43 *American University LR* (Washington DC) 1993, pp.277-323

VON ZEBINSKY, A.M. – The General Agreement on Trade in Services: its implications for air transport. –
18 *AASL* 1993, vol. I, pp.359-405

GERACI, Th.A. – Overflight, landing rights, customs, and clearances. –
37 *Air Force LR* (Washington DC), annual 1994, pp.155-168

GIALLORETO, L. – A retrospective on the reinvention of international civil air transport economic regulation: circa 1994-2004. –
19 *AASL* 1994, vol. II, pp.327-347

GUNTHER, J. – Multilateralism in international air transport – the concept and the quest. –
19 *AASL* 1994, vol. I, pp.259-278

HAANAPPEL, P.P.C. – Multilateralism and economic bloc forming in international air transport. –
19 *AASL* 1994, vol. I, pp.279-320

HAMMARSKJÖLD, K. – Turning science fiction into science fact – challenge to international governance. –
19 *AASL* 1994, vol. I, pp.321-336

HEDLUND, D.C. – Toward open skies: liberalizing trade in international airline services. –
3 *Minnesota J of Global Trade* (Minneapolis MN) 1994, pp.259-299

KRÄMER, P.M. – Kapazitätsengpässe im Luftraum. –
Diss. Köln. Schriften zum Luft- und Weltraumrecht Bd. 12. Köln 1994, xviii-225 pp.

MENDES DE LEON, P. – Air transport as a service under the Chicago Convention: the origins of cabotage. –
19 *AASL* 1994, vol. II, pp.523-565

Multilateral age approaches. –
Airline Business, Febr. 1994, pp.44-45, 47

POONOOSAMY, V. – Developing countries in the wake of aeropolitical changes. –
19 *AASL* 1994, vol. II, pp.589-632

SCHLESS, A.L. – Open skies: loosening the protectionist grip on international civil aviation. –
8 *Emory ILR* (Atlanta GA) 1994, pp.435-471

WASSENBERGH, H.A. – The right of States to participate in air and space transportation activities. –
Valedictory lecture Univ. of Leiden, 2 Sept. 1994. Deventer 1994, 29 pp.

WASSENBERGH, H.A. – World air transport regulatory reform. –
19 *AASL* 1994, vol. I, pp.491-529

ABEYRATNE, R.I.R. – The air traffic rights debate – Where does everyone stand? –
14 *Lloyd's Aviation Law*, 1 Sept. 1995, no. 17, pp.1-8

ABEYRATNE, R.I.R. – The liberalization of air transport services with GATT – Some legal issues. –
Trading Law and Trading Reports, Jan.-Febr. 1995, pp.165-181

ABEYRATNE, R.I.R. – The world-wide air transport conference and air traffic rights. – A commentary. –
30 *ETL* 1995, pp.131-147

EBDON, R. – A consideration of GATS and of its compatibility with the existing regime for air transport. –
20 *Air and Space Law* 1995, pp.71-75

KATZ, R. – The great Gats. –
11 *Airline Business*, Sept. 1995, pp.81-82

LEVINE, M.E. – Government policy and commercial strategy in the 21st century. –
In: The use of airspace and outer space, The Hague 1995, pp.11-21

WASSENBERGH, H.A. – The future of international air transportation law: A philosophy of law and the need for reform of the economic regulation of international air transport in the 21st century. –
20 *AASL* 1995, vol. II, pp.383-415

WASSENBERGH, H.A. – Future regulation to allow multi-national arrangements between air carriers (cross-border alliances), putting an end to air carrier nationalism. –
20 *Air and Space Law* 1995, pp.164-166

WASSENBERGH, H.A. and MENDES DE LEON, P. – Impressions from the fourth ICAO World-wide Air Transport Conference, Montreal, 23 November-6 December 1994. –
20 *Air and Space Law* 1995, pp.22-31

b. Bilaterals

FELDMAN, J.M. – On getting from here to there. –
27 *Air Transport World*, July 1990, pp.26-28

PINO ICHAZO, R. – Los convenios bilaterales en América. –
La Paz 1990, 206 pp.

CREEDY, K.B. – The cost of restrictive bilaterals. –
46 *Interavia Aerospace Review*, March 1991, pp.19-21

GERTLER, J.Z. – ICAO and bilateralism: the case of standard bilateral clauses. –
16 *AASL* 1991, pp.57-78

KRÄMER, P.M. – Conference: Beyond bilaterals. New directions in global air transport negotiations. Brussels, 30-31 May 1991. –
40 *ZLW* 1991, pp.289-293

KIM, J.S. – Bilateralism v. multilateralism in the international aviation order: historical & analytical aspects, and Korean responses. –
4 *Korean JAL* 1992, pp.139-153 (in Korean)

THAKER, J.S. – Model clause on aviation security for bilateral air transport agreements. –
17 *AASL* 1992, vol. II, pp.403-440

TZOU, C.-K. and CHENG, C.-J. – New types of agreements in international air transport. –
In: The highways of air and outer space, Dordrecht 1992, pp.299-310

WEBER, L. – Air transport agreements. –
In: Encyclopedia of Public Int. Law, Amsterdam 1992, vol. I, pp.75-78

HEERE, W.P. – Luchtvaartverdragen – een overbodig kwaad. –
25 *Just* (Utrecht) 1994, pp.132-136

c. The Bermuda type

FELDMAN, J.M. – The bilateral shuffle. –
27 *Air Transport World*, Dec. 1990, pp.26-29, 32

NUUTINEN, H. – US-Europe aviation negotiations: Bermuda 3 – or the end of bilateralism? –
10 *The Avmark Aviation Economist*, May 1993, pp.5-7

POGUE, L.W. – The International Civil Aviation Conference (1944) and its sequel the Anglo-American Bermuda Air Transport Agreement (1946). –
19 *AASL* 1994, vol. I, pp.1-54

SEKIGUCHI, M. – The need to revise the Bermuda capacity principle. The need to update the Chicago Convention. –
In: The use of airspace and outer space, The Hague 1995, pp.23-34

SHANE, J.N. – The Bermuda capacity principle: does it still work? –
In: The use of airspace and outer space, The Hague 1995, pp.35-42

d. Change of gauge

DIERIKX, M.L.J. – Shaping world aviation: Anglo-American civil aviation relations, 1944-1946. Change of gauge. –
57 *JALC* 1992, pp.795-840, at pp.833-834

e. Code sharing

DE GROOT, J.E.C. – Code-sharing. United States' policies and the lessons for Europe. –
19 *Air and Space Law* 1994, pp.62-74

HUMPHREYS, B.K. – The implications of international code sharing. –
1 *J of Air Transport Management* 1994, pp.195-207

VÁSQUEZ ROCHA, E. – Los acuerdos de código compartido – un moderno sistema de cooperación entre líneas aéreas. –
In: La aviación civil internacional, XVIII Jornadas latinoamericanas, Buenos Aires 1994, pp.127-132

WEBER, L. – IATA. II. Implications of code sharing practices. –
19 *AASL* 1994, vol. II, pp.678-679

ABEYRATNE, R.I.R. – Legal and regulatory aspects of computer reservation systems and code sharing agreements in air transport. –
Gif/Yvette (France) 1995

JENNINGS, M. – What's in a code? –
11 *Airline Business*, June 1995, pp.64-65, 67

WEBER, L. – Legal activities of the International Air Transport Association (IATA) 1993-1994. 2. Implications of code sharing practices. –
20 *Air and Space Law* 1995, pp.32-34, at p.33

49. Cabotage

Inter-governmental relations in air transport between EEC and non-EEC countries (cabotage issues).

MENDES DE LEON,P.	Euro-cabotage: a lever for liberalization of international civil aviation, pp.191-198
GERTLER, J.Z.	Towards a new, rational and fair exchange of opportunities for airlines, pp.199-210
SCOCOZZA, M.V.	EEC-US aviation relations and cabotage, pp.211-216

In: EEC air transport policy and regulation, Deventer 1990

SCOCOZZA, M.V. – EEC-US aviation relations and cabotage. –
ITA Magazine, Jan./Febr. 1990, no. 59, pp.3-5

AGNEW, D.P. – US cabotage policy. –
European infrastructure development, London/Hong Kong 1991, pp.14-24

FOLLIOT, M.G. – L'espace aérien européen en formation. –
45 *RFDAS* 1991, pp.11-25

FOLLIOT, M.G. – Une évolution en cours dans les relations aériennes internationales: l'ouverture du droit de cabotage. –
Revue des Affaires Européennes 1991, no. 3, pp.35-44

GORMLEY, M. – Avoiding the cabotage snare. –
68 *Business & Commercial Aviation*, June 1991, pp.86-88

HONG, S.K. – Freedoms of the air and air cabotage: their legal concept and problems of expanded applications. –
4 *Korean JAL* 1992, pp.37-48 (in Korean)

MENDES DE LEON, P. – Le cabotage aérien dans les Communautés Européennes. –
Revue du Marché Commun, juillet/août 1992, no. 360, pp.631-636

MENDES DE LEON, P.M.J. – Cabotage in air transport regulation. –
Diss. Leiden. Dordrecht etc. 1992, xxiii-264 pp.

PLATT, J.R. – The creation of a Community cabotage area in the European Community and its implications for the US bilateral aviation system. –
17 *Air and Space Law* 1992, pp.183-198. See also: 22 *Transportation LJ* 1994, pp.61-85

REED, A. – Not quite cabotage. –
29 *Air Transport World*, Sept. 1992, pp.66-68. 70

VILAO, C. – Air cabotage: current legal issues. –
Diss. McGill. Montreal 1992

WEBER, L. – EEC air transport liberalization and the Chicago Convention. –
17 *AASL* 1992, vol. I, pp.245-262

TRENT, J. – Cabotage rights: the minimal impact of opening up cabotage. –
10 *The Avmark Aviation Economist*, May 1993, pp.7-10

WARNER, S.M. – Liberalize open skies: foreign investment and cabotage restrictions keep noncitizens in second class. –
43 *American University LR* (Washington DC) 1993, pp.277-323

GAU, M.S. – The future Taiwan-Mainland China air links and the cabotage concept under current international air law. –
19 *Air and Space Law* 1994, pp.317-325

KASS, H.E. – Cabotage and control: bringing 1938 U.S. aviation policy into the jet age. –
26 *Case Western Reserve JIL* (Cleveland Ohio) 1994, pp.143-181

MENDES DE LEON, P. – Air transport as a service under the Chicago Convention: the origins of cabotage. –
19 *AASL* 1994, vol. II, pp.523-565

PLATT, J. – European Community cabotage. –
22 *Transportation LJ* 1994, pp.61-85

BLISS, F.A. – Rethinking restrictions on cabotage: moving to free trade in passenger aviation. –
33 *Duquesne LR* (Pittsburgh PA) 1995, pp.283-307

SHIN, H.-K. – Multilateralism and nationality of aircraft and airlines and its implications with respect to Article 7 of the Chicago Convention. –
7 *Korean JAL* 1995, pp.151-173 (in Korean) and pp.174-175 (English summary)

50. Aviation policy

PINO MUÑOZ, J.H. – La política aérea en América Latina. Perspectivas. –
XIX Jornadas iberoamericanas, Madrid 1989, pp.59-63

WASSENBERGH, H.A. – The future of East-West civil aviation in Europe. –
15 *Air Law* 1990, pp.149-156

ALBANO DA SILVEIRA, E. – Política aeronáutica de transporte aéreo. –
RBDAE, July-Dec. 1991, no. 55, pp.8-15

DOBSON, A.P. – Peaceful air warfare. The United States, Britain, and the politics of international aviation. –
Oxford 1991, xiii-307 pp.

DUTHEIL DE LA ROCHÈRE, J. – Le contrôle communautaire des restructurations d'entreprises comme instrument d'une politique de l'aviation civile. –
46 *RFDAS* 1993, pp.389-400

FIORE, D.R. – Expanding international air service opportunities to more U.S. cities. –
22 *Transportation LJ* (Denver CO) 1994, pp.327-364

GULDIMANN, W. – Luftverkehrspolitik. –
42 *ZLW* 1993, pp.369-385 and 43 *ZLW* 1994, pp.11-29

SHELTON, H. – US international aviation policy: the last of Yankee imperialism? –
11 *The Avmark Aviation Economist*, Nov. 1994, pp.2-5

VIDELA ESCALADA, F. and PERUCCHI, H.A. – Les problèmes juridiques et administratifs de la déréglementation du transport aérien. –
19 *AASL* 1994, vol. II, pp.633-649

WASSENBERGH, H.A. – World trends in air transport policies. –
19 *Air and Space Law* 1994, pp.174-178

NAYAR, B.R. – Regimes, power, and international aviation. –
49 *Int. Organization* (Los Angeles CA) 1995, pp.139-170

51. State responsibility – FTCA

STIVEN, J.F. – Recent cases and developments in aviation law. III. Federal Tort Claims Act. –
55 *JALC* 1989, pp.1-121, at pp.29-39

ALLEN, G.W. – The FAA's designee program: a system under pressure. –
5 *Air and Space Lawyer* (ABA) 1990, no. 2, pp.3-5

PETKOFF, G.S. – Recent cases and developments in aviation law. I.B.3 Federal Tort Claims Act. –
56 *JALC* 1990, pp.1-91, at pp.17-20

PETKOFF, G.S. – Recent cases and developments in aviation law. V. Federal Tort Claims Act. –
56 *JALC* 1990, pp.491-556, at pp.492-509

CRAFT JR, R.R. – Aviation liability law developments in 1990. V. Liability of the United States: the Federal Tort Claims Act. –
57 *JALC* 1991, pp.1-172, at pp.125-139

HARRINGTON, M.J. – A review of state, diversity jurisdiction, and FTCA decisions concerning choice of law rules in the United States. –
5 *ASL* (ABA) 1991, no. 4, pp.3-11

HOFFMAN, J.M. and HARRIS, P.S. – Recent developments in aviation case law. III. Federal Tort Claims Act (FTCA). –
58 *JALC* 1992, pp.1-101, at pp.31-38

KIM, D.H. – Liability of governmental bodies in international civil aviation. –
In: The highways of air and outer space, Dordrecht 1992, pp.177-193

KOLCZYNSKI, P.J. a.o. – Aviation and space law: annual survey. III. Governmental liability. –
27 *Tort & Insurance LJ* (ABA) 1992, pp.156-172, at pp.161-165

STROUD, J.C. – Recent developments in aviation case law. III. Federal Tort Claims Act. –
59 *JALC* 1993, pp.1-75, at pp.27-36

SWIECICKI, E.M. – Liability of the Canadian government for the negligent enforcement of aviation safety legislation. –
18 *AASL* 1993, pp.275-313

ABEYRATNE, R.I.R. – General principles of liability of States as providers of space technology in the field of air navigation. –
29 *ETL* 1994, pp.553-569

ANDERSEN, D.R. – Recent cases and developments in aviation law. V. Federal Tort Claims Act (FTCA). –
60 *JALC* 1994, pp.3-178, at pp.106-120

GROSS, R.J. – Special considerations in military flying club litigation. –
59 *JALC* 1994, pp.561-586

HARRIS, R. – Liability of government agencies for negligent non-enforcement of Air Navigation Orders. –
43 *ZLW* 1994, pp.199-202

MINTER, V.L. – Certification of unfit pilots: is the United States flying blind? –
59 *JALC* 1994, pp.763-811

ALIMONTI, F.P. – Death by misinformation? Governmental liability for faulty FAA weather information. –
60 *JALC* 1995, pp.961-996

KENNEY, S.C. – Recent developments in aviation law. V. United States Government tort liability and defenses. –
61 *JALC* 1995, pp.89-99

52. Air rescue services

ABEYRATNE, R.I.R. – Relief flights and humanitarian intervention. Perspectives in international law. –
44 *ZLW* 1995, pp.3-20

53. Extraterritorial consequences of domestic legislation

GULDIMANN, W. – Die extraterritoriale Anwendung nationaler Wettbewerbsgesetze im Luftverkehr. –
ASDA Bulletin 1990-1, no. 108, pp.5-7

Chapter IV. The aviation industry

61. General

KANE, R.M. and VOSE, A.D. – Air transportation.
Dubuque (Iowa) 1987, 9th ed.

ESER, G.O. – Air traffic congestion – Meeting the challenge. –
15 *AASL* 1990, pp.47-57

VELLAS, P. – Tendances du transport aérien 1988-1990. –
Paris 1990, 128 pp.

VELLAS, P. a.o. – La vie de l'avion commercial. –
Paris 1990, 244 pp.

ZUBKOV, V.D. – Major problems associated with the continued development in the air transport field in the 1990ies. –
2 *Korean JAL* 1990, pp.160-188

BENEISH, M.D. – The effect of regulatory changes in the airline industry on shareholders' wealth. –
34 *J of Law & Economics* (Chicago IL) 1991, pp.395-430

ELLETT, E.T. – International and U.S. legal and policy impediments to the growth of the airline industry: time for a change in the world order? –
5 *Air and Space Lawyer* (ABA) 1991, no. 3, pp.3-11

WASSENBERGH, H.A. – The globalization of international air transport. –
ITA Magazine, July/August 1991, no. 67, pp.3-8

DEMPSEY, P.S. – The state of the airline, airport & aviation industries. –
21 *Transportation LJ* 1992, pp.129-213

GOLICH, V.L. – From competition to collaboration: the challenge of commercial-class aircraft manufacturing. –
46 *Int. Organization* (Cambridge MA) 1992, pp.899-934

ICAO. World-wide air transport colloquium, Montreal, 6-10 April 1992. Proceedings. Exploring the future of international air transport regulation. –
ICAO, Montreal 1992

KAWANO, M. – Environment, congestion and the development of international civil aviation. –
In: The highways of air and outer space, Dordrecht 1992, pp.195-201

ŻYLICZ, M. – Towards a new world air transport system. –

19 *Polish YbIL* 1991-1992, pp.241-253

SHEARMAN, P. – Air transport: strategic planning and development. –
London 1992, xii-291 pp.

WASSENBERGH, H. – Principles and practices in air transport regulation. –
ITA, Paris 1993, viii-268 pp.

BOCK, A.K. – How to restore the airline industry to its full upright position: an analysis of the National Commission to ensure a strong, competitive airline industry report. –
59 *JALC* 1994, pp.663-707

DEMPSEY, P.S. – The prospectus for survival and growth in commercial aviation. –
19 *AASL* 1994, vol. II, pp.163-219

GRIGOLI, M. – La rilevazione del profilo economico nella evoluzione normativa e sistematica della materia di navigazione. –
Trasporti 1994, no. 62/63, pp.3-27

MENDES DE LEON, P. – Future trends in civil aviation from a European perspective. –
6 *Korean JAL* 1994, pp.97-107

NUÑEZ SARDÁ, A. – Aviación civil. –
Instituto de Investigaciones Aeroespaciales, Lima 1994, 114 pp.

POONOOSAMY, V. – Developing countries in the wake of aeropolitical changes. –
19 *AASL* 1994, vol. II, pp.589-632

ŻYLICZ, M. – Key problems to the future international air transport regime. –
19 *Air and Space Law* 1994, pp.185-188

DEMPSEY, P.S. – Airlines in turbulence: strategies for survival. –
23 *Transportation LJ* 1995, pp.15-98

MAPELLI, E. – Sobre los problemas del transporte aéreo. –
Empuje-50, marzo 1995, pp.22-23

SMIT, H.G. – Prospects for the aviation industry: has the recession ended? –
In: Aircraft finance, The Hague 1995, pp.53-69

WASSENBERGH, H.A. and MENDES DE LEON, P. – Impressions from the fourth ICAO World-wide Air Transport Conference, Montreal, 23 November-6 December 1944. –
20 *Air and Space Law* 1995, pp.22-31

63. Companies

b. Private or State companies

MUJICA SERELLE, F. – La línea de bandera. Apuntes sobre aviación comercial. –
Lima 1990

RAPP, L. – La privatisation des compagnies aériennes en Europe et ses problèmes. –
44 *RFDAS* 1990, pp.145-154

RAPP, L. and VELLAS, F. – La privatisation des compagnies aériennes en Europe. Airline privatisation in Europe. –
Paris, ITA Studies & reports/Études & documents 92/4, vol. 28, 164 pp., 2nd ed.

c. Competition

FORSYTH, P. – Airlines and airports: privatisation, competition and regulation. –
5 *Fiscal Studies* 1984, pp.61-75

STIVEN, J.F. – Recent cases and developments in aviation law. XI. Antitrust. –
55 *JALC* 1989, pp.1-121, at pp.115-118

ELLIG, J. – Airline competition: a consumer perspective. –
Washington DC 1990, Citizens for a Sound Economy Foundation, 32 pp.

The implications of EEC and North American competition law for air transport

ARGYRIS, N.	EEC competition law rules and their impact on air transport services ancillary thereto, pp.73-80
WINTER, J.A.	EC supervision of State aids in the air transport sector, pp.81-98
RULE, C.F.	Deregulation of US airlines and the continuing role of the antitrust law, pp.99-126
CHANDLER, H.	Note for an address to the McGill Conference, pp.127-131

In: EEC air transport policy and regulation, Deventer 1990

MORINI, A. – Qualche riflessione su di un provvedimento in materia di concorrenza sleale nel trasporto aereo di linea. –
92 *Diritto Marittimo* 1990, pp.1116-

PHILLIPS, A. – Antitrust principles and regulatory needs. –
35 *Antitrust Bulletin* 1990, pp.631-675

Airline deregulation. International experiences

PICKRELL, D.	The regulation and deregulation of US airlines, pp.5-47

PICKRELL, D. — The regulation and deregulation of Australia's domestic airline industry, pp.48-84
BUTTON, K. and SWANN, D. — Aviation policy in Europe, pp.85-123
OUM, T.; STANBURY, W. and TRETHEWAY, M. — Airline deregulation Canada, pp.124-187
London 1991, x-191 pp.

Antitrust lessons from the airline industry
NANNES, J.M. — Introduction
LEVINE, M.J. — Airline deregulation: a perspective, pp.687-694
WILLIG, R.D. - The DoJ experience
HIRST, R.B. — An insider's view
WILSON , B.B. — Railroads, airlines, and the antitrust laws
60 *Antitrust LJ* (Chicago IL) 1991, pp.685-721

British competition policy: an interventionist policy to ensure competition. –
8 *The Avmark Aviation Economist*, Jan, 1991, pp.3-6

DODGSON, J.S.; KATSOULACOS, Y. and PRYKE, R.W.S. – Predatory behaviour in aviation. –
Luxembourg, EC, 1991, [8]-102 pp.

FLEMING, D.K. – Competition in the US airline industry. –
45 *Transportation Quarterly*, April 1991, pp.181-210

GALLACHER, J. – Going for the kill. –
Airline Business, Sept. 1991, pp.88-90

GESELL, L. and FARRIS, M.T. – Antitrust irrelevance in air transportation and the redefining of price discrimination. –
57 *JALC* 1991, pp.173-197

GLISSON, L.M. – Is U.S. domestic airline competition on a flight to oblivion? –
58 *Transportation Practitioners Quarterly* (Washington DC) 1991, pp.217-230

GRAY, F. – European airlines in competition. –
1 *European government: the key to Europe* 1991, pp.72, 76-77

SINCLAIR, R.A. – Airport dominance and state action antitrust immunity for airport operators. –
96 *Dickinson LR* (Carlisle, PA), fall 1991, pp.1-10

DE WIT, J.G. – Luchtvaartliberalisatie: op weg naar een werkzame mededinging? –
Ts voor Vervoerswetenschap 1991, pp.457-468

SONNTAG, I. – La concurrence et le transport aérien en Europe. –
Diss. McGill. Montreal 1991, 141 pp.

BAUER, R. – Tariff coordination – can airlines live without it? –
IATA Review, Oct./Nov. 1992, pp.11-13

CALLOW JR, J.M. – Cut-throat competition in the friendly skies: Alaska Airlines v. United Airlines. –
61 *Univ. of Cincinnati LR* 1992, pp.682-713

FELDMAN, J.M. – A trust buster by any other name ... –
29 *Air Transport World*, March 1992, pp.40-42, 44

GOH, J. – Fear and loathing in the air. –
142 *New LJ* (UK) 1992, pp.822, 868

HARDAWAY, R.M. and DEMPSEY, P.S. – Airlines, airports and antitrust: a proposed strategy for enhanced competition. –
58 *JALC* 1992, pp.455-507

VAN HOUTTE, B. – Competition issues. –
In: External aviation relations of the EC, Deventer/Boston 1992, pp.21-29

JACCHIA, R.A. and MORETTO, M. – Trasporto aereo e normativa communitaria antitrust. –
19 *Giurisprudenza Commerciale* 1992, p.370

KLINGAMAN, R.A. – Predatory pricing and other exclusionary conduct in the airline industry: is antitrust law the solution? –
4 *dePaul Business LJ* (Chicago IL) 1992, pp.281-343

KLM/Northwest – Antitrust immunity the key to link-up. –
10 *The Avmark Aviation Economist*, Dec. 1992, pp.6-7

RAKOWSKI, J.P. and BEJOUR, D. – Structural change and the nature of competition in the deregulated U.S. airline industry. –
59 *Transportation Practitioners J* (Washington DC) 1992, pp.241-262

ROBERTS, M.J. – Congressional proposals to enhance airline competition and passenger protection. –
59 *Transportation Practitioners J* 1992, pp.292-295

ANN, C. – Deregulierung in der Luft, Monopole auf dem Boden. Zur kartellrechtlichen Situation und Problematik der Märkte für Bodendienste auf deutschen Verkehrsflughäfen. –
48 *Betriebsberater* 1993, Beilage 16 zu Heft 23, 12 pp.

COOPER, R.E. – Communication and cooperation among competitors: the case of the airline industry. –
61 *Antitrust LJ* (Chicago IL) 1993, pp.549-557

HENRY, L.-C. – La concurrence et la politique communautaire du transport aérien. –
Diss. Nice. Nice 1993, 800 pp.

VAN HOUTTE, B. – Community competition law in the air transport sector. –
18 *Air and Space Law* 1993, pp.61-70 and 275-287

JOHNSON, M.A. – Removing barriers to market entry in the air transport industry: the application of EC competition rules. –
Legal issues of European integration (Netherl.) 1993, no. 2, pp.1-35

US anti-trust action: the silent conversations issue: farce or tragedy? –
10 *The Avmark Aviation Economist*, May 1993, pp.2-4

WILLIAMS, G. – The airline industry and the impact of deregulation. –
Aldershot 1993, xii-188 pp.

ADKINS, B. – Air transport and E.C. competition law. –
London 1994, xxxiii-330 pp.

BALFOUR, J. – EC Commission: competition rules – a seven year assessment. –
11 *The Avmark Aviation Economist*, Dec. 1994, pp.8-11

BRACHMANN, U. – Die rechtlichen und tatsächlichen Möglichkeiten zugunsten eines effektiven Wettbewerbs trotz überlasteter Flughäfen im europäischen Luftverkehr. –
Diss. Konstanz. Konstanz 1994, xiii-311 pp.

DOGANIS, R.S. – Effectiveness of the competition rules within the Single Market. –
19 *Air and Space Law* 1994, pp.131-137

DUTHEIL DE LA ROCHÈRE, J. – Control of competition as a tool of civil aviation policy. –
6 EALA Conference Papers 1994, pp.39-49

HAANAPPEL, P.P.C. – Les activités de l'IATA (hiver 1994). 3. La coordination tarifaire, l'immunité 'antitrust' aux États-Unis et les exemptions de groupe dans l'Union européenne. –
47 *RFDAS* 1994, pp.139-142, at pp.140-142

VAN HOUTTE, B. – Some comments on the application of the competition rules. –
6 EALA Conference Papers 1994, pp.107-115

HUNT, A. – Assault on the airline industry: private antitrust litigation and the problem of settlement. –
59 *JALC* 1994, pp.983-1021

SHIN, D.-C. – The deregulation of the air transport industry in the world. –
6 *Korean JAL* 1994, pp.217-237 (in Korean)

Always carry a spare. –
Airfinance J, Febr. 1995, no. 170, p.10

HAANAPPEL, P.P.C. – IATA tariff co-ordination and competition law. –
20 *Air and Space Law* 1995, pp.82-86

LOWENFELD, A.F. – Competition in international aviation: the next round. –
In: The use of airspace and outer space, The Hague 1995, pp.175-184

SHIN, D.C. – Competition law. Application to air transport. –
7 *Korean JAL 1995, pp.135-150*

WEBER, L. – Modern trends in the antitrust/competition law governing the aviation industry. –
20 *Air and Space Law* 1995, pp.101-109

WASSENBERGH, H. – 'Open skies'/'Open markets': the limits to competition. –
In: The use of airspace and outer space, The Hague 1995, pp.195-204

d. Collaboration

COSENTINO, E.T. – Fórmulas de colaboración interempresaria en el transporte aéreo. –
La Ley 1988 C, 726-737

GARLAND COMBE, J. – La cooperación en el campo de la aeronáutica civil en América Latina y sus posibilidades en el siglo XXI. –
40 *Revista Peruana de Derecho Internacional* 1988, pp.211-224

GROSBOIS, T. – Liberté du trafic aérien et intégration aérienne. La première tentative de rapprochement entre la KLM et la SABENA (1946-1950). –
6 *Lettre d'information des Historiens de l'Europe contemporaine* (Louvain), déc. 1991, no. 3/4, pp.84-148

RECKEWERTH, S. – Zusammenarbeit der Luftverkehrsgesellschaften nach europäischem und US-amerikanischem Recht. –
Diss. Göttingen. Studien zum int. Wirtschaftsrecht und Atomenergierecht Bd. 85. Köln etc. 1993, 437 pp.

VELLAS, P. – Coopération internationale et stratégies des compagnies aériennes dans une conjoncture de crise. –
46 *RFDAS* 1993, pp.15-32

BALFOUR, J. – Airline mergers and marketing alliances – Legal constraints. –
20 *Air and Space Law* 1995, pp.112-117

WASSENBERGH, H.A. – Future regulation to allow multi-national arrangements between air carriers (cross-border alliances), putting an end to air carrier nationalism. –
20 *Air and Space Law* 1995, pp.164-166

e. Nationality – Multinational companies

UMBRICHT, V.R. – Multilateral mediation. Practical experiences and lessons. 14.2 East African Airways. –
Dordrecht 1989, xiv-429 pp., at pp.167-171

BALFOUR, J. – Flying the flag – The role of nationalism in air transport. –
3 EALA Conference Papers 1990, pp.53-68

WASSENBERGH, H.A. – Euro-deregulation and Asian air carriers' operations after 1992. (The 'nationality' criterion in international civil aviation regulation.) –
Symposium proceedings Lahore, 11-12 December 1989. ITA Études & documents/Studies & reports 90/2, vol. 19, iv-104 pp., at pp.31-40

STEWART JR, J.T. – United States citizenship requirements of the Federal Aviation Act – A misty moor of legalisms or the rampart of protectionism? –
55 *JALC* 1990, pp.685-724

BALFOUR, J. – Factortame: the beginning of the end for nationalism in air transport? –
16 *Air Law* 1991, pp.251-266

PACHECO, J. DA SILVA – A transnacionalização do transporte aéreo. –
RBDAE, May-June 1991, no. 54, pp.14-18

VAN FENEMA, H.P. – Substantial ownership and effective control as airpolitical criteria. –
In: Essays in honour of Henri A. Wassenbergh, Dordrecht etc. 1992, pp.27-41

Ownership trend creates need for new links between States and airlines. –
47 *ICAO J*, June 1992, pp.14-15

DIEDERIKS-VERSCHOOR, I.H.Ph. – International cooperation and its implications for aircraft registration and nationality. –
19 *AASL* 1994, vol. I, pp.145-159

GERTLER, J.S. – Nationality of airlines: is it a Janus with two (or more) faces? –
19 *AASL* 1994, vol. I, pp.211-258

SOAMES, T. and RYAN, A. – Unlicensed premises. –
Airfinance J, April 1994, no. 161, pp.50-51

SHIN, H.-K. – Multilateralism and nationality of aircraft and airlines and its implications with respect to Article 7 of the Chicago Convention. –
7 *Korean JAL* 1995, pp.151-173 (in Korean) and pp.174-175 (English summary)

f. Corporate aviation

HALLIDAY, S.D. – Tax issues arising from the use of non-commercial aircraft. –
46 *Tax Executive* (Washington DC) 1994, pp.190-197

g. Mergers

European airline mergers – implications for passengers and policy options. –
IFAPA, June 1988, 51 + 47 pp.

BALFOUR, J. – Cross-border airline mergers and acquisitions in the EC. –
1 EALA Conference Papers 1989, pp.61-76

O'FARRELL, J.E. – El caso Aerolíneas-SAS; enfoque jurídico. –
La Ley 1989, A 1195-1203

RULE, Ch.F. – Antitrust and airline mergers: a new era. –
57 *Transportation Practitioners J* 1989, pp.62-76

Airline mergers and cooperation in the European Community.

NEVE, E.C.	The British Government's position, pp.11-14
DENZA, E.	The interface between the Chicago Convention and the European Community, pp.15-26
ARGYRIS, N.	Costs and benefits of airline mergers and strategic cooperation – an economic analysis, pp.27-39
RICHARDS, S.	The EC merger regulation, pp.41-48
ELLAND, W.	The Merger Control Regulation and its effect on national merger controls, pp.49-70
SOAMES, T.	Joint ventures and cooperation agreements in the air transport sector, pp.70-98
BURNSIDE, A.J.	A fable of parallel proceedings (or CAT and MAUS go shopping), pp.99-105
EASTON, R.L.	Airline mergers and acquisitions: the U.S. experience and likely trends, pp.107-114
PERKINS, D.	What is best for the airline industry and the passenger, pp.115-122

2 EALA Conference Papers 1991

BROWN, J.D. – Foreign investment in U.S. airlines: what limits should be placed on foreign ownership of U.S. carriers? –
41 *Syracuse LR* (Syracuse NY) 1990, pp.1269-1291

CURTIS, E.F. – Negative impacts of leveraged buyouts on the domestic airline industry. –
44 *Transportation Quarterly*, Oct. 1990, pp.517-532

DEMPSEY, P.S. – Robber barons in the cockpit: the airline industry in turbulent skies. –
18 *Transportation LJ* 1990, pp.133-171

JOCHNER, M.M. – The detrimental effects of hostile takeovers, leveraged buyouts, and excessive debt on the airline industry. –
19 *Transportation LJ* 1990, pp.219-245

MIFSUD, P.V. – The KLM/Northwest Airlines case and general principles applicable to all investments and cooperative arrangements between U.S. air carriers and foreigners. –
15 *Air Law* 1990, pp.36-44

SOAMES, T. – Air transport mergers and joint ventures. –
87 *The Law Society's Gazette* (London) 1990, no. 13, pp.33-36

WILSON, J.B. – The lessons of airline deregulation and the challenge of foreign ownership of U.S. air carriers. –
24 *George Washington JIL and Economics* 1990, pp.103-147

CREEDY, K.B. – Foreign money lures US airlines. –
46 *Interavia Aerospace Review*, Febr. 1991, pp.48-50

DIERIKX, M.L.J. – Bermuda bias: substantial ownership and effective control 45 years on.
16 *Air Law* 1991, pp.118-124

FELDMAN, J.F. – The foreign-ownership dilemma. –
28 *Air Transport World*, Jan. 1991, pp.19-20 and 22-24

Foreign investment in US airlines: DoT relaxes rules; foreigners not impressed. –
8 *The Avmark Aviation Economist*, Febr. 1991, pp.4-5

GALLACHER, J. – Controlling interests. –
Airline Business, March 1991, pp.22-24

GJERSET, J.E. – Crippling United States airlines: archaic interpretations of the Federal Aviation Act's restriction on foreign capital investments. –
7 *The American University JIL and Policy* (Washington DC) 1991, pp.173-196

GRAHAM, B.L. – Navigating the mists of metaphor: an examination of the doctrine of piercing the corporate veil. –
56 *JALC* 1991, pp.1135-1183

JENNINGS, M. – A foot in the door. –
Airline Business, May 1991, pp.43-44

VON KISTOWSKY, Th. – Ausländische Mehrheitsbeteiligung an einem deutschen Luftfahrtunternehmen. –
40 *ZLW* 1991, pp.132-136

ROBERTS, M.J. – Foreign investment in US airlines: change in the wings? –
58 *Transportation Practitioners J* 1991, pp.251-253

WALLS, J. – Airline mergers, acquisitions and bankruptcies: will the collective bargaining agreement survive? –
56 *JALC* 1991, pp.847-893

WASSENBERGH, H.A. – 1990/91, the airline industry in distress? –
16 *Air Law* 1991, pp.82-92

WILSON, J.B. – The new limits on foreign investment in U.S. air carriers: the continuing challenge of foreign ownership. –
24 *George Washington JIL and Economics* 1991, pp.713-721

Merger control in the air transport sector.

RUPPELT, H.-J.	Natinonal merger control for international airlines, pp.43-50
STOFFREGEN, K.	Application of the EC Merger Regulation in the air transport sector, pp.51-62
MONTAG, F.	Problems of the application of the EC Merger Regulation to airlines, pp.63-74

4 EALA Conference Papers 1992

LANGE, D.G. and WEITBRECHT, A. – European merger control in the air transport industry. –
41 *ZLW* 1992, pp.41-50

MIFSUD, P.V. – Airline concentrations and cross border arrangements. –
In: External aviation relations of the EC, Deventer 1992, pp.11-20

PICKIN, K. – An identity crisis. –
Airline Business, May 1992, pp.32-35

TRINDER, R.B. – A perspective on the US approach to international civil aviation in the Pacific. –
In: The highways of air and outer space, 1992, pp.19-32

US rules on foreign investment: why delay the inevitable. –
10 *The Avmark Aviation Economist*, July/Aug. 1992, pp.9-11

WOOD, B. – The ownership of international airlines: a European view. –
In: The highways of air and outer space, 1992, pp.311-327

ARLINGTON, D.T. – Liberalization of restrictions on foreign ownership in U.S. air carriers: the United States must take the first step in aviation globalization. –
59 *JALC* 1993, pp.133-192

DUTHEIL DE LA ROCHÈRE, J. – Le contrôle communautaire des restructurations d'entreprises comme instrument d'une politique de l'aviation civile. –
46 *RFDAS* 1993, pp.389-400

FLANAGAN, A. and MARCUS, M. – Airline alliances: the secrets of a successful liaison. –
10 *The Avmark Aviation Economist* 1993, no. 1, pp.20-23

SHIN, D.-C. – Foreign ownership of airlines. –
5 *Korean JAL* 1993, pp.207-262

VELLAS, P. – Coopération internationale et stratégies des compagnies aériennes dans une conjoncture de crise. –
46 *RFDAS* 1993, pp.15-32

WARNER, S.M. – Liberalize open skies: foreign investment and cabotage restrictions keep noncitizens in second class. –
43 *American University LR* (Washington DC) 1993, pp.277-323

ALEXANDRAKIS, C.G. – Foreign investment in U.S. airlines: restrictive law is ripe for change. –
4 *Business LJ* (Miami), fall 1994, pp.71-92

DONATO, A.M. and RAVINA, A. – Propiedad sustancial y control efectivo de las empresas de transporte aéreo y marítimo internacionales. –
RBDAE, May-Sept. 1994, no. 66, pp.35-44; XIII Jornadas latinoamericanas, Buenos Aires 1994, pp.101-117

GLISSON, L.M. and JONES, M.K. – Analyzing the U.S. domestic airline industry, part 3: A model for airline mergers. –
61 *Transportation Practitioners J* 1994, pp.307-319

GRANT, Th.D. – Foreign takeovers of United States airlines: free trade process, problems, and progress. –
31 *Harvard J on Legislation*, winter 1994, pp.63-151

HARPER, G.R. – Cambios en la ley estadounidense: inversión extranjera en líneas aéreas de dominio extranjero. –
Aviación comercial, turismo, etc.; Buenos Aires 1994, pp.215-217

KASS, H.E. – Cabotage and control: bringing U.S. aviation policy into the jet age. –
26 *Case Western Reserve JIL* (Cleveland Ohio) 1994, pp.143-181

VITALE, R. – US ownership rules hang in the air on the issue of control. – *Airfinance J*, Febr. 1994, no. 159, pp.38-40

BALFOUR, J. – Airline mergers and marketing alliances – Legal constraints. – 20 *Air and Space Law* 1995, pp.112-117

MIFSUD, P.V. – Foreign investment in air transport in the emerging multilateral era. –
In: The use of airspace and outer space, The Hague 1995, pp.161-166

64. Economic problems

a. Financing

BRADLEY, F.W. – The impact of air transport liberalization on aircraft financing. Les effets de la libéralisation du transport aérien sur le financement des flottes. –
Symposium proceedings Dubrovnik, 9-10 November 1989. ITA Études & documents/Studies & reports 89/5, vol. 17, iv-183 pp., at pp.169-176

BUTLER, W. – Legal considerations to aircraft financing in the USSR. – *Airfinance J*, April 1990, no. 113, pp.40-41

Legal aspects of air finance.

THORNE, P. and FARRELL, P.	Salvage or survival when an airline crashes, pp.2-7
COLEMAN, C.P.	Aircraft hull, liability and repossession insurance: issues for the financier/lessor, pp.8-12
O'ROURKE, S. and MERRYWEATHER, P.	Tailwinds – Australian aircraft financing takes a new direction, pp.14-17
THAINE, C.	Asset value support in aircraft financing: the role of manufacturers and others, pp.18-25
GAUNT, I.	Aircraft operating leases – meeting the needs of the parties involved, pp.26-29
PEASE, A. and PETERSON, J.	Leases – protecting the airline lessee, pp.30-32
STRIVENS, R. and WEIGHTMAN, E.	Liberalisation of air transport within the European Community, pp.33-36

Airfinance J, supplement, Febr. 1990, no. 111

VAN BAKELEN, F.A. – De financiering van luchtvaartuigen en het NBW. – In: 85 jaar Nederlandse Vereniging van Hypotheekbanken, Deventer 1991, pp.207-238

BUNKER, D.D. – Aircraft financing and drugs. –
16 *AASL* 1991, pp.31-40

DIEDERIKS-VERSCHOOR, I.H.Ph. – Aircraft financing and international law. –

In: 85 jaar Nederlandse Vereniging van Hypotheekbanken, Deventer 1991, pp.181-205

DOGANIS, R. – Flying off course: the economics of international airlines. –
London 1991, 2nd ed., xv-362 pp.; 1st ed. 1985

FELDMAN, M.K. – Legal opinions in secured aircraft financing transactions. –
6 *Banking & Finance LR* 1991, pp.127-149

JENKS, C. – Asset-based finance: some new factors. –
IATA Review 1991, no. 1, pp.8-13

LIU, Y. – Legal issues on aircraft finance in China. –
44 *RFDAS* 1991, pp.2-8

RICE, M.D. – Current issues in aircraft finance. –
56 *JALC* 1991, pp.1027-1092

ROSALES, R.K. – Legal aspects of asset based aircraft financing. –
Diss. McGill. Montreal 1991

VERCHÈRE, I. – Closing the Hong Kong window. –
46 *Interavia Aerospace Review* 1991, pp.43-45

VIDAL, E. and WARD, S. – Preventive medicine for pre-delivery finance. –
Airfinance J, March 1991, no. 124, pp.40-41

Aircraft financing: recent developments and prospects. –
17 *Air and Space Law* 1992, special issue, pp.42-124

Financing air transport developments poses serious worldwide challenge. –
47 *ICAO J*, June 1992, pp.16-20

GITTLEMAND, R.M. and ROXAN, I. – Securitization financing in the European aircraft industry. –
Legal aspects of aviation finance, supplement of *Airfinance J*, Sept. 1992, pp.2-6

HOLLOWAY, St. – Aircraft acquisition finance. –
London 1992, xvii-358 pp.

ZACHARY, Z.M. and GREENWALD, J. – Aircraft financing with an FSC: a tax analysis. –
Airfinance J, March 1992, no. 136, pp.38-41

Aids for the aviation financier.
Aircraft detention: the draconian rights of airport operators and Eurocontrol, pp.1-17.
A primer for bankers and lawyers on maintenance parlance, pp.19-59.

The essential features of residual value support, pp.61-80.
Can one be serious about secured financing of spare engines?, pp.82-99.
Political risk: a necessary cover?, pp.101-126.
Wilde Sapte, London 1993, 126 pp.

Seminar : Topics of aircraft finance.

CRANS, B.J.H.	The third EC aviation package: its impact on the leasing industry, 18 pp.
JACOBSON, M.D.	Lessons learned from recent airline bankruptcies in the United States, 10 pp.
THAINE, C.	What to expect from manufacturers' residual value support, 13 pp.
BRANDON, D.R.	Rule 144A and aircraft financing, 21 pp.

De Brauw Blackstone Westbroek, Amsterdam 1993

GARABGA, T. – Air finance for Africa, legal issues. The airline perspective. – 20 *Air and Space Law* 1995, pp.18-21

JIANDUAN, W. – Investment in China civil air transportation. Some legal aspects. –
20 *Air and Space Law* 1995, pp.201-205

WOOL, J. – Unidroit's proposed convention on security interests in, and leasing of, mobile equipment: recommendations of an aviation working group. – *Airfinance J*, July-Aug. 1995, no. 175, pp.32-35

CRANS, B.J.H., ed. – Aircraft finance. Recent developments and prospects.

CRANS, B.J.H.	Selected pitfalls and booby-traps in aircraft finance, pp.1-21
WALTON, S.M.	Review of important funding sources, pp.23-31
GÜNTHER, K. and ERBACHER, P.	Aspects of aircraft leasing in Germany, pp.33-51
SMIT, H.G.	Prospects for the aviation industry: has the recession ended, pp.53-69
VAN MIERLO, T.I.M.	Security rights in aircraft and engines under Netherlands law, pp.71-82
FALCÓN RAVELO, J.F.	An overview on aircraft leasing in Spain, pp.83-94
HOFLAND, D.A.	Recent developments in tax law, pp.95-101
EKBOM, P.G.	Legal status of aircraft finance in Sweden, pp.103-108
LE GALL, J.-P. and REEB, S.	Highlighting various tax and security law aspects of aircraft financing – France, pp.109-115
CRANS, B.J.H.	The third EC aviation package: its impact on the leasing industry, pp.117-125
GORIS, W.	Security rights in aircraft under Belgian law, pp.127-138
CLUMPKENS, R.	The role of the notary under the law of the Netherlands with respect to the transfer of title and encumbrance of registered aircraft, pp.139-147

PIJNACKER HORDIJK, E.H., Relevant EC-law topics, pp.149-154

The Hague 1995, viii-154 pp.

b. Subsidies

DEHOUSSE, F. – Le conflit entre les États-Unis et la Communauté dans le secteur aéronautique: un révélateur des paradoxes du GATT. –
25 *Revue belge de droit international* 1992, pp.536-564

EC-US agreement. A deal at last – but no fanfare? –
10 *The Avmark Aviation Economist*, May 1992, pp.4-6

State aids in the air transport sector.
MANNIN, C. Should the GATT Civil Aircraft Code be revised?, pp.95-116
DUTHEIL de la ROCHÈRE, J. Commission policy towards national aid to airlines, pp.117-127
4 EALA Conference Papers 1992

MANNER, J.A. – How to avoid Airbus II: a primer for domestic industry. –
23 *California Western ILJ* 1992, pp.139-176

BALFOUR, J. – The control of State aids in the air transport sector. –
18 *Air and Space Law* 1993, pp.199-204

BANGMA, K.L. and BONESCHANSKER, E. – Steunverlening aan de luchtvaart. –
25 *Openbare Uitgaven* 1993, pp.143-152

LEVICK, M.J. – The production of civil aircraft: a compromise of two world giants. –
21 *Transportation LJ* 1993, pp.433-467

COSENTINO, E.T. – Las ayudas estatales a las empresas de transporte aéreo en la Unión europea. –
XXIV Jornadas iberoamericanas, Salamanca 1994, pp.175-183

State aids to airlines.
SLOT, P.J. EC State aids: a general introduction, pp.15-23
HILBRECHT, H. The DG VII perspective, pp.25-32
SOAMES, T. and RYAN, A. The practical application of the State aid rules to the air transport sector, pp.33-73
FLYNN, J. Is air transport special?, pp.75-84
ALLEN, Chr. Contribution, pp.85-87
NAVEAU, J. Contribution, pp.89-91
DAGTOGLOU, P.D. Closing remarks, pp.93-94
7 EALA Conference Papers 1994, 94 pp.

BALFOUR, J. – The EC Commission's policy on State aid for airline restructuring: is the bonfire alight? –
20 *Air and Space Law* 1995, pp.60-67

CRANS, B.J.H. – EC aviation scene. –
20 *Air and Space Law* 1995, pp.206-213, at pp.208-212

KOHL, N.E.M. – Herziene richtsnoeren in de luchtvaartsector. –
1 *Nederlands Ts voor Europees Recht* 1995, pp.11-13

SOAMES, T. and RYAN, A. – State aid to air transport. –
16 *European Competition LR* (UK) 1995, pp.290-309

SPRADLIN, S. – The aircraft subsidies dispute in the GATT's Uruguay round. –
60 *JALC* 1995, pp.1191-1218

c. Fiscal problems. Taxes. Customs

FRISQUE, M. – The impact of the EC 1992 fiscal harmonization on air transport in Europe. Les conséquences, pour le transport aérien européen, de l'harmonisation fiscale dans la Communauté en 1992. –
Symposium proceedings Dubrovnik 1989, ITA Études & documents/Studies & reports 89/5, vol. 17, pp.129-147

RATLIFF, A.G. – Congress deals aviation a bad hand: time to learn how to play the ace. –
55 *JALC* 1990, pp.1159-1215

ABEYRATNE, R.I.R. – Taxation in the field of international air transport – Legal aspects. –
16 *Air Law* 1991, pp.106-117

BOIDMAN, N. – Proposed exemption for U.S. and other foreign aircraft lessors. –
21 *Tax Management IJ* (Washington DC) 1992, pp.88-91

LANG, D. – Taxation of international aviation: a Canadian perspective. –
40 *Canadian Tax J* 1992, pp.881-901

MANDEL, R.L. – Jet fuel taxation: current state approach and the need for Congressional limitations. –
58 *JALC* 1992, pp.103-218

GOLDING, J. – Cleared for take-off: various tax implications concerning flying and the operation of aircraft. –
132 *Taxation* (UK), 9.2.1993, pp.216-218

ABEYRATNE, R.I.R. – Taxation consequences attendant upon privileged travel of airline employees. A potential problem. –
13 *Lloyd's Aviation Law*, 15 Febr. 1994, no. 4, pp.2-6

DONSIMONI, P. – TVA intracommunautaire. Acquisition des aéronefs neufs et location d'aéronefs en provenance d'un autre État membre de l'Union européenne par des assujettis établis en France. –
47 *RFDAS* 1994, pp.127-138

GRIESSHAMMER, E.R. – Ausländische Fluggesellschaften: Mehrwertsteuerpflichtig! –
ASDA Bulletin 1994-2, no. 117, pp.5-10

HALLIDAY, St.D. – Tax issues arising from the use of non-commercial aircraft. –
46 *Tax Executive* (Washington DC) 1994, pp.190-197

ABEYRATNE, R.I.R. – Recent developments in the taxation of air transport – The ICAO-IATA symbiosis. –
20 *Air and Space Law* 1995, pp.48-59

HEILBRONN, G.N. and BONSALL, C.J. – Aeronautical charges: the need for a more specific legislative context. –
20 *Air and Space Law* 1995, pp.125-136

d. Tariffs

DE CONINCK, F. – De mededingingsregels van het E.E.G.-verdrag en de Europese luchtvaarttarieven. –
53 *Rechtskundig Weekblad* (Belgium) 1990, pp.1073-1086

OTT, J. – Justice Dept investigates carriers' pricing practices. –
133 *AW&ST*, 16 July 1990, pp.18-20

KRÄMER, P.M. – Tarife im europäischen Luftlinienflugverkehr. –
2 *Europäische Zs für Wirtschaftsrecht* 1991, pp.15-19

BAUER, R. – Tariff coordination – can airlines live without it? –
IATA Review, Oct./Nov. 1992, pp.11-13

The ECAC/US Memorandum of Understanding: end of MoU could lead to end of IATA. –
9 *The Avmark Aviation Economist*, April 1992, pp.2-4

HAANAPPEL, P.P.C. – Tariff coordination: a bilateral or multilateral framework? –
In: External aviation relations of the EC, Deventer 1992, pp.31-38

MARLOWE, A.N. – Something special in the fares? Regulating commercial airlines advertising. –
58 *JALC* 1992, pp.605-642

ACHTNICH, H. – Neues Flugpreisrecht: Anwendungsvorrang der EWG-VO 2409/92 vor LuftVG, RabG, Zugabe VO. –
39 *Wettbewerb in Recht und Praxis* 1993, pp.731-736

HAANAPPEL, P.P.C. – Fares. –
5 EALA Conference Papers 1993, pp.37-42

HAANAPPEL, P.P.C. – Pricing. –
In: The new legal framework for aviation in the European Community; ICC, Paris 1993, pp.53-62

STUYCK, J. – An aspect of fair competition: pricing. –
5 EALA Conference Papers 1993, pp.57-73

US anti-trust action: the silent conversations issue: farce or tragedy? –
10 *The Avmark Aviation Economist*, May 1993, pp.2-4

COSENTINO, E.T. – Nuevos desarrollos normativos de la Unión europea en materia de transporte aéreo. La cuestión tarifaria. –
XXIV Jornadas iberoamericanas, Salamanca 1994, pp.407-414

FRUEHE, C. – Tariff realities in a liberalized single European market. –
6 EALA Conference Papers 1994, pp.117-120

HAANAPPEL, P.P.C. – Les activités de l'IATA (hiver 1994). La coordination tarifaire, l'immunité 'antitrust' aux États-Unis et les exemptions de groupe dans l'Union européenne. –
47 *RFDAS* 1994, pp.139-142, at pp.140-142

SOAMES, T. and RYAN, A. – Predatory pricing in air transport. –
15 *European Competition LR* (UK) 1994, pp.151-164

CLOUATRE, M.T. – The legacy of Continental Airlines v. American Airlines: a re-evaluation of predatory pricing theory in the airline industry. –
60 *JALC* 1995, pp.869-915

HAANAPPEL, P.P.C. – IATA tariff co-ordination and competition law. –
20 *Air and Space Law* 1995, pp.82-86

e. Fuel

MANDEL, R.L. – Jet fuel taxation: current state approach and the need for Congressional limitations. –
58 *JALC* 1992, pp.103-218

f. Bankruptcy. Insolvency

GIDDENS, J.W. and SCHICK, S.E. – Section 1110 of the Bankruptcy Code: time for refueling? –

64 *American Bankruptcy LJ* (Lexington KY) 1990, pp.109-132

PAPAIOANNOU, A. – The duty to bargain and rejection of collective agreements under Section 1113 by a bankrupt airline: trying to reconcile R.L.A. with Bankruptcy Code. –
18 *Transportation LJ* 1990, pp.219-253

BLOOMER JR, H.F. – Bankruptcy protection for aircraft financiers. –
10 *Int. Financial LR* (UK) 1991, no. 4, pp.20-24

CARVELL, J. – Continental causes havoc with Chapter 11. –
Airfinance J, March 1991, no. 124, pp.42-43

FELDMAN, J. – Chapter 11: balancing the scales of justice. –
Airfinance J, May 1991, no. 126, pp.36-39

HALLAM, R. – Keeping out of bankruptcy courts. –
Legal aspects of aircraft finance, supplement of *Airfinance J*, May 1991, no. 126, pp.17-19

MORGAN, E.L. – Section 1110: the impact of the Pan Am and Continental bankruptcies. –
Legal aspects of aircraft finance, supplement of *Airfinance J*, May 1991, no. 126, pp.3-7

RICE, M.D. – Current issues in aircraft finance. Bankruptcy. –
56 *JALC* 1991, pp.1027-1092, at pp.1058-1092

WALLS, J. – Airline mergers, acquisitions and bankruptcies: will the collective bargaining agreement survive? –
56 *JALC* 1991, pp.847-893

HOFFMAN, J.M. and HARRIS, Ph.S. – Recent developments in aviation case law. XIV.B. Bankruptcy. –
58 *JALC* 1992, pp.1-101, at pp.97-98

MILLER, B.F. – The airline industry: labor relations in the era of deregulation, mergers, bankruptcies, and layoffs. –
43 *Labor LJ* (Chiacgo IL) 1992, pp.388-394

SABINO, A.M. – Flying the unfriendly skies: a year of reorganizing aircraft lessors, and the Bankruptcy Code. –
57 *JALC* 1992, pp.841-903

SCHICK, S.E. – When airlines crash: Section 1110 revisited. –
48 *Business Lawyer* (ABA), Nov. 1992, pp.277-314

The bankruptcy virus in the US airline industry: causes and cures. –
Washington DC, George Washington University, April 1993

Financial crisis in the aviation industry.

FARRELL, P.	United Kingdom, pp.153-167
JACOBSON, M.D. and THOMPSON, M.J.	United States, pp.168-182
LE GALL, J.-P. and REEB, S.	France, pp.183-191
GÜNTHER, K.	Germany, pp.192-198

18 *Air and Space Law* 1993

JACOBSON, M.D. – Lessons learned from recent airline bankruptcies in the United States. –
Topics of aircraft finance, Amsterdam 1993, 10 pp.

Repossession of aircraft and insolvency in EC countries. An industry report edited by Sinclair Roche & Temperley. –
Lloyd's of London Press 1993, xii-162 pp.

SABINO, A.M. – Protecting airport operators' terminal and gate leases from airline bankruptcies. –
2 *J of Bankruptcy Law and Practice* (Boston MA), March/April 1993, pp.75-78

STROUD, J.C. – Recent developments in aviation case law. IX.A. Bankruptcy. –
59 *JALC* 1993, pp.1-75, at pp.64-66

ANDERSEN, D.R. – Recent cases and developments in aviation law. IV.D. Bankruptcy. –
60 *JALC* 1994, pp.3-178, at pp.99-101

HOFF-PATRINOS, K. – The last chapter. –
Airfinance J, Dec. 1994, no. 168, pp.34-35

SCHROEDER, J.L. and CARLSON, D.G. – Airplanes in bankruptcy. –
3 *J of Bankruptcy Law and Practice* (Boston MA) 1994, pp.203-264

65. Aviation and the European Union

CASTEJÓN, B. – La desreglementación en los Estados Unidos. El movimiento hacia la liberalización en Europa. Sus consecuencias en la región iberoamericana en relación con el transporte aéreo. –
XVII Jornadas iberoamericanas, Rio de Janeiro 1987, pp.26-33

COSENTINO, E.T. and CASTELLI, L. – Enfoques sobre la 'deregulación' en la Comunidad Económica Europea y América Latina. –
XVII Jornadas iberoamericanas, Rio de Janeiro 1987, pp.54-59

UTTON, M. – The likely impact of deregulation on industrial structures and competition in the Community. –
Commission of the European Communities 1987, CB-87-251-EN-C

VÁSQUEZ ROCHA, E. – La desreglementación en los Estados Unidos. El movimiento hacia la liberalización en Europa. –
XVII Jornadas iberoamericanas, Rio de Janeiro 1987, pp.46-53

BASEDOW, J. – National authorities in European airline competition law. –
9 *European Competition LR* (YK) 1988, pp.342-355

La Comunità Economica Europea e la struttura del trasporto aereo italiano. –
12 *DPAC* 1988, pp.319-385

DAGTOGLOU, P. – EEC transport policy – a survey with special reference to air transport.
In: J.Schwarze and H.G.Schermers, eds. – Structure and dimensions of European Community policy, Baden-Baden 1988, pp.127-138

KARK, A. – Prospects for a liberalization of the European air transport industry: a study of commercial air transport policy for the European Community. –
8 *Northrop Univ. LJ of Aerospace, Business & Taxation* (Inglewood CA) 1988, pp.1-34

La libéralisation du transport dans la CEE: le point de vue des pays voisins. Air transport liberalization in the EEC: the viewpoint of neighbouring countries.

SØRENSEN, F.	The achievement of the Community dimension in air transport, pp.79-90
RABEN, H.	Air transport liberalisation in the EEC: present and future characteristics, pp.91-94
RIVOAL, C.	The relations between the EC and non-EC airlines in Europe

Symposium proceedings Marrakech. ITA Études & documents/Studies & reports 88/4, vol. 11

WHITELEGG, J. – Transport policy in the EEC. –
London 1988, xvi-233 pp.

ANDRÉU MUSTÉ, N. – La nueva política aérea de la CEE y su relación con Iberoamérica. –
XIX Jornadas iberoamericanas, Madrid 1989, pp.23-28

BAUZÁ ARAÚJO, A. – La nueva política aérea en la Comunidad Económica Europea y su relación con Iberoamérica. –
XIX Jornadas iberoamericanas, Madrid 1989, pp.29-34

BUSTI, S. – La nuova disciplina della concorrenza nel trasporto aereo intracomunitario. –
28 *Diritto Comunitario e degli Scambi Internazionali* 1989, pp.685-694

DAGTOGLOU, P. – Air transport after the Nouvelles Frontières judgment. – In: Liber amicorum Pierre Pescatore, Baden-Baden 1987, pp.115-137. Slot and Dagtoglou, Toward a Community air transport policy, Deventer 1989, pp.115-138

DIEDERIKS-VERSCHOOR, I.H.Ph. – Spotlight on liberalisation. –
Nomos (Saloniki) 1989, pp.293-305

Euro-deregulation as seen by Asia.

VINCENT, D.	The foreign policy of the EC, pp.5-13
WASSENBERGH, H.A.	Euro-deregulation and Asian air carriers' operations after 1992, pp.31-40
RIVOAL, C.	An essential point of strategy for European Community airlines: an appropriate definition of the external Community policy, pp.41-46

Symposium proceedings Lahore 1989, ITA Études & documents/Studies & reports 90/2, vol. 19, iv-104 pp.

Air transport and the European Community. Recent developments.

BRITTAN, Sir Leon	Civil aviation and 1992, pp.11-18
LENZ, C.O.	The contribution of the Court of Justice to the common air transport policy, pp.19-34
CLOSE, G.L.	Case 66/86 – Ahmed Saeed, pp.35-46
HALL, D.F.	Ahmed Saeed and the legal situation now, pp.47-54
STUYCK, J.	Analysis of Ahmed Saeed and the legal situation now, pp.55-60
BALFOUR, J.M.	Cross-border airline mergers and acquisitions in the EC, pp.61-76
LANG, J.T.	European Community competition law and air transport, pp.77-99
STANBROOK, C. and ADAMANTOPOULOS, K.	Comments on the proposed second Air Transport Liberalisation Package, pp.101-115
SLOT, P.J.	European Community competition law. Air transport, pp.117-123

1 EALA Conference Papers 1990

FOSMAN, J. – Nuevas directivas del Mercado Común Europeo respecto a paquetes turísticos. ¿Lesionan el sistema de Varsovia? –
XIX Jornadas iberoamericanas, Madrid 1989, pp.35-40

FRIEND, M. – Competition in the air transport sector. –
14 *European LR* 1989, pp.424-428

GIARDINA, A. – La disciplina comunitaria del trasporto aereo: gli sviluppi a seguito della sentenza nel caso Saeed. –
3 *Diritto del Commercio Internazionale* 1989, pp.77-

KARK, A. – Prospects for a liberalization of the European air transport industry – A study of commercial air transport policy for the European Community. –

10 *European Competition LR* 1989, pp.377-406

PINA, D. – Os transportes aéreos face ao direito comunitario da concorrencia. –
XIX Jornadas iberoamericanas, Madrid 1989, pp.55-58

PIZZINO, A. – Verso la seconda fase di liberalizzazione del trasporto aereo comunitario: le proposte della Commissione CEE. –
3 *Diritto del Commercio Internazionale* 1989, pp.703-

I riflessi sul trasporto aereo del processo di liberalizzazione del Mercato Comune Europeo: opportunità e prospettive.
I. Profili di carattere generale di diritto comunitario in relazione ai trasporti, pp.9-68

SAULLE, M.R.	L'unificazione delle legislazioni in materia di servizi, pp.11-16
GIARDINA, A.	Attuali prospettive della liberalizzazione, pp.19-26
ROMANELLI, G.	Recenti orientamenti giurisprudenziali della Corte di Giustizia in materia di trasporto aereo, pp.27-31
GAETANI D'ARAGONA, G.	L'Atto Unico Europeo ed alcuni effetti sull'economia italiana sui trasporti, pp.32-42
GUILLAUME, G.	Le pouvoir de représentation de la Commission des Communautés Européennes en matière de service aérien vis-à-vis des États tiers, pp.52-64

II. I servizi aerei, pp.69-138

DUTHEIL DE LA ROCHÈRE	Les tarifs de transport aérien en Europe, pp.102-121
LIOI, L.	Problematiche aperte dalla prima fase del processo di liberalizzazione del trasporto aereo in Europa, pp.122-128
LASSANDRO, A.	Le attuali esperienze in materia di liberalizzazione comunitaria, pp.129-138

III Le gestioni aeroportuali, pp.139-221
IV. Assistenza al volo, pp.222-283
13 *DPAC* 1989, pp.1-294

SCOCOZZA, M.V. – Air transport liberalization in the Common Market. –
4 *Air and Space Lawyer* (ABA) 1989, no. 2, pp.3-6, 12

SØRENSEN, F. – As mudanças no cenário da aviação européia e sus efeitos. –
RBDAE 1989, no. 46, pp.19-22

STANBROOK, C. – Application of European Community competition law to civil aviation. –
20 *CMLR* 1989, pp.535-550

STYNES, E. and BLACKLOCK, M. – 1992 and all that. –
Flight International, 20 May 1989, pp.55-56, 58, 60-62

Air transport: 1,000 days to get Europe off the ground? Transport aérien: 1000 jours pour faire l'Europe?

TENENBAUM, D. European liberalization: an ECAC perspective, pp.15-18
La libéralisation européenne: le point de vue de l'ECAC, pp.15-18

VINCENT, D. European civil aviation policy, pp.23-28
La politique européenne de l'aviation civile, pp.23-28

SAMOROUKOV, V. European deregulation and the outlook for a single market of international air services, pp.57-63
La déréglementation en Europe et le perspective d'un marché unique des services aériens, pp.57-63

FRISQUE, M. The impact of the EC 1992 fiscal harmonization on air transport in Europe, pp.129-147
Les conséquences, pour le transport aérien européen, de l'harmonisation fiscale dans la Communauté en 1992, pp.129-147

HUMPHREYS, B. Airline computer reservation systems, pp.149-157
Les systèmes informatisés de réservation dans les compagnies aériennes, pp.149-157

BRADLEY, F.W. The impact of air transport liberalization on aircraft financing, pp.169-176
Les effets de la libéralisation du transport aérien sur le financement des flottes, pp.169-176

Symposium proceedings Dubrovnik 1989. ITA Études & documents/Studies & reports 89/5, vol. 17, iv-183 pp.

Airline mergers and cooperation in the European Community.

NEVE, E.C. The British Government's position, pp.11-14

DENZA, E. The interface between the Chicago Convention and the European Community, pp.15-26

ARGYRIS, N. Costs and benefits of airline mergers and strategic cooperation – an economic analysis, pp.27-39

RICHARDS, S. The EC merger regulation, pp.41-48

ELLAND, W. The Merger Control regulation and its effect on national merger controls and the residual application of Articles 85 and 86, pp.49-70

SOAMES, T. Joint ventures and cooperation agreements in the air transport sector, pp.70-98

BURNSIDE, A.J. A fable of parallel proceedings (or CAT and MAUS go shopping), pp.99-105

EASTON, R.L. Airline mergers and acquisitions: the U.S. experience and likely trends, pp.107-114

PERKINS, D. What is best for the airline industry and the passenger, pp.115-122

2 EALA Conference Papers 1991

ANSPACH, P. – L'idée de la déréglementation du transport aérien en Europe a dix ans ... mais le plus dur reste à faire. –
Aviastro, mai 1990, pp.18-22

ATTALI, B. – The future of air transport in Europe: three scenarios for the year 2000. –
ITA Magazine, July/August 1990, no. 62, pp.3-7

AUSSANT, J.; FORNASIER, R. a.o. – Libre circulation des personnes, des services et des capitaux. Transports. Chapitre II. Section II. Les transports aériens. – Brussels 1990, Commentaire Megret. Le droit de la CEE, 2nd, tome 3, pp.294-323

BALFOUR, J. – EEC legislation: beyond the Second Package. –
7 *The Avmark Aviation Economist*, July 1990, pp.2-4

BANOWSKY, D. – Cutting drag and increasing lift: how well will a more competitive EEC air transport industry fly? –
24 *International Lawyer* (ABA) 1990, pp.179-206

BOOTH, M. – Removal of physical frontiers at airports. –
ITA Magazine, May/June 1990, no. 61, pp.14-16

BUTTERWORTH-HAYES, P. – Europe's single market will bring radical changes. –
45 *Interavia Aerospace Review* 1990, pp.1099-1102

CARLUCCI, F. – Trasporto aereo: liberalizzazione comunitaria in una visione di industria 'contestabile'. –
Trasporti 1990, no. 50-52, pp.181-191

CLOSE, G. – External relations in the air transport sector: air transport policy or the common commercial policy? –
27 *CMLR* 1990, pp.107-127

Communication 'des griefs' à la SABENA: le texte intégrale. –
Aviastro, juin 1990, pp.15-24

DE CONINCK, F. – De mededingingsregels van het E.E.G.-verdrag en de Europese luchtvaarttarieven. –
53 *Rechtskundig Weekblad* (Belgium) 1990, pp.1073-1086

CLAVERIE, B. – Expérience et stratégie de la coopération européenne dans le domaine de l'aéronautique. –
Revue du Marché Commun 1990, no. 333, pp.18-24

DAGTOGLOU, P. – Luftverkehr und europäisches Recht. –
Universität des Saarlandes, Vorträge Reden und Berichte aus dem Europa-Institut, 1990, no. 217, 13 pp.

MAJONE, G., ed. – Deregulation or re-regulation? Regulatory reform in Europe and in the United States.

BREYER, S. Regulation and deregulation in the United States: airlines, telecommunications and antitrust, pp.7-58
STOETZER, M.-W. Efficiency and prices in the European air transport market: some further evidence, pp.124-138
London/New York 1990, 262 pp.

EBKE, W.F. and WENGLORZ, G. – Die zweite Stufe der Liberalisierung des Luftlinienverkehrs in der EG: open skies in Europe. –
36 *Recht der internationalen Wirtschaft* 1990, pp.468-478

EC – civil aviation 1993.
SUTHERLAND, P. Editorial, pp.233-235
BALFOUR, J. Airline mergers and acquisitions: what controls does EEC law provide?, pp.237-251
JASINSKI, P.C. Commentary, pp.253-255
KALSHOVEN, E. The EEC Commission as the European version of the CAB?, pp.257-271
ESPÉROU, R. Commentary: A Europe full of suspicion?, pp.273-275
WEBER, L. External aspects of EEC air transport liberalization, pp.277-287
DUTHEIL DE LA ROCHÈRE Commentary, pp.289-293
CLOSE, G.L. External competence for air policy in the third phase – trade policy or transport policy?, pp.295-305
WASSENBERGH, H.A. Opening the skies – the EEC and third countries, pp.307-316
HAANAPPEL, P.P.C. The future relations between EEC institutions and international organizations in the field of civil aviation, pp.317-323
SØRENSEN, F. Commentary, pp.325-326
EVERITT, R.L. The pros and cons of airport privatisation in the EEC after 1992, pp.327-334
JEANDRAIN, P. Commentary, pp.335-336
15 *Air Law* 1990, pp.231-336

HAANAPPEL, P.P.C.; PETSIKAS, G.; ROSALES, R. and THAKER, J., eds. – EEC air transport policy and regulation, and their implications for North America. Proceedings of a conference held at McGill University, Montreal, Canada, September 1989. –
Deventer/Boston 1990, ix-216 pp.

EEC external relations: who negotiates? The Commission or ECAC? –
7 *The Avmark Aviation Economist*, May 1990, pp.2-4

The EEC legal instruments relevant to air transport policy and regulation.
WILLIAMS, S.A. Internal market and Common market – the Single European Act versus the Treaty of Rome, pp.3-32

LENZ, C.O. The decisions of the European Court of Justice on the applicability of the rules of the Treaty of Rome to air transport, pp.33-48
WEBER, L.J. The EEC internal air transport market and its impact on the airline industry, pp.49-64
LIPMAN, G.H. The impact of Europe's internal market on the airlines, pp.65-70
In: EEC air transport policy and regulation, Deventer 1990

WEBER, L. EEC liberalisation policy and the Chicago Convention, pp.17-30
CLOSE, G.L. External competence for air policy in the third phase – trade policy or commercial policy?, pp.31-44
STÅHLE, B. Non EEC carriers and the EEC aviation policy, pp.45-52
BALFOUR, J. Flying the flag – The role of nationalism in air transport, pp.53-68
ADAMANTOPOULOS, K. Block exemptions in the air transport sector, pp.73-84
SØRENSEN, F. A third package: what remains to be done?, pp.87-95
VAN MIERT, K. The way forward, pp.97-101
3 EALA Conference Papers 1991

EWERS, H.-J. – Institutional requirements for a Common Market in transport services. –
In: The completion of the internal market, Symposium 1989; Tübingen 1990, pp.150-164

GAILLARD, E. and PINGEL, I. – La libéralisation des transports aériens dans la Communauté Économique Européenne. –
44 *RFDAS* 1990, pp.9-32

GIEMULLA, E. and SCHMID, R. – Europäisches Luftverkehrsrecht. –
Frankfurt am Main 1990, loose-leaf

GRIGOLI, M. – Incidenza della liberalizzazione del trasporto aereo in Europa sulla sicurezza nautica. –
14 *DPAC* 1990, pp.14-18

Istituto per la Documentazione e gli Studi Legislativi – Gruppo di studio per l'esame degli aspetti connessi alla liberalizzazione del trasporto aereo in Europa. –
14 *DPAC* 1990, pp.19-56

KALSHOVEN-VAN TIJEN, E.L.M. – Recent developments in EEC aviation law: 'the second phase'. –
15 *Air Law* 1990, pp.122-139

KATZ, R. – Fortress Brussels? –
Airline Business, May 1990, pp.32-34, 37-38

KEHRBERGER, H.P. – EG-Luftverkehrspolitik und -Recht und deren Auswirkung auf Nordamerika. Symposium in Montreal, 12.-15. September 1989. –
39 *ZLW* 1990, pp.79-82

LASSANDRO, A. – Il pacchetto di misure comunitarie sulla 2a fase della liberalizzazione dei servizi di trasporto aereo. –
14 *DPAC* 1990, pp.1-13

Liberalisatie EG-luchtvaart. Advies tweede liberalisatiefase EG-burgerluchtvaart. Uitgebracht door de Commissie Vervoersvraagstukken aan de Minister van Verkeer en Waterstaat. –
SER-advies, publikatie nr. 9, 1 juni 1990

LUEBKER, M.L. – The 1992 European unification: effects in the air transport industry. –
56 *JALC* 1990, pp.589-639

NAVEAU, J. – The incentive role of the Court of Justice of the European Communities. –
ITA Magazine, Jan./Febr. 1990, no. 59, pp.12-13

NAVEAU, J. – Legal issues concerning the application of the EEC treaty to air transport. –
ITA Magazine, Dec. 1990, no. 64, pp.14-17

PERROTT, D.L. – The European Communities. –
24 *International Lawyer* (ABA) 1990, pp.553-558

PIZZINO, A. – EEC air transportation law and its implications for the member States: focus on Italy. –
Diss. McGill. Montreal 1990

SANTORO, F. – Il Mercato Unico Europeo ed i trasporti. –
Trasporti 1990, no. 50-52, pp.21-52

SCOCOZZA, M.V. – EEC-US aviation relations and cabotage. –
ITA Magazine, Jan./Febr. 1990, no. 59, pp.3-5

SIMONS, J.G.W. – De Europese luchtvervoersintegratie, in het bijzonder: de luchtvaart. –
26 *Ts voor Vervoerswetenschap* 1990, pp.236-246

SOCHOR, E. – Air transport in the European Community: the hard-core problem. –
45 *ICAO J*, Dec. 1990, pp.15-18

STRIVENS, R. and WEIGHTMAN, E. – Liberalisation of air transport within the European Community. –

In: Legal aspects of air finance, supplement to *Airfinance J*, Febr. 1990, no. 111, pp.33-36

VINCENT, D. and STASINOPOULOS, D. – The aviation policy of the European Community. 24 *J of Transport Economics and Policy*, Jan. 1990, pp.95-100

WHEATCROFT, S. and LIPMAN, G. – European liberalisation and world air transport. –
The Economist Intelligence Unit, Special report 2015, London 1990, 11-213 pp.

WOOLLEY, D. – EC Commissioners want immediate bilateral authority. –
14 *Airline Executive International*, July 1990, pp.22-23, 26

YOUNG, Y.W. – What will be the effects of EC market unification on intercontinental air services after 1992? –
45 *ICAO Bulletin*, Jan. 1990, pp.25-28

ADENAUER-FROWEIN, B. – Aktuelle luftrechtliche Probleme in der Europäischen Gemeinschaft. –
40 *ZLW* 1991, pp.236-249

MENDES DE LEON, P. and ABERSON, E., eds. – Air transport law in the 1990s. Controlling the boom. Proceedings of an international symposium held in Delft on 4 and 5 October 1990. –
Dordrecht etc. 1991, xiv-160 pp.

BALFOUR, J. – Factortame: the beginning of the end for nationalism in air transport? –
16 *Air Law* 1991, pp.251-266

BEYEN, R.K. and HERBERT, J. – Deregulierung des amerikanischen und EG-europäischen Luftverkehrs: theoretische Grundlagen und Analyse der verkehrspolitischen Umsetzung. –
Giessener Studien zur Transportwirtschaft und Kommunikation, No. 5. Hamburg 1991, xlvi-146 pp.

BORRMANN, J. – Zur Allokation von Start- und Landerechten: eine Kritik an den Regulierungsvorschlagen der EG-Kommission. –
41 *Wirtschaft und Wettbewerb* 1991, pp.678-688

BURTON, R. – The deregulation of air transport law within the European Community. –
13 *Liverpool LR* 1991, pp.139-149

BUSTI, S. – Verso un mercato comune aeronautico. –
Trasporti 1991, no. 53-55, pp.49-77

BUTTON, K. and SWANN, D. – Aviation policy in Europe. –
In: Airline deregulation. International experiences. London 1991, pp.85-123

Conduct of the Community's external aviation relations. –
London 1991, House of Lords, Select Committee on the European Communities, HL paper 39, 128 pp.

CRANS, B.J.H. – EC aviation scene. –
16 *Air Law* 1991, pp.287-292

CRANS, B.J.H. and BIESHEUVEL, M.B.W. – EC aviation scene. –
16 *Air Law* 1991, pp.133-141

CRANS, B.J.H. and LOOZEN, E.M.H. – EC aviation scene. –
16 *Air Law* 1991, pp.178-194

DOLFEN, M. – Der Verkehr im europäischen Wettbewerbsrecht. –
Diss. Augsburg 1990. R.v.Deckers rechts- und sozialwissenschaftliche Abhandlungen Band 48; Abteilung Verkehrsrecht und Verkehrspolitik Band 1. Heidelberg 1991, xx-309 pp.

EBKE, W.F. and WENGLORZ, G.W. – Liberalizing scheduled air transport within the European Community: from the first phase to the second and beyond. –
19 *Transportation LJ* 1991, pp.417-452; 19 *Denver J of Int. Law and Policy* 1991, pp.493-527

FELDMAN, J.M. – Will EC burst the bilateral bubble? –
28 *Air Transport World*, June 1991, pp.33-35

FOLLIOT, M.G. – L'espace aérien européen en formation. –
45 *RFDAS* 1991, pp.11-25

FOUILLOUX, G. – Les systèmes informatisés de réservation dans la Communauté Économique Européenne. –
In: L'Europe et le droit: mélanges en hommage à Jean Boulouis, Paris 1991, pp.265-284

GALLACHER, J. – Controlling interests. –
Airline Business, March 1991, pp.22-24

GALLACHER, J. – Going for the kill. –
Airline Business, Sept. 1991, pp.88-90

GOTSAKOS, C.M. – Blue skies and red tape. –
European infrastructure development 1991, London/Hong Kong, pp.71-76

GRAY, F. – European airlines in competition. –
European Government: the key to Europe 1991, pp.72, 76-77

GREAVES, R. – Transport law of the European Community. Part IV: Air transport. –
London 1991, xii-241 pp., at pp.163-199

GRIFFIN, R. – The European dream come true: what will become of American business (Boeing) after EEC '92? –
18 *Northern Kentucky LR* (Highland Heights KY) 1991, pp.431-455

GUILLAUME, G. – Vers l'Europe du transport aérien. –
44 *RFDAS* 1991, pp.339-357

HAANAPPEL, P.P.C. – Recent regulatory developments in Europe. –
16 *AASL* 1991, pp.107-123

KAISER, S.A. – Die Neuregelung der Slotvergabe. –
14 *Transportrecht* 1991, pp.266-276

KRÄMER, P.M. – Europe 1992: a single aeropolitical market? Washington DC, November 15-16, 1990. –
40 *ZLW* 1991, pp.39-43

KRÄMER, P.M. – Tarife im europäischen Linienflugverkehr. –
2 *Europäische Zs für Wirtschaftsrecht* 1991, pp.15-19

LOEWENSTEIN, A. – European air law. Towards a new system of international air transport regulation. –
Baden-Baden 1991, 264 pp.

MCMULLAN, K. – EC policy: should Euro-majors ever be subsidised? –
8 *The Avmark Aviation Economist*, Febr. 1991, pp.2-4

MAPELLI, E. – Regulación de sobreventa (overbooking) en la Comunidad Económica Europea. –
RBDAE, May-June 1991, no. 54, pp.32-38

Overboeking op lijndienstvluchten. –
19 *Consumenten-reisgids*, mei 1991, pp.14-15

PELKMANS, J. – The internal EC market for air transport: issues after 1992. –
In: Transport in a free market economy, London 1991, pp.195-219

PILLING, M. – Airlines have new fair play policeman. –
46 *Interavia Aerospace Review*, March 1991, pp.11-13

PRYKE, R. – American deregulation and European liberalisation. –
In: Transport in a free market economy, London 1991, pp.220-248

RINALDI BACCELLI, G. – La terza fase della liberalizzazione del trasporto aereo nella Comunità Economica Europea. –
15 *DPAC* 1991, pp.237-252

VAN RIJN, Th. – EC-Kommission. Flugzeuglärm. –
2 *Europäische Zs für Wirtschaftsrecht* 1991, p.418

ROUAUD, H. – The end of Community controls in air transport. –
ITA Magazine, July/August 1991, no. 67, pp.9-15

RUHNAU, H. – The challenge of air transport deregulation in a European perspective. –
RBDAE, May-June 1991, no. 54, pp.10-13

SCHMID, R. – EG-Binnenmarkt: der Kommissions-Vorschlag zur Abschaffung von Gepäckkontrollen auf innergemeinschaftlichen Flug- und Seereisen. –
14 *Transportrecht* 1991, pp.90-91

SCHMID, R. – Der europäische Luftverkehr auf dem Weg in den Binnenmarkt. –
2 *Europäische Zs für Wirtschaftsrecht* 1991, pp.19-25

SONNTAG, I. – La concurrence et le transport aérien en Europe. –
Diss. McGill. Montreal 1991, 141 pp.

VERES, R. – Política aérea da C.E.E. –
XXI Jornadas iberoamericanas, Lisboa 1991, pp.101-108

VILLIERS, J. – Competition and efficiency. Which policy for which objectives for European air transport? Concurrence et efficacité. Quelle politique européenne de transport aérien? Pour quels objectifs et quelle efficacité? –
ITA Studies & reports/Études & documents 91/2, vol. 23, Paris 1991

WEINBERG, S.K. – Liberalization of air transport: time for the EEC to unfasten its seatbelt. –
12 *Univ. of Pennsylvania J of Int. Business Law* 1991, pp.433-455

DE WIT, J.G. – Luchtvaartliberalisatie: op weg naar een werkzame mededinging? –
Ts voor Vervoerswetenschap 1991, pp.457-468

XUEREB, P.G. – Transport. A.1. Air transport. –
40 *ICLQ* 1991, pp.224-227

BLATTNER, L. and ROSENBERG, B. – US aviation and Europe 1992. –
Washington DC 1992, iv-147 pp.

BUSTI, S. – I sistemi telematici di prenotazione per il trasporto aereo nella disciplina comunitaria. –
Diritto dei Trasporti 1992, pp.15-

BUSTI, S. – Verso un mercato comune aeronautico. –
31 *Diritto comunitario e degli scambi internazionali* 1992, pp.439-465

CHENG, C-J. – The possible impact of the European Community air transport policy on the aviation industry in Asia. –
4 *Korean JAL* 1992, pp.170-176

CHRONAS, A.D. – Certain recent developments in Greek aviation law under a Community law perspective. –
17 *Air and Space Law* 1992, pp.297-309

CRANS, B.J.H. – EC aviation scene. –
17 *Air and Space Law* 1992, pp.217-223

CRANS, B.J.H. and LOOZEN, E.M.H. – EC aviation scene. –
17 *Air and Space Law* 1992, pp.160-163

DE CONINCK, F. – European air law. New skies for Europe. –
Paris 1992, 335 pp.

DEMPSEY, P.S. – European aviation regulation: flying through the liberalization labyrinth. 15 *Boston College ICLR* 1992, pp.311-374

DUTHEIL DE LA ROCHÈRE, J. – The contribution of the European Court of Justice to the implementation of the EEC Treaty in the field of air transport: past and future. –
In: Essays in honour of Henri A. Wassenbergh, Dordrecht 1992, pp.161-172

DUTHEIL DE LA ROCHÈRE, J. – La libéralisation du transport aérien communautaire et les relations avec les pays tiers. L'accord de 'ciel ouvert' Pays-Bas/États-Unis, un contre-exemple? –
38 *AFDI* 1992, pp.983-998

EC external aviation policy – negotiating with one voice. –
10 *The Avmark Aviation Economist*, Oct. 1992, pp.6-7

ENCAOUA, D. and PERROT, A. – Concurrence et coopération dans le transport aérien en Europe. –
EEC, Luxembourg 1992, 162 pp.

ESPÉROU, R. – L'Europe du transport aérien au seuil de 1992. –
45 *RFDAS* 1992, pp.119-130

Euro-liberalisation. The Third Package – final version. –
10 *The Avmark Aviation Economist*, July/August 1992, pp.2-4

RUPPELT, H.-J. National merger control for international airlines, pp.43-50
STOFFREGEN, K. Application of the EC Merger Regulation in the air transport sector, pp.51-62
MONTAG, F. – Problems of the application of the EC Merger Regulation to airlines, pp.63-74
4 EALA Conference Papers 1992

Ramifications of the establishment of the Internal Market on the relationship with third countries.
BARNUM, J. Prospects for a new relationship between the EC and the US, pp.81-84
VEENSTRA, K. Problems arising from the negotiation of air transport agreements by the EC Commission, pp.85-92
4 EALA Conference Papers 1992

State aids in the air transport sector.
MANNIN, C. Should the GATT Civil Aircraft Code be revised?, pp.95-116
DUTHEIL DE LA ROCHÈRE Commission policy towards national aid to airlines, pp.117-127
4 EALA Conference Papers 1992

The future of European air transport policy.
KNITTEL, W. EC air transport policy: the German view, pp.131-137
4 EALA Conference Papers 1992

FRIZ, E. – Brevi note sul Mercato Unico nel settore dei trasporti aerei. –
31 *Diritto comunitario e degli scambi internazionali* 1992, pp.433-438

GIEMULLA, E.; SCHMID, R. and MÖLLS, W. – European air law. –
Deventer/Boston/Berlin 1992, loose-leaf

GOH, J. – Air transport competition in the European Economic Community: the antitrust procedures. –
21 *Transportation LJ* 1992, pp.91-103

GOH, J.M.S. – Regulating the skies of Europe: air transport competition. –
27 *ETL* 1992, pp.295-314

HAANAPPEL, P. – Airlines and the 'New Europe'. –
IATA Review, Oct./Nov. 1992, pp.8-10

HAANAPPEL, P.P.C. – Bilateralism and multilateralism in EEC-non-EEC commercial air transport relations. –
In: Essays in honour of Henri A. Wassenbergh, Dordrecht 1992, pp.173-188

HAANAPPEL, P.P.C. – Europe 1992 and airline (de)regulation. –
17 *AASL* 1992, vol. I, pp.271-280

HAANAPPEL, P.P.C. – Recent European air transport developments. –
17 *AASL* 1992, vol. II, pp.217-235

HACKET, G. – Liberalization of air transport in the EEC and its implications for non-EEC countries. –
Diss. McGill. Montreal 1992

JACCHIA, R.A. and MORETTO, M. – Trasporto aereo e normativa comunitaria antitrust. –
19 *Giurisprudenza Commerciale* 1992, pp.370-

KRÄMER, P.M. – European Air Law Association. 1991 Annual conference: Recent developments in EC air transport law and policy. Berlin, 15 November 1991. –
41 *ZLW* 1992, pp.89-92

LANGE, D.G. and WEITBRECHT, A. – European merger control in the air transport industry. –
41 *ZLW* 1992, pp.41-50

LENZ, C.O. – Die Rechtsprechung des Gerichtshofes der Europäischen Gemeinschaften zur Anwendung des EWG-Vertrages auf den Luftverkehr. –
In: Festschrift für Bodo Börner zum 70. Geburtstag, Köln 1992, pp.179-194

LIZARRAGA LACALLE, M.D. – Hacia la libre circulación del personal de vuelo entre los Estados de la Comunidad Económica Europea. –
8 *Revista europea DNMA* 1992, pp.1287-1296

LOOZEN, E.M.H. – EC aviation scene. –
17 *Air and Space Law* 1992, pp.28-29

MANNIN, C. – The Warsaw dilemma within the European Community. An E.E.C. air travel protection directive? –
Brussels symposium, April 1992, 12 pp.

MAZZARELLA, D. – The integration of aviation law in the EC: teleological jurisprudence and the European Court of Justice. –
20 *Transportation LJ* 1992, pp.353-372

MEIER, U. – Kritische Erwägungen zur europäischen Luftverkehrspolitik. –
41 *ZLW* 1992, pp.203-218

MENDES DE LEON, P. – Le cabotage aérien dans les Communautés Européennes. –
Revue du Marché Commun, juillet/août 1992, no. 360, pp.631-636

VAN MIERT, K. – Air transport policy in the European Community. –
Airport Technology International 1992, pp.15-17

MURIEL, A. – European air transport – the third phase. –
Legal aspects of aviation finance, supplement of *Airfinance J*, Sept. 1992, pp.24-29

NAVEAU, J. – Droit aérien européen. Les nouvelles règles du jeu. –
ITA, Paris 1992, 326 pp.

NAVEAU, J. – The Single European Market and the air carriers' liability regime. –
Brussels symposium, April 1992, 6 pp.

PLATT, J.R. – The creation of a Community cabotage area in the European Community and its implications for the US bilateral aviation system. –
17 *Air and Space Law* 1992, pp.183-198

Politique extérieure de la Communauté Européenne relative aux transports par air: vues de la CCI. –
45 *RFDAS* 1992, pp.203-207

REED, A. – Not quite cabotage. –
29 *Air Transport World*, Sept. 1992, pp.66-68, 70

REIMER, G. – Deutsche Flughafenpolitik ohne europäische Dimension? –
41 *ZLW* 1992, pp.142-153

ROSENBAUM, A. – Unscheduled moves. –
29 *Air Transport World,* March 1992, pp.30-32

SCHMID, R. – Air transport within the European Single Market – how will it look after 1992? –
17 *Air and Space Law* 1992, pp.199-205

SMIT-KROES, N. – The impact of European liberalization on operations between Asia and Europe. –
In: The highways of air and outer space, Dordrecht 1992, pp.3-9

SØRENSEN, F. – EEC internal and external aviation policy. –
In: External aviation relations of the EC, Deventer 1992, pp.1-10

STASINOPOULOS, D. – The second aviation package of the European Community. –
26 *J of Transport Economics and Policy* 1992, pp.83-87

VAN DE VOORDE, E.E. – European air transport after 1992: deregulation or reregulation? –
37 *Antitrust Bulletin* (NY) 1992, pp.507-528

WASSENBERGH, H.A., ed. – External aviation relations of the EC.
SØRENSEN, F. EEC internal and external aviation policy, pp.1-10

MIFSUD, P.V. Airline concentrations and cross border arrangements, pp.11-20
VAN HOUTTE, B. Competition issues, pp.21-29
HAANAPPEL, P.P.C. Tariff coordination: a bilateral or multilateral framework?, pp.31-38
Deventer/Boston 1992, xi-124 pp.

WEBB, R.S. – Significant legal developments in aviation and insurance law in the United Kingdom and Europe. –
Brussels symposium, April 1992, 8 pp.

WEBER, L. – EEC air transport liberalization and the Chicago Convention. –
17 *AASL* 1992, vol. I, pp.245-262

WENGLORZ, G.W. – Die Deregulierung des Luftlinienverkehrs im europäischen Binnenmarkt., –
Diss. Konstanz. R.v.Decker's rechts- und sozialwissenschaftliche Abhandlungen, Bd. 55. Abteilung Verkehrsrecht und Verkehrspolitik Bd. 4. Heidelberg 1992, xvi-166 pp.

WOOD, B. – The ownership of international airlines: a European view. The European Economic Community. –
In: The highways of air and outer space, Dordrecht 1992, pp.324-326

ZAFRA RIASCOS, M. – La influencia de las normas comunitarias sobre competencias en los servicios de asistencia en tierra ('handling'). Sus repercusiones respecto a los servicios aéreos intra-extra comunitarios. –
8 *Revista europea DNMA* 1992, pp.1369-1378

ACHTNICH, H. – Neues Flugpreisrecht: Anwendungsvoorang der EWG-VO 2409/92 vor LuftVG, RabG, Zugabe VO. –
39 *Wettbewerb in Recht und Praxis* 1993, pp.731-736

Airline competition in the Single European Market. –
CAA, London 1993, CAP 623, vi-216 pp.

ANN, Chr. – Deregulierung in der Luft, Monopole auf dem Boden. Zur kartellrechtlichen Situation and Problematik der Märkte für Bodendienste auf deutschen Verkehrsflughäfen. –
48 *Betriebsberater* 1993, Beilage 16 zu Heft 23, 12 pp.

BALDWIN, M. and CONLON, M. – Lessors face VAT penalty. –
Airfinance J, March 1993, no. 148, p.43

BALFOUR, J. – The control of State aids in the air transport sector. –
18 *Air and Space Law* 1993, pp.199-204

BÖCKSTIEGEL, K.-H. – Rahmenbedingungen für einen zukünftigen Luftverkehr auf dem Marktplatz EG. –
42 *ZLW* 1993, pp.117-120

BUSTI, S. – La nuova disciplina comunitaria dei servizi aerei. –
Trasporti 1993, no. 61, pp.71-103; 32 *Diritto comunitario e degli Scambi internazionali* 1993, pp.187-211

CAMERON, D. and ODELL, M. – Brussels enters handling debate. –
Airline Business, July 1993, pp.20-21

CAVALLI, M. – Rifiuto all'imbarco e overbooking: problemi di diritto interno e di diritto comunitario. –
32 *Diritto comunitario e degli Scambi internazionali* 1993, pp.377-379

CHENG, B. – Air carriers' liability for passenger injury or death: the Japanese initiative and response to the recent EC Consultation Paper. –
18 *Air and Space Law* 1993, pp.109-122, 182

Commission asked to review ground handling monopolies. –
5 *Jane's Airport Review*, Sept. 1993, p.3

CRANS, B.J.H. – The third EC aviation package: its impact on the leasing industry. –
18 *Air and Space Law* 1993, pp.102-108; Topics of aircraft finance, Amsterdam 1993, 18 pp.

DAVIES, P. and GOH, J. – EC law on aircraft noise: recent developments. –
2 *European Environmental LR* 1993, pp.229-232, 241-242

DUTHEIL DE LA ROCHÈRE, J. – Le contrôle communautaire des restructurations d'entreprises comme instrument d'une politique d'aviation civile. –
46 *RFDAS* 1993, pp.389-400

SLOT, P.J.	Harmonised licensing agreements, pp.21-36
HAANAPPEL, P.	Fares, pp.37-42
BALFOUR, J.	The slot problem – can competition rules help?, pp.45-46
STUYCK, J.	An aspect of fair competition: pricing, pp.57-73
SAGGIO, A.	Legal problems relating to the European Economic Area Agreement and in particular to its effect on air transport, pp.83-104
CHENG, B.	EEC aviation policy: an international law perspective, pp.105-130

5 EALA Conference Papers 1993

GIRARDI, P. – La liberalizzazione dei traffici aerei in vista del completamento del mercato unico europeo e suoi riflessi sul trasporto aereo nell'area del Mediterraneo. –
Trasporti 1993, no. 59, pp.61-73

GIRARDI, P. and COLETTA, C. – La nuova disciplina dell'assegnazione delle bande orarie negli aeroporti comunitari. –
Diritto dei Trasporti 1993, pp.705-

GOLDA, C. – Verso la 'deregulation' anche nei servizi aeroportuali. –
95 *Il Diritto Marittimo* 1993, pp.1003-1007

GRIGOLI, M. – Liberalizzazione e sicurezza nel trasporto aereo comunitario. –
Trasporti 1993, no. 59, pp.3-15

HAANAPPEL, P. – As linhas aéreas e a 'nova Europa'. –
RBDAE, Jan./Febr. 1993, no. 61, pp.8-10

HAANAPPEL, P.P.C. – Recent European air transport developments: 1992-93. –
18 *AASL* 1993, pp.133-152

HENRY, L.-C. – La concurrence et la politique communautaire du transport aérien. –
Diss. Nice. Nice 1993, 800 pp.

HÖFER, B.J. – Strukturwandel im europäischen Luftverkehr: marktstrukturelle Konsequenzen der Deregulierung. –
Frankfurt am Main 1993, 765 pp.

VAN HOUTTE, B. – Community competition law in the air transport sector. –
18 *Air and Space Law* 1993, pp.61-70 and 275-287

JOHNSON, M.A. – Removing barriers to market entry in the air transport industry: the application of EC competition rules. –
Legal issues of European integration 1993, no. 2, pp.1-35

KUNZ, D. – Rechtliche Aspekte der neueren Luftraumorganisation und der internationalen Flugsicherungszusammenarbeit. –
ASDA Bulletin 1993-1, no. 114, pp.19-44

LEVICK, M.J. – The production of civil aircraft: a compromise of two world giants. –
21 *Transportation LJ* 1993, pp.433-467

MAPELLI, E. – La Comunidad Europea y el transporte aéreo. –
Revista general del Derecho (Valencia), junio 1993, no. 585, pp.6103-6112

MEIER, U. – Die Gestaltung der Luftverkehrsbeziehungen der Mitgliedstaaten der Europäischen Gemeinschaft mit Drittstaaten – eine gemeinschaftliche Aufgabe? –
42 *ZLW* 1993, pp.3-20

MORALES RODRÍGUEZ, J.R. – El transporte aéreo y la Comunidad Europea. – Madrid 1993, 470 pp.

The new legal framework for aviation in the European Community. Proceedings of the International Colloquium in Paris on 17 June 1993, edited by K.-H. BÖCKSTIEGEL.
EBDON, R.J.C. Market access, pp.31-37
BALFOUR, J. Licensing, pp.39-51
HAANAPPEL, P.P.C. Pricing, pp.53-62
KANDULSKI, G. Slot allocation, pp.63-68
ICC, Paris 1993, 273 pp.

PASCALL, S.C. – The ATLAS study. –
35 *J of ATC* 1993, no. 3, pp.78, 80-82

RECKEWERTH, S. – Zusammenarbeit der Luftverkehrsgesellschaften nach europäischem und US-amerikanischem Recht. –
Diss. Göttingen. Studien zum int. Wirtschaftsrecht und Atomenergierecht, Bd. 85. Köln 1993, 437 pp.

REYMOND, C. – Analysis and developments of the EC aircraft noise directive. –
18 *Air and Space Law* 1993, pp.2-15

RICKETTS, R. and BALFOUR, J. – Aircraft use, registration and leasing in the EC. –
18 *Air and Space Law* 1993, pp.25-28

RINALDI BACCELLI, G. – Concorrenza e liberalizzazione nel trasporto aereo: profili giuridici. –
Trasporti 1993, no. 59, pp.17-26

RINALDI BACCELLI, G. – La terza fase della liberalizzazione del trasporto aereo nella Comunità Economica Europea. –
Trasporti 1993, no. 60, pp.35-51

SAGGIO, A. – Legal problems relating to the European Economic Area Agreement and in particular to its effect on air transport. –
5 EALA Conference papers 1993, pp.83-104

SCHMID, R. – Das dritte Massnahmenbündel der EG-Kommission zur Errichtung des Binnenmarktes im Luftverkehr (Juni 1992). –
16 *Transportrecht* 1993, pp.89-93

Sinclair Roche & Temperley eds – Repossession of aircraft and insolvency in EC countries. An industry report. –
Lloyd's of London Press 1993, 162-xii pp.

STASINOPOULOS, D. – The third phase of liberalisation in Community aviation and the need for supplementary measures. –
27 *J of Transport Economics and Policy* 1993, pp.323-328

TOSI, J.-P. – Le droit d'établissement est-il effectif en matière de transport aérien? –
Mélanges offerts à André Colomer, Paris 1993, pp.503-516

WASSENBERGH, H. – Principles and practices in air transport regulation. –
ITA, Paris 1993, viii-268 pp.

ADKINS, B. – Air transport and E.C. competition law. –
London 1994, xxxiii-330 pp.

AUER, A. – Das Verhältnis der Schweiz zur Europäischen Gemienschaft im Bereich des Luftverkehrs. –
ASDA Bulletin 1994-2, no. 117, pp.11-17

BALFOUR, J. – Air transport – A Community success story? –
31 *CMLR* 1994, pp.1025-1053

BALFOUR, J. – The battle of Orly: the legal dimension. –
1 *J of Air Transport Management* 1994, no. 3, pp.161-164

BALFOUR, J. – The changing role of regulation in European air transport liberalization. –
1 *J of Air Transport Management*, March 1994, pp.27-36

BALFOUR, J. – EC Commission: competition rules – a seven year assessment. –
11 *The Avmark Aviation Economist*, Dec. 1994, pp.8-11

BASEDOW, J. – Airline deregulation in the European Community – Its background, its flaws, its consequences for EC-US relations. –
German national reports in civil law matters for the XIVth Congress of Comparative Law in Athens, 1994, pp.41-66. 13 *J of Law and Commerce* (Pittsburgh PA) 1994, pp.247-277

BASS, T.C. – Infrastructure constraints and the EC. –
1 *J of Air Transport Management* 1994, no. 3, pp.145-150

BÖCKSTIEGEL, K.-H. and KRÄMER, P.M. – Filling in the gaps of the Chicago Convention: main features of the new legal framework for aviation in the European Community. –
19 *AASL* 1994, vol. I, pp.127-143

BONNET, D. and SCAPEL, C. – Droit européen de l'aviation civile. –
IFURTA, Aix-en-Provence 1994, loose-leaf

BRACHMANN, U. – Die rechtlichen und tatsächlichen Möglichkeiten zugunsten eines effektiven Wettbewerbs trotz überlasteter Flughäfen im europäischen Luftverkehr. –
Diss. Konstanz. Konstanz 1994, xiii-311 pp.

CAVANI, R. – Computerized reservation systems for air transport: remarks on the European Community legislation. –
17 *Fordham Inernational LJ* (NY) 1994, pp.441-457

COSENTINO, E.T. – Las ayudas estatales a las empresas de transporte aéreo en la Unión Europea. –
XXIV Jornadas iberoamericanas, Salamanca 1994, pp.175-183

COSENTINO, E.T. – Nuevos desarrollos normativos de la Unión europea en materia de transporte aéreo. La cuestión tarifaria. –
XXIV Jornadas iberoamericanas, Salamanca 1994, pp.407-414

CRANS, B. – EC aviation scene. –
19 *Air and Space Law* 1994, pp.232-234

CRANS, B.J.H. and CRAS, S.P. – EC aviation scene. –
19 *Air and Space Law* 1994, pp.31-39

DAGTOGLOU, P.D. – Air transport and the European Union. –
Athens/Deventer 1994, 2nd ed., 375 pp.

DODGSON, J.S. – Competition policy and the liberalisation of European aviation. –
21 *Transportation LJ* 1994, pp.355-370

DOGANIS, R.S. – Effectiveness of the competition rules within the Single Market. –
19 *Air and Space Law* 1994, pp.131-137

DONSIMONI, P. – TVA intracommunautaire. Acquisition des aéronefs neufs et location d'aéronefs en provenance d'un autre État membre de l'Union européenne par des assujettis établis en France. –
47 *RFDAS* 1994, pp.127-138

DRIVEN, M. – Liberalization and privatization in European Community air transport law. –
6 *International Legal Perspectives* (Portland Oregon), spring 1994, pp.97-129

DUCREST, J. – L'Union Européenne, futur membre de l'Organisation de l'Aviation civile internationale? –
19 *AASL* 1994, vol. II, pp.239-281

DUSSART-LEFRET, C. and FEDERLIN, C. – Ground handling services and EC competition rules. –
19 *Air and Space Law* 1994, pp.50-61

DUTHEIL DE LA ROCHÈRE, J. – L'accés des transporteurs aériens au marché communautaire. Le règlement 2408/92 et son interprétation. –
47 *RFDAS* 1994, pp.389-401

DUTHEIL DE LA ROCHÈRE, J. – Les problèmes juridiques et administratifs de la déréglementation en matière de transport aérien. –
46 *Revue int. de Droit comparé* (France) 1994, pp.543-555

VINCENT, D.	After the third package: tasks for the future in European civil aviation, pp.31-35
DUTHEIL DE LA ROCHÈRE	Control of competition as a tool of civil aviation policy, pp.39-49
ESPÉROU, R.	Prospects for a common external policy, pp.89-98
VAN FENEMA, P.	Perspectives for an EU external aviation policy, pp.99-104
VAN HOUTTE, B.	Some comments on the application of the competition rules, pp.107-115
FRUEHE, C.	Tariff realities in a liberalized single European market, pp.117-120
BAUCHET, P.	The effect of computerisation on the pricing policies of public services, pp.121-129
BENADON, D.	The view of France on the third package, pp.133-138

6 EALA Conference Papers 1994

Expanding horizons. A report by the Comité des Sages for air transport to the European Commission, pp.136-207
DE CONINCK, F. – The report of the 'Comité des Sages': the right remedies for the European airlines' woes?, pp.209-243
29 *ETL* 1994, pp.136-243

FOBE, J.-M. – Aviation products liability and insurance in the EU. –
Deventer 1994, xv-172 pp.

GALÁN CORONA, E. – Nuevos desarrollos normativos de la Unión europea en materia de transporte aéreo. –
XXIV Jornadas iberoamericanas, Salamanca 1994, pp.381-403

GIRARDI, P. and COLETTA, C. – La nuova ed attuale disciplina dell'assegnazione delle bande orarie negli aeroporti comunitari. –
Trasporti 1994, no. 64, pp.43-135

HAANAPPEL, P.P.C. – Les activités de l'IATA (hiver 1994). 3. La coordination tarifaire, l'immunié 'antitrust' aux États-Unis et les exemptions de groupe dans l'Union européenne. –
47 *RFDAS* 1994, pp.139-142, at pp.140-142

HAANAPPEL, P. – European regulatory framework in transition. –
IATA Review, March/April 1994, pp.9-11

HAANAPPEL, P.P.C. – Multilateralism and economic bloc forming in international air transport. –
19 *AASL* 1994, vol. I, pp.279-320

MALANIK, P. – The report of the European 'Comité des Sages'. –
19 *Air and Space Law* 1994, pp.75-80

MESMIN, O. – La satisfaction des besoins de l'État au regard de la nouvelle donne du transport aérien. –
47 *RFDAS* 1994, pp.117-126

NAVEAU, J. – The report of the Comité des Sages. –
ITA Press, February 1994, no. 209, supplement Viewpoint, 8 pp.

PLATT, J. – European Community cabotage. –
22 *Transportation LJ* 1994, pp.61-85

POONOOSAMY, V. – Challenges facing African countries in the field of civil aviation and the impact of European aeropolitical developments on African countries. –
29 *ETL* 1994, pp.245-256

RITTNER, F. – Zur Neuordnung der Bodenverkehrsdienste (groundhandling) auf den Flughäfen der Europäischen Union. –
13 *Neue Zs für Verwaltungsrecht* 1994, pp.429-435

SCHMID, T. – Flying the Euro-skies: the changing face of European aviation. –
39 *J of the Law Society of Scotland* 1994, pp.465-467

State aids to airlines.

SLOT, P.J.	EC State aids: a general introduction, pp.15-23
HILBRECHT, H.	The DG VII perspective, pp.25-32
SOAMES, T. and	The practical application of the State aid rules to the
RYAN, A.	air transport sector, pp.33-73
FLYNN, J.	Is air transport special?, pp.75-84
ALLEN, Chr.	Contribution, pp.85-87
NAVEAU, J.	Contribution, pp.89-91
DAGTOGLOU, P.D.	Closing remarks, pp.93-94

7 EALA Conference Papers 1994, 94 pp.

TEUSCHER, R.R. – Zur Liberalisierung des Luftverkehrs in Europa. –
Göttingen 1994

WEBER, L. – The European Union and the Chicago Convention of 1944. –
19 *Air and Space Law* 1994, pp.179-184

WITTMANN, M. – Die Liberalisierung des Luftverkehrs in der Europäischen Gemeinschaft. –
Konstanz 1994

BALFOUR, J. – Airline mergers and marketing alliances – Legal constraints. –
20 *Air and Space Law* 1995, pp.112-117

BALFOUR, J. – The EC Commission's policy on State aid for airline restructuring: is the bonfire alight? –
20 *Air and Space Law* 1995, pp.60-67

BAUMANN, J.M. – Die Luftverkehrspolitik der Europäischen Union. –
Berlin 1995, 205 pp.

BLISS, F.A. – Rethinking restrictions on cabotage: moving to free trade in passenger aviation. –
33 *Duquesne LR* (Pittsburgh PA) 1995, pp.283-307

CRANS, B.J.H. – Aircraft finance. Recent developments and prospects.
CRANS, B.J.H. The third EC aviation package: its impact on the leasing industry, pp.117-125
HOFLAND, D.A. Recent developments in tax law, pp.95-101
PIJNACKER HORDIJK, E.H. Relevant EC-law topics, pp.149-154
The Hague 1995, viii-154 pp.

CRANS, B. and RIJSDIJK, O. – EC aviation scene. –
20 *Air and Space Law* 1995, pp.328-335

DUCHENE, D.A. – The third package of liberalization in the European air transport sector: shying away from full liberalization. –
23 *Transportation LJ* 1995, pp.119-161

European Parliament: report on civil aviation – the way forward. –
Transport Europe, Febr. 1995, 18 pp.

GIEMULLA, E. and SCHMID, R. – Nochmals – Wem gehört die Zeit? –
44 *ZLW* 1995, pp.259-268

GOH, J. – Problems of transnational regulation: a case study of aircraft noise regulation in the European Community. –
23 *Transportation LJ* 1995, pp.277-300

GRIEF, N. – New E.C. directive on the investigation of air accidents and incidents. –
J of Business Law (UK) 1995, pp.422-429

HEERKENS, H. – De grenzen van liberalisering: Europese Commissie wil hoofdrol bij sluiten luchtvaartverdragen. –
12 *Maandblad Luchtvaart*, jumi 1995, pp.4-6

HUGHES, N. – Investigation of civil aviation accidents and incidents in Europe. –
3 *Transport Law and Policy* 1995, pp.87-88

JENNINGS, M. and ODELL, M. – A definitive lesson in competence. –
11 *Airline Business*, April 1995, pp.22-23

KOHL, N.E.M. – Herziene richtsnoeren in de luchtvaartsector. –
1 *Nederlands Ts voor Europees Recht* 1995, pp.11-13

MAPELLI, E. – El incidente aeronáutico en la Unión Europea. –
XX Jornadas latinoamericanas, Buenos Aires 1995, 13 pp.

RACIC, M.A. – Opinion 1/94 of the European Court of Justice and its implications for European external aviation relations. –
20 *AASL* 1995, vol. II, pp.291-323

REED, A. and CRUMLEY, B. – EC liberalization after two years. –
32 *Air Transport World*, Jan. 1995, pp.45-47, 50, 53

SHIN, H.-K. – Multilateralism and nationality of aircraft and airlines and its implications with respect to Article 7 of the Chicago Convention. –
7 *Korean JAL* 1995, pp.151-173 (in Korean) and pp.174-175 (English summary)

SLOT, P.J. – Het Europese luchtvervoerbeleid: eindelijk los van de grond? –
43 *Sociaal-Economische Wetgeving* 1995, pp.683-705

SOAMES, T. and RYAN, A. – State aid and air transport. –
16 *European Competition LR* (UK) 1995, pp.290-309

WEBER, L. – Modern trends in the antitrust/competition law governing the aviation industry. –
20 *Air and Space Law* 1995, pp.101-109

66. Aviation and the consumer

SARAF, D.N. – Public utility services with special reference to air services and the consumer. –
31 *J of the Indian Law Institute* 1989, pp.136-153

PETROSKI, D. – Airlines' response to the DPTA Section 1305 preemption. –
56 *JALC* 1990, pp.125-153

THIELER, V. – Recht und Rat für Flugpassagiere. –
Bastei-Lübbe Taschenbücher 66900. Bergisch-Gladbach 1990, 176 pp.

PINTO DE CARVALHO, L.C. – O código do consumidor e o direito aeronáutico. –
RBDAE, March-April 1991, no. 53, pp.41-43

STAEHELIN, B. – Gewerbsmässiger Luftverkehr und Konsumentenschutz. –
ASDA Bulletin 1991-1, no. 110, pp.5-46

ROBERTS, M.J. – Congressional proposals to enhance airline competition and passenger protection. –
59 *Transportation Practitioners J* (Washington DC) 1992, pp.241-262

ELLIG, J. and WINEGARDEN, W.H. – Airline policy and consumer welfare. –
61 *Transportation Practitioners J* 1994, pp.411-430

GILES, L. – Interpreting the Airline Deregulation Act of 1978: federal preemption over state deceptive advertising laws. –
22 *Transportation LJ* 1994, pp.87-103

PARR, J. – The customer of the future. –
20 *Air and Space Law* 1995, pp.97-100

67. Aviation and tourism

HERRERA ESTEBAN, L. – Turismo y transporte aéreo desde la experiencia española. –
Fundación Actilibre, Cuadernos del tiempo libre, Madrid 1991, 47 pp.

PALACÍN FERNÁNDEZ, J. – Transporte aéreo internacional y turismo. –
Revista cubana de derecho 1992, no. 2, pp.128-136

ABEYRATNE, R.I.R. – Air transport tax and its consequences on tourism. –
20 *Annals of Tourism Research* 1993, pp.450-460

LIPMAN, G. – Multilateral liberalisation – the travel and tourism dimension. –
19 *Air and Space Law* 1994, pp.152-157

68. Aviation and automatization

ARCADU, G. – Informatica e aviazione civile: aspetti relativi alla responsabilità. –
14 *DPAC* 1990, pp.375-381

ABEYRATNE, R.I.R. – The role of automation in facilitation of air transport into the 21st century. –
20 *AASL* 1995, Vol. I, pp.259-282

Chapter V. Aircraft

71. Definitions

a. General aviation

EICHENBERGER, J.A. – General aviation law. –
TAB Practical Flying Series. Blue Ridge Summit PA 1990, xiv-222 pp.

WELLS, G.P. – General aviation accident liability standards: why the fuss? –
56 *JALC* 1991, pp.895-935

ANDREOTTI, R.J. – Promoting general aviation safety: a revision of pilot negligence law. –
58 *JALC* 1993, pp.1089-1148

YODICE, J.S. – Product liability on trial. –
36 *The AOPA Pilot*, May 1993, pp.123-124

ARMSTRONG, A. – Navigating in the zone of confusion – reflections on illegal air taxi operations. –
21 *Transportation LJ* 1994, pp.329-357

GREINER, H.W. – Die Betriebspflicht von Flugplätzen. Rechtliche Grundlagen und 'Kleinflieger-Problematik'. –
Bayerische Verwaltungsblätter 1994, pp.449-457

MCQUILLEN, M.G. – The deception about the inception rule: coverage for VFR pilots under IFR conditions. –
60 *JALC 1994*, pp.179-235

VANWORMER, J.A. – Federal preemption of aircraft design certification standards after Cleveland v. Piper Aircraft Corp.: can general aviation manufacturers recover? –
19 *J of Corporation Law* (Iowa City) 1994, pp.665-679

BOSWELL, J.H. and COATS, G.A. – Saving the general aviation industry: putting tort reform to the test. –
60 *JALC* 1995, pp.533-574

KENNEY, S.C. – Recent developments in aviation law. IV.A. General Aviation Revitalization Act of 1994. –
61 *JALC* 1995, pp.80-82

MCALLISTER, T.S. – A 'tail' of liability reform: the General Aviation Revitalization Act of 1994 and the general aviation industry in the United States. –
23 *Transportation LJ* 1995, pp.301-322

McNatt Jr, C.C. and England, S.L. – The push for statutes of repose in general aviation. –
23 *Transportation LJ* 1995, pp.323-343

Tarry, S.E. and Truitt, L.J. – Rhetoric and reality: tort reform and the uncertain future of general aviation. –
61 *JALC* 1995, pp.163-201

b. Helicopters

Hur, J. – Helicopter operation/transportation business under regulation. –
7 *Korean JAL* 1995, pp.85-100 (n Korean)

d. Hovercraft

Kaiser, S.A. – The legal status of ekranoplanes. –
17 *Air and Space Law* 1992, pp.286-290

l. Microlights – ULM

Chamberlain, D. – Ultralights. –
31 *FAA Aviation News*, March-April 1992, pp.4-10

n. Spaceplane

Colloque 'L'avion spatial et le droit'.

	Aspects généraux et programmes, pp.435-484
Böckstiegel, K.-H.	Conditions d'utilisation de l'avion spatial, pp.485-486
Frankle, E.A.	Exemple de la navette spatiale américaine, pp.487-493
Montlivault, J.-L. de	Immatriculation et certification, pp.495-500
Lambert, Y.	Règles de la circulation aérienne: conditions de navigation, pp.501-505
Frantzen, C.	Utilisation de l'avion spatial et droit aérien, pp.507-514
Vereshchetin, V.S.	Utilisation de l'avion spatial et droit de l'espace, pp.515-524
du Pontavice, E.	Détermination de l'exploitant, pp.531-533
Webb, R.	Étendue de la responsabilité de l'exploitation vis-à-vis du personnel de bord, des passagers et des tiers, pp.535-540
Braure, E.	Responsabilité du constructeur et assurance, pp.541-542
Garnault, F.	Responsabilité du constructeur, pp.543-547
Clerc, A.	Couverture des responsabilités par les assurances, pp.549-557
Guillaume, G.	Conclusion générale sur le régime juridique de l'avion spatial, pp.563-568

44 *RFDAS* 1991

HINTZ, M. – International colloquium: The spaceplane and the law. Paris, 14-15 May 1991. –
40 *ZLW* 1991, pp.287-289

VAN DER LAAN, S.A.L.B. – The aerospace plane. Collisions and damage to a third party on the surface of the earth: which liability regime will rule? –
4 *Leiden JIL* 1991, pp.249-279

CHRISTOL, C.Q. – The aerospace plane and the definition and delimitation of outer space. 16 *Revista de la CIDA-E* 1992, no. 17, pp.13-34

CHRISTOL, C.Q. – Legal aspects of aerospace planes. –
In: The highways of air and outer space, 1992, pp.77-90

VON DER DUNK, F.G. and YAN, L. – The spaceplane and the law – A dream come true? Colloquium of May 1991. –
17 *Air and Space Law* 1992, pp.20-21

HASHIMITO, Y. – The space plane and international space law. –
35 Colloquium on the law of outer space, Washington 1992, pp.378-381

MASSON-ZWAAN, T.L. – The aerospace plane: an object at the cross-roads between air and space law. –
In: Essays in honour of Henri A. Wassenbergh, Dordrecht 1992, pp.247-261

CHRISTOL, C.Q. – The aerospace plane – its legal and political future. –
9 *Space Policy* 1993, pp.35-43

KAYSER, V. – Aux confins de l'air et de l'espace – d'Accursius à l'avion spatial. –
19 *AASL* 1994, vol. II, pp.465-500

o. Home-built aircraft

LANGE, P.A. – Tort liability surrounding homebuilt, amateur-built, and experimental aircraft. –
60 *JALC* 1995, pp.575-606

72. State v. private aircraft

GEUT, H. – IFALPA, Legal Committee meeting, Cape Town, South Africa, 19-20 October 1992. Status of aircraft civil/State. –
18 *Air and Space Law* 1993, pp.97-98

73. Legal status of aircraft

GRIGOLI, M. – L'aeromobile nella giurisprudenza. –
14 *DPAC* 1990, pp.154-198

MAPELLI, E. – El concepto legal de la aeronave. –
11 *Anuario hispano-luso-americano de derecho internacional* 1994, pp.189-201

PELÁEZ, M.J. a.o. – Notas sobre la conceptualización jurídica de la aeronave. Perspectiva histórica y regulación normativa en derecho común y comparado, preferencialmente italiano y francés, en relación al derecho español. –
In: Historia del derecho de la navegación I, Barcelona 1994, pp.633-721. *Cuadernos informativos de derecho histórico público, procesal y de la navegación* 2/3 (1986), pp.223-299 and 6/7 (1987), pp.1095-1109

SCHWENK, W. – Luftsportgerät, Luftfahrzeug und Luftfahrtgerät – eine Standortbestimmung. –
43 *ZLW* 1994, pp.143-155

ELBING, G. – Sind Triebwerke wesentliche Bestandteile von Flugzeugen? –
44 *ZLW* 1995, pp.387-395

74. Nationality of aircraft

VIDELA ESCALADA, F. – La nacionalidad de las aeronaves: una visión hacia el futuro. –
In: Aviación comercial, turismo, etc., Buenos Aires 1994, pp.185-192

VIDELA ESCALADA, F. – Nationality of aircraft: a vision of the future. –
In: Essays in honour of Henri A. Wassenbergh, Dordrecht 1992, pp.185-192

WHALEN, Th.J. and LYNES, T.J. – Foreign ownership of US registered aircraft: the voting trust. –
17 *Air and Space Law* 1992, pp.153-159

DE CASTRO FARIAS, H. – A verdadeira nacionalidade da aeronave. –
RBDAE, May-Sept. 1994, no. 66, pp.9-10

DIEDERIKS-VERSCHOOR, I.H.Ph. – International cooperation and its implications for aircraft registration and nationality. –
19 *AASL* 1994, vol. I, pp.145-159

SHIN, H.-K. – Multilateralism and nationality of aircraft and airlines and its implications with respect to Article 7 of the Chicago Convention. –
7 *Korean JAL* 1995, pp.151-173 (in Korean) and pp.174-175 (English summary)

75. Registration of aircraft

HEPPER, G. and MÜLLER, R. – Das Registerprinzip im See-, Luft- und Weltraumrecht – eine rechtsvergleichende Betrachtung. –
39 *ZLW* 1990, pp.256-269

DE MONTLIVAULT, J.-L. – Immatriculation et certification. –

44 *RFDAS* 1991, pp.495-500

VIDAL, E. – Registering aircraft in the US: the legal requirements. –
Legal aspects of aircraft finance, supplement of *Airfinance J*, May 1991, no. 126, pp.12-15

WENZLER, Th. – Die Registrierung von Luftfahrzeugen in der Luftfahrzeugrolle nach dem 'Leasingerlass' des Bundesministers für Verkehr vom 12. Februar 1991. –
40 *ZLW* 1991, pp.276-277

FIORITA, D.M. – The registration of aircraft and the recordation of security interests in aircraft (Canadian practice). –
18 *Oklahoma City Univ. LR*, spring 1993, pp.57-85

RICKETTS, R. and BALFOUR, J. – Aircraft use, registration and leasing in the EC. –
18 *Air and Space Law* 1993, pp.25-28

SÖZER, B. – Aircraft registration in Turkey. –
18 *Air and Space Law* 1993, pp.76-84

BOSTON, W.C. – Registration of aircraft and recording of security instruments under federal law. –
48 *Consumer Finance Law Quarterly Report* (Oklahoma City) 1994, pp.466-475

DIEDERIKS-VERSCHOOR, I.H.Ph. – International cooperation and its implications for aircraft registration and nationality. –
19 *AASL* 1994, vol. I, pp.145-159

77. Construction of aircraft

a. Liability of the manufacturer – Product liability

DANN, D.L. – Present trends in products liability insurance. –
4 *Air and Space Lawyer* (ABA) 1989, no. 3, pp.8-9

GIEMULLA, E. and WENZLER, Th. – Produkthaftpflicht in der Luftfahrt. Der ausländische Kläger vor US-amerikanischen Gerichten. –
35 *Recht der internationalen Wirtschaft* 1989, pp.946-951

LINK II, J.E. – Placards, warning labels & operation manuals: an aircraft manufacturer's duty to warn. –
55 *JALC* 1989, pp.265-302

STIVEN, J.F. – Recent cases and developments in aviation law. II. Product liability. –
55 *JALC* 1989, pp.1-121, at pp.9-29

CARDILLO, S. – La responsabilità del costruttore dell'aeromobile nella prassi contrattuale. –
14 *DPAC* 1990, pp.369-374

CHOI, W.-S. – Aviation products liability in tort – with particular reference to aviation case law in the United States. –
35 *Korean JIL* 1990, pp.59-79 (in Korean

GIEMULLA, E. and WENZLER, Th. – Product liability in the field of aviation – the foreign plaintiff in the U.S.-American court. –
15 *Air Law* 1990, pp.110-121

Oriental Fire & Marine Insurance Co., Ltd. Aircraft product liability insurance. –
2 *Korean JAL* 1990, pp.313-323 (in Korean) and pp.324-339 (in English)

PETKOFF, G.S. – Recent cases and developments in aviation law. II. Products liability. –
56 *JALC* 1990, pp.1-91, at pp.37-49

RINALDI BACCELLI, G. – La responsabilità del costruttore aerospaziale secondo la giurisprudenza comparatistica e la direttiva CEE in materia di responsabilità per prodotto difettoso. –
14 *DPAC* 1990, pp.358-366

SPAIRANI, F. – Controllo di navigabilità e responsabilità del costruttore. –
14 *DPAC* 1990, pp.340-347

BONNEAU, B. – Liability fight goes on. –
5 *Aerospace World*, March 1991, pp.9-10

BRAURE, E. – Responsabilité du constructeur et assurance. –
44 *RFDAS* 1991, pp.541-542

CHOI, W.-S. – A study on aviation products liability in tort – with particular reference to avaition case law in the United States. –
3 *Korean JAL* 1991, pp.113-141 (in Korean)

CRAFT JR, R.R. – Aviation liability law developments in 1990. IV. Liability of manufacturers and suppliers. –
57 *JALC* 1991, pp.1-172, at pp.93-124

GARNAULT, F. – Responsabilité du constructeur. –
44 *RFDAS* 1991, pp.543-547

GOODRICH, M.H. – State-of-the-art aviation technology: a myth. –
27 *Trial* (Washington DC), Febr. 1991, pp.34-38

KRAUSE, C.F. – The impact of disaster litigation on airline and aircraft technology. –
20 *Transportation LJ* 1991, pp.77-87

WELLS, G.P. – General aviation accident liability standards: why the fuss? –
56 *JALC* 1991, pp.895-935

ASSELTA, J.J. – Products liability: new ball games in the United States and Europe. A United States view. –
Brussels symposium, April 1992, 18 pp.

CHRISTIE, J. – The plane truth: thanks largely to the aviation bar, small-plane manufacturing in the United States has all but disappeared. –
12 *California Lawyer*, April 1992, p.19

COOK, J.T. – The product liability crisis: is it the demise of aviation manufacturers? Two myths from hell. –
6 *Air and Space Lawyer* (ABA) 1992, no. 4, pp. 1 and 11

FERRELL JR, W.E. – Aircraft manufacturer's liability. –
17 *AASL* 1992, vol. I, pp.97-136

HOFFMAN, J.M. and HARRIS, P.S. – Recent developments in aviation case law. II. Products liability. –
58 *JALC* 1992, pp.1-101, at pp.18-31

HUON, C. – La responsabilité des fabricants de matériel aéronautique en Europe. –
Diss. McGill. Montreal 1992

KOLCZYNSKI, P.J. a.o. – Aviation and space law: annual survey. I. Aviation product liability. –
27 *Tort & Insurance LJ* (ABA) 1992, pp.156-172, at pp.156-158

PINO JR, J.V. – The product liability crisis and the demise of aviation manufacturers? –
6 *Air and Space Lawyer* (ABA) 1992, no. 3, pp.12-14

SLIJPER, D. – Recent European developments concerning product liability. –
In: The highways of air and outer space, 1992, pp.203-243

STERNS, G.C. – The law of products liability in the United States and Europe. –
Brussels symposium, April 1992, 14-38 pp.

STROUD, J.C. – Recent developments in aviation case law. V. Products liability. –
59 *JALC* 1993, pp.1-75, at pp.46-53

WOLK, A.A. – Product liability: a plaintiff's lawyer responds. –
36 *The AOPA Pilot*, June 1993, pp.117-119

YODICE, J.S. – Product liability on trial. –
36 *The AOPA Pilot*, May 1993, pp.123-124

ABEYRATNE, R.I.R. – The evolution from FANS to CNS/ATM and products liability of technology providers in the United States. –
43 *ZLW* 1994, pp.156-186

ANDERSEN, D.R. – Recent cases and developments in aviation law. IV. Products liability. 60 *JALC* 1994, pp.3-178, at pp.80-106

FOBE, J.-M. – Aviation products liability and insurance in the EU. Legal aspects and insurance of the liability of civil aerospace products manufacturers in the EU, for damage to third parties. –
Deventer 1994, xv-172 pp.

HARVEY, L.M. – The Tenth Circuit holds that the Federal Aviation Act of 1958 does not preempt state common law claims for negligent design. Cleveland v. Piper Aircraft Corp. 985 F.2d 1438 (10th Cir. 1993). –
46 *Baylor LR* (Waco TX) 1994, pp.485-507

KAISER, S.A. – What can be done against bogus aircraft parts? –
19 *Air and Space Law* 1994, pp.298-300

VANWORMER, J.A. – Federal preemption of aircraft design certification standards after Cleveland v. Piper Aircraft Corp.: can general aviation manufacturers recover? –
19 *J of Corporation L* (Iowa City) 1994, pp.665-679

BOSWELL, J.H. and COATS, G.A. – Saving the general aviation industry: putting tort reform to the test. –
60 *JALC* 1995, pp.533-574

GUERRERI, G. – An overview of Italian product liability law. –
44 *ZLW* 1995, pp.21-28

HAND, G.M. – Should juries decide aircraft design? Cleveland v. Piper Aircraft Corp. and federal preemption of state tort law. –
29 *Univ. of San Francisco LR* 1995, pp.741-807

KENNEY, S.C. – Recent developments in aviation law. IV. Sellers' and manufacturers' liability and defenses. –
61 *JALC* 1995, pp.80-89

MCALLISTER, T.S. – A 'tail' of liability reform: the General Aviation Revitalization Act of 1994 and the general aviation industry in the United States. –
23 *Transportation LJ* 1995, pp.301-322

MCNATT Jr, C.C. and ENGLAND, S.L. – The push for statutes of repose in general aviation. –
23 *Transportation LJ* 1995, pp.323-343

PYNE, T. – An historical overview and recent developments in products liability law in Australia. –
44 *ZLW* 1995, pp.413-443

SAVITT, L.J. and COLLERAN, M.J. – Recent developments in aviation and space law. I. Aviation products liability. –
30 *Tort & Insurance LJ* 1995, pp.249-254

d. The Bureau Veritas

DOMAGE, G. – International Aeronautical Register and Pegase computer data base. –
73 *Bulletin Technique du Bureau Véritas* 1991, no. 1, pp.36-39

BOURGEOIS, J.C. and SADIN, J.F. – Surveying air carriers. –
75 *Bulletin Technique du Bureau Véritas*, June 1993, pp.43-54

78. Airworthiness

RINALDI BACCELLI, G. – Attuali tendenze relative al decentramento del controllo di navigabilità dell'aeromobile in occasione della costruzione e dell'esercizio. –
11 *DPAC* 1987, pp.285-311

SPAIRANI, F. – Controllo di navigabilità e responsabilità del costruttore. –
14 *DPAC* 1990, pp.340-347

BRANNEN, E. – The problem of aging aircraft: is mandatory retirement the answer? –
57 *JALC* 1991, pp.425-467

HARRIS, R. – Service bulletins and airworthiness certificates. –
17 *Air and Space Law* 1992, pp.235-236

BERMANN, G.A. – Regulatory cooperation with counterpart agencies abroad: the FAA's aircraft certification experience. –
24 *Law and Policy in Int. Business* (Washington DC) 1993, pp.669-781

DESBIENS, C. – Government liability for the control of air traffic as well as the inspection and certification of aircraft. –
Diss. McGill. Montreal 1993

FOGLIANI, E. – Il controllo della R.a.i. sulla costruzione di aeromobile e cooperazione internazionale. –
Diritto dei Trasporti 1993, pp.505-

MARTIN, P. – Aircraft accident investigation and airworthiness – A practical example of the interaction of two disciplines with some reflections on possible legal consequences. –
19 *Air and Space Law* 1994, pp.158-163

VANWORMER, J.A. – Federal preemption of aircraft design certification standards after Cleveland v. Piper Aircraft Corp.: can general aviation manufacturers recover? –
19 *J of Corporation L* (Iowa City) 1994, pp.665-679

PARKE, R.B. – FAA/JAA harmonization still off-key. –
77 *Business & Commercial Aviation*, July 1995, pp.60-64

SLIJPER, D.J. – Standardization of safety requirements. –
In: The use of airspace and outer space, The Hague 1995, pp.185-193

80. Sale of aircraft

DONSIMONI, P. – TVA intracommunautaire. Acquisition des aéronefs neufs et location des aéronefs en provenance d'un autre État membre de la Union européenne par des assujettis établis en France. –
47 *RFDAS* 1994, pp.127-138

ABEYRATNE, R.I.R. – Dispute resolution in trading in civil aircraft and related services. A comparative study with other aviation issues. –
14 *Trading Law and Trading Law Reports*, July/Aug. 1995, no. 4, pp.284-299

81. Precautionary arrest

ARANGO RODRÍGUEZ, A.J. – Consideraciones sobre el embargo preventivo de aeronaves. –
18 *Revista cubana de derecho* 1989, no. 36, pp.139-150

CRANS, B.J.H. – EC aviation scene. 4. Irish Aerospace (Belgium) N.V. v. Eurocontrol and CAA. –
16 *Air Law* 1991, pp.287-292, at pp.291-292

DAVIES, J.G. – Eurocontrol keeps its powers. –
Airline Business, Sept. 1991, p.110

GUERRERI, G. – Seizure and arrest of aircraft in Italy: unique protection for the airline. –
16 *AASL* 1991, pp.460-462

CHRISTOPHERSON, T. and BAX, J.-H. – Eurocontrol: U.K. detention rights. –
17 *Air and Space Law* 1992, pp.2-8

HUGHES, N. – Eurocontrol and airport liens and some other rights of detention/forfeiture of aircraft. –

17 *Air and Space Law* 1992, pp.137-146

THAINE, C. – Aircraft detention – the draconian rights of airport operators and Eurocontrol. –
Legal aspects of aviation finance, supplement of *Airfinance J*, Sept. 1992, pp.39-44

Aircraft detention: the draconian rights of airport operators and Eurocontrol. –
In: Wilde Sapte – Aids for the aviation financier, London 1993, pp.1-17

VAN BAREN, W.H. – Recent aviation case law from the Benelux. 3. The 1933 Rome Convention on precautionary arrest. –
18 *Air and Space Law* 1993, pp.29-35, at p.34

MIRABELLI, Ph. and PHIPPARD, S. – Rights and remedies open to airlines and other operators for non-payment of route navigation charges, with particular reference to the position in Italy. –
18 *Air and Space Law* 1993, pp.141-147

Repossession of aircraft and insolvency in EC countries. An industry report edited by Sinclair Roche & Temperley. –
Lloyd's of London Press 1993, xii-162 pp.

HERTWIG, A. – Eurocontrol's exercise of detention rights in the United Kingdom illegal? –
20 *Air and Space Law* 1995, pp.277-287

MOUSSÉ, J. – The recovery of route charges and the exercise of the right of detention in the United Kingdom. –
20 *Air and Space Law* 1995, pp.137-145

82. Rights in aircraft

a. General

CRABBE, M. – The power market. –
Airfinance J, Nov. 1990, no. 120, pp.30-31

MCBAIN, G.S. – Aircraft liens under English law. –
15 *Air Law* 1990, pp.79-86

SCHÖLERMANN, H. and SCHMID-BURGK, K. – Flugzeuge als Kreditsicherheit. –
44 *Wertpapier Mitteilungen* 1990, pp.1137-

BUTLER-SLOSS, F. – Engine swapping among financed fleet aircraft. –
Legal aspects of aircraft finance, supplement of *Airfinance J*, May 1991, no. 126, pp.21-23

CUPERFAIN, J. – A Canadian central registry for security interests in aircraft: a good idea but will it fly? –
17 *Canadian Business LJ* 1991, pp.380-414

PACHECO, J DA SILVA – Especulações sobre a hipoteca de aeronave em costrução. –
RBDAE, Jan./Febr. 1991, no. 52, pp.14-20

ROSALES, R.K. – Recordation of rights in aircraft and international recognition: a comparison between the American and Canadian situations. –
16 *AASL* 1991, pp.195-241

SVERNLÖV, C. – Security in aircraft: the Scandinavian systems. –
17 *AASL* 1992, vol. II, pp.369-401

Can one be serious about secured financing of spare engines? –
Wilde Sapte – Aids for the aviation financier, London 1993, pp.82-99

FIORITA, D.M. – The registration of aircraft and the recordation of security interests in aircraft (Canadian practice). –
18 *Oklahoma City Univ. LR*, spring 1993, pp.57-85

SPANÒ, A. – Considerazioni in tema di ipoteca aeronautica. –
Diritto dei Trasporti 1993, pp.854-

Repossession of aircraft and insolvency in EC countries. An industry report edited by Siclair Roche & Temperley. –
Lloyd's of London Press 1993, xii-162 pp.

ANDERSEN, D.R. – Recent cases and developments in aviation law. IX. Debtor-creditor. –
60 *JALC* 1994, pp.3-178, at pp.177-178

BOSTON, W.C. – Registration of aircraft and recording of security instruments under federal law. –
48 *Consumer Finance Law Quarterly Report* (Oklahoma City) 1994, pp.466-475

ELBING, G. – Sind Triebwerke wesentliche Bestandteile von Flugzeugen? –
44 *ZLW* 1995, pp.387-395

c. Spare parts

KAISER, S.A. – What can be done against bogus aircraft parts? –
19 *Air and Space Law* 1994, pp.298-300

Always carry a spare. –
Airfinance J, Febr. 1995, no. 170, p.10

KJELGAARD, C. – Buddy, can you spare the time. –
Airfinance J, Febr. 1995, no. 170, pp.34-35

83. Maintenance – Repairs

SCHUPP, T.R. – Liability of mechanics and repair facilities in general aviation cases. –
57 *Defense Counsel J* (Chicago IL), Jan. 1990, pp.81-84

VERCHÈRE, I. – Lessors look out. –
Airfinance J, Dec. 1990, no. 121, pp.52 and 54

PARRISH, R.L. – Maintenance: new challenges, new solutions. –
68 *Business & Commercial Aviation*, Febvr. 1991, pp.60-62

VERCHÈRE, I. – Leased aircraft need new service law. –
46 *Interavia Aerospace Review*, March 1991, pp.41-44

HARRIS, R. – Service bulletins and airworthiness certificates. –
17 *Air and Space Law* 1992, pp.235-236

A primer for bankers and lawyers on maintenance parlance. –
Wilde Sapte – Aids for the aviation financier, London 1993, pp.19-59

KENNEY, S.C. – Recent developments in aviation law. VI.C. Mechanic's liens. –
61 *JALC* 1995, pp.117-118

LEARMOUNT, D. – Licence to change. –
148 *Flight International*, 26 July-1 August 1995, pp.25-27

Chapter VI. Aviation personnel

91. Labour conditions

RINALDI BACCELLI, G. – Il diritto alla mobilità dei cittadini e lo sciopero nei pubblici servizi di trasporto. –
12 *DPAC* 1988, pp.311-318

COHEN, I. – Political climate and two airlines strike: Century Air in 1932 and Continental Airlines in 1983-85. –
43 *Industrial and Labor Relations R* (Ithaca NY) 1990, pp.308-323

COLEMAN, J.M. – Labor law: settling labor-management disputes: has the Railway Labor Act become obsolete? –
58 *George Washington LR* (Washington DC) 1990, pp.1073-1099

DESJARDINS, M. – L'importance de la gestion des ressources humaines dans l'avenir de l'industrie de l'aviation. –
15 *AASL* 1990, pp.37-44

DONN, C.B. and MARETT, P.C. – Deregulation and the future of transportation trade unionism in the United States. –
41 *Labor LJ* (Chicago IL) 1990, pp.492-497

MCEVOY, K. and OWENS, R. – The flight of Icarus: legal aspects of the pilots' dispute. –
3 *Australian J of Labour Law*, August 1990, pp.87-129

PAPAIOANNOU, A. – The employer's duty to bargain over lay-offs in the airline industry: how the courts have distorted the Railway Labor Act. –
55 *JALC* 1990, pp.939-1008

Railway and airline labor law. –
6 *The Labor Lawyer* (ABA) 1990, pp.611-640

REIS, J. VEILLARD – O acidente de trabalho no direito aeronáutico. –
RBDAE 1990, no. 51, pp.22-23

THOMS, W.E. and DOOLEY, F.J. – Airline labor law. –
Westport CT 1990, 193 pp.

VAN WEZEL STONE, K. – Labor relations of the airlines: the Railway Labor Act in the era of deregulation. –
42 *Stanford LR* 1990, pp.1485-1547

WHITESIDES, P. – Flight attendant weight policies: a Title VII wrong without a remedy. –

64 *Southern California LR* (LA) 1990, pp.175-233

L'esercizio del diritto di scopero nei servizi aerei, aeroportuali e di assistenza al volo, pp.1-31.
La tutela del servizio pubblico essenziale di trasporto aereo in Italia ed in Europa, pp.32-65. –
15 *DPAC* 1991, pp.1-65

DE FUSCO, R.A. and FUESS JR, S.M. – The effects of airline strikes on struck and nonstruck carriers. –
44 *Industrial and Labor Relations R* (Ithaca NY) 1991, pp.324-333

EBERTS, D. – The Mackay doctrine: the grand dame of labor clashes with the current state of the union. –
57 *JALC* 1991, pp.257-296

NAY, L.A. – The determinants of concession bargaining in the airline industry. –
44 *Industrial and Labor Relations R* 1991, pp.307-323

MOROCCO, M. – Weighty discrimination; TWA flight attendants contest weight limits after American settlement. –
77 *ABAJ* 1991, p.34

PARADA VÁZQUEZ, J.D. – Régimen jurídico del personal de vuelo. –
XXI Jornadas iberoamericanas, Lisboa 1991, pp.29-78

RINALDI BACCELLI, G. – La réglementation du droit de grève et le transport aérien en Italie. Considérations sur la Loi 194 sur la grève dans les services publics essentiels. –
16 *AASL* 1991, pp.3-10

DE STEFANI, G. – L'esercizio del diritto di sciopero nei servizi aerei. –
15 *DPAC* 1991, pp.253-261

DE STEFANI, G. – Il diritto di sciopero nei servizi aerei, aeroportuali e di assistenza al volo. –
Trasporti 1991, no. 53/55, pp.89-96

BECHTLOFF, G. – Die Auswirkungen des ÖTV-Streiks 1992 auf den Luftverkehr. Zur Rechtmässigkeit der Streikmassnahmen der Bediensteten des öffentlichen Dienstes auf den Flughäfen. –
41 *ZLW* 1992, pp.226-239

DELUCA, H.O. – El derecho de huelga: alcances. Los servicios públicos esenciales. Situación en la República Argentina, España e Italia. –
8 *Revista europea DNMA* 1992, pp.1411-1418

GRAHAM, B. – Protecting airline employees, protecting the public interest. –
10 *Hofstra Labor LJ* (Hampstead NY), fall 1992, pp.1-21

MILLER, B.F. – The airline industry: labor relations in the era of deregulation, mergers, bankruptcies, and layoffs. –
43 *Labor LJ* (Chicago IL) 1992, pp.388-394

MONSTER, M. – Met de vrucht op de vlucht. Vliegverbod voor zwangere vrouwen. –
8 *Nemesis* (Neth.), juli-aug. 1992, pp.1-3

REED, T.S. – Flight attendant furies: is Title VII really the solution to hiring policy problems? –
58 *JALC* 1992, pp.267-343

Régimen jurídico-laboral del personal de vuelo.

PELÁEZ, M.J.	Notas para una historia del derecho laboral aeronáutico español (1911-1946), pp.1165-1176
GONZÁLEZ DE MANSILLA	Régimen jurídico laboral del personal de vuelo en Venezuela, pp.1185-1209
BALIAN, E.N.	Aspectos jurídicos del personal de vuelo. Modalidad de trabajo. Algunos problemas actuales, pp.1211-1236
FERNÁNDEZ, R.A.	Régimen jurídico-laboral del personal de vuelo, pp.1245-1258
CANTIANO, M.E.	Interpretación normativa del régimen jurídico del personal de vuelo, pp.1259-1264
HARBI, A.B.	La relación laboral del personal de vuelo, pp.1265-1275
LIZARRAGA LACALLE, M.D.	Hacia la libre circulación del personal de vuelo entre los Estados de la Comunidad Económica Europea, pp.1287-1296

8 *Revista europea DNMA* 1992

SCHMID, R. – Flugdienst- und Ruhezeiten von Flugbesatzungsmitgliedern. Ein Kommentar zur 2.DV LuftBO. –
Neuwied etc. 1992, 64 pp.

STORM VAN 'S GRAVESANDE, J.W.E. – Work and rest periods in aviation – A need for safety or a threat to deregulation/liberalisation? –
In: Essays in honour of Henri A. Wassenbergh, Dordrecht 1992, pp.189-200

TILLHET-PRETNAR, J. – La spécificité du droit de travail aérien. –
45 *RFDAS* 1992, pp.353-364

WELLS, S.T. – From the cockpit to the nursing home: a look at the recent developments in the law concerning the age-60 rule. –
57 *JALC* 1992, pp.755-793

ABEYRATNE, R.I.R. – Pepper (Inspector of Taxes) v. Hart and related appeals and privileged travel of airline employees. –
18 *AASL 1993*, vol. I, pp.453-466

DRISCOLL, D.L. – A comparative analysis of the labor statutes which govern the United States and Canadian airline industries and how the relationship may be affected by a new bilateral air agreement. –
60 *Transportation Practitioners J* (Washington DC) 1993, pp.119-142

GUEST, A. – European unions: stern resistance to deregulated strategies. –
10 *The Avmark Aviation Economist*, March 1993, pp.13-14

MCEVOY, K.P. and OWENS, R.J. – On a wing and a prayer: the pilots' dispute in the international context. –
6 *Australian J of Labour Law*, March 1993, pp.1-30

MAPELLI, E. – El sexo, la aviación y el derecho aeronáutico. –
Airline Ninety Two (Spain), dic. 1992/enero 1993, nos. 48-49, pp.38-43

MASINI, L. – Brevi considerazioni sull'ammissibilità della stipulazione di contratti a tempo determinato per il personale di volo. –
95 *Il Diritto Marittimo* 1993, pp.63-67

MASINI, L. – Problematiche attinenti all'applicazione della legge 146/90 relativa all'esercizio del diritto di sciopero nei servizi pubblici essenziali. –
95 *Il Diritto Marittimo* 1993, pp.464-473

YODICE, J.S. – The FAA expunction program. –
36 *The AOPA Pilot*, March 1993, pp.109-110

ABEYRATNE, R.I.R. – Taxation consequences attendant upon privileged travel of airline employees – A potential problem. –
13 *Lloyd's Aviation Law*, 15 Febr. 1994, no. 4, pp.2-6

CHUN, S.-H. – Die Rechtsstellung des Personals im Luftrecht. –
6 *Korean JAL* 1994, pp.239-264 (in Korean) and 265-266 (German summary)

CONWAY, J.A. – The Americans with Disabilities Act: new challenges in airline hiring practices. –
59 *JALC* 1994, pp.945-982

MOORE, M.F. – Hit and run strikes. Protected activity or suicidal actions under the Railway Labor Act? –
59 *JALC* 1994, pp.867-903

SCHODER, L. – Flying the unfriendly skies: the effect of airline deregulation on labor relations. –
22 *Transportation LJ* 1994, pp.105-132

McCormack, B.C. – HIV employment discrimination in air transportation. – 61 *JALC* 1995, pp.287-328

Thomas, S.L.; Officer, D. and Johnson, N.B. – The capital market response to wage negotiations in the airlines. –
34 *Industrial Relations* (Cambridge MA) 1995, pp.203-217

92. Aircraft commander

Metsälampi, V.-M. – The aircraft commander: some observations concerning his legal status. –
In: Essays in honour of Berndt Godenhielm, Helsinki 1984, pp.71-77

Minale Costa, E. – Comandante di aeronave ed equivalenza delle mansioni. –
90 *Il Diritto Marittimo* 1988, pp.1088-1091

Geut, H. – The pilot and the air traffic controller. Division of responsibilities. –
IFALPA Quarterly Review, March 1990, no. 17, pp.6-13

Giemulla, E. and Schmid, R. – Der Luftfahrzeugführer: seine Rechte und Pflichten. –
Neuwied/Frankfurt 1990, 152 pp.

Giemulla, E. and Schmid, R. – Die Verantwortlichkeit der 'Sicherheitspiloten'. –
Neue Zs für Verkehrsrecht 1990, pp.298-301

Malcher, J. Lisboa da Gama – O poder de policía do comandante de aeronave. –
RBDAE 1990, no. 51, p.11

Rüegger, B. – Human error in the cockpit. –
Swiss Re, Zürich 1990, 43 pp.

Rüegger, B. – Menschliches Fehlverhalten im Cockpit. –
Schweizer Rück, Zürich 1990, 43 pp.

Venet, M. – Statut juridique et responsabilités du commandant de bord. –
44 *RFDAS* 1990, pp.169-195

Yodice, J.S. – FAA flight test: who is pilot in command? –
33 *The AOPA Pilot*, August 1990, pp.112 and 114

Farias, H. de Castro – Noções práticas de direito aeronáutico para comandante de aeronave. –
RBDAE, Jan./Febr. 1991, no. 52, pp.11-13

Holmes, J. – Is the Federal Aviation Administration 'kicking the dog?': pilot disciplinary proceedings and the self-incrimination privilege. –
57 *JALC* 1991, pp.297-356

Mapelli, E. – La intimidad del comandante de aeronave. –
Airline (Madrid), May 1991, no. 29, pp.4-9

van Wijk, A. – International Federation of Airline Pilots' Associations (IFALPA). B.2.5. Delegation of command in augmented crew situations. –
16 *AASL* 1991, pp.440-442

Yodice, J.S. – Who's in command, anyway? –
34 *The AOPA Pilot*, June 1991, pp.125-126

Scheer, K.J. – Verantwortung und Rollenverteilung an Bord bei überlangen Flügen. –
41 *ZLW* 1992, pp.377-386

Scofield, D.U. – Knowing when to say when: federal regulation of alcohol consumption by air pilots. –
57 *JALC* 1992, pp.937-979

Yodice, J.S. – The pilot's emergency authority. –
35 *The AOPA Pilot*, Oct, 1992, pp.132 and 134

El comandante de aeronave.

Pérez San Emeterio, C.	Indalecio Rego, in memoriam, pp.17-30
Tapia Salinas, L.	Concepto general de comandante de aeronave, pp.31-37
Fernández Pérez, J.L.	El comandante de aeronave como piloto al mando, pp.39-45
Herrera Esteban, L.	El comandante de aeronave como autoridad pública, pp.47-58
Cembranos Miranda, A.	El comandante de aeronave como piloto, pp.59-64
Loustau Ferrán, F.	El comandante de aeronave como mandatario del operador, pp.65-78
Parada Vázquez, J.D.	El comandante de aeronave, aspectos jurídicos aeronáuticos, civiles y laborales, pp.79-94
Bartolomé Izquierdo, A.	El humanismo del comandante de aeronave, pp.95-103
Aparicio Gallego, J.	Comandante de aeronave militar: comandante militar de aeronave. Su concepto en el derecho español, pp.105-134
Mapelli, E.	El comandante de aeronave en el convenio de Tokio, pp.135-154
Bravo Navarro, M.	Estatuto internacional del comandante de aeronave, pp.155-182

NAVARRETE CASAS, F. Estatuto de comandante de aeronave de la compañía Iberia, pp.183-198
El comandante de aeronave, Madrid 1993, 205 pp.

HIBBS, L.R. and SWEET, J.W. – Aircraft with dual controls: who is flying the plane? –
1 *Nevada Lawyer*, June 1993, pp.16-17

BARKLOW, B.K. – Rethinking the age sixty mandatory retirement rule: a look at the newest movement. –
60 *JALC* 1994, pp.329-368

BOCKSTHALER, K.B. – Der Sicherheitspilot: wer hat die Entscheidungsgewalt im Cockpit? 38 *Aerokurier*, Febr. 1994, pp.31-32

KANE, R. and PYNE , T. – The legal status and liability of the copilot. –
19 *Air and Space Law* 1994, pp.290-297 and 20 *Air and Space Law* 1995, pp.2-17

YODICE, J.S. – Careless or reckless? –
38 *The AOPA Pilot*, April 1995, pp.142 and 144

93. Licences

YODICE, J.S. – New medical application form. –
324 *The AOPA Pilot*, August 1991, pp.117-119

SWIECICKI, E. – Legal aspects of licensing of airline transport pilots: international standards versus Canadian aviation safety regulations. –
Diss. McGill. Montreal 1992, xx-180 pp.

FRANK, D.C. – Drunk driving offenses and pilots: special problems representing holders of FAA pilots licenses. –
72 *Michigan Bar J*, Jan. 1993, pp.64-65

YODICE, J.S. – The FAA expunction program. –
36 *The AOPA Pilot*, March 1993, pp.109-110

MINTER, V.L. – Certification of unfit pilots: is the United States flying blind? –
59 *JALC* 1994, pp.763-811

KENNEY, S.C. – Recent developments in aviation law. X. FAA enforcement/local regulation. –
61 *JALC* 1995, pp.142-155

95. Liability

VAN WIJK, A. – IFALPA Legal Committee meeting, Montreal, Canada, 6-7 September 1989. 2. Criminal liability of pilots. –
15 *Air Law* 1990, p.157

GUILLAUME, G. – Responsabilité pénale du commandant de bord en droit français. –
16 *AASL* 1991, pp.79-92

Legal liability of the pilot. –
IFALPA Quarterly Review, June 1991, 28 pp.

VAN WIJK, A. – IFALPA. B.2.1. Legal liability of pilots. –
16 *AASL* 1991, pp.436-439

ANDREOTTI, R.J. – Promoting general aviation safety: a revision of pilot negligence law. –
58 *JALC* 1993, pp.1089-1148

Chapter VII. Airports and air navigation facilities

101. Airports

a. General

HARDAWAY, R. – Economics of airport regulation. –
20 *Transportation LJ* 1991, pp.47-75

RINALDI BACCELLI, G. – Sintesi delle informazioni relative ad alcuni principali aeroporti europei. –
DPAC 1993, no. 1, pp.15-40

GIL, A. – The outcome of the 4th Air Transport Conference and its implications for airports. –
20 *Air and Space Law* 1995, pp.76-81

102. Regulations

a. General

DAVISON, C. and HALLOWAY, L.B. – The two faces of Section 105 – Airline shield or airport sword. –
56 *JALC* 1990, pp.93-123

RUSSELL, A.S. and FLUEGEL, L. – Airport law (regulation of commercial activity; pilot sanctions). –
22 *The Urban Lawyer* (ABA) 1990, pp.331-332

BALFOUR, J. – The battle of Orly: the legal dimension. –
J of Air Transport Management 1994, no. 3, pp.161-164

POLLAK VARELA, J.P. – Aeropuertos. Aspectos jurídicos. –
Aviación comercial, turismo, etc. Buenos Aires 1994, pp.159-165

b. International

STAEHELIN, B. – Rechtszuständigkeit der Schweiz auf den Flughafen Basel-Mulhouse. –
ASDA Bulletin 1990-2, no. 109, pp.25-30

BENTZIEN, J. – Die völkerrechtliche Sonderstellung des Flughafens Basel-Mülhausen. –
42 *ZLW* 1993, pp.401-423

SPOENDLIN, K. – Schweizerische Lufthoheit und Fluglärm um den Flughafen Basel-Mulhouse. –

94 *Schweizerisches Zentralblatt für Staats- und Verwaltungsrecht* 1993, pp.285-297

c. National

MARCHETTI, M. – L'infrastruttura aeroportuale. Accelerazione dei lavori e programmazione degli interventi. –
13 *DPAC* 1989, pp.322-348

STIVEN, J.F. – Recent cases and developments in aviation law. V. Airports. –
55 *JALC* 1989, pp.41-58

ANDERSON, T.W. and RASMUSSEN, P.J. – Recent developments in airport law. –
22 *The Urban Lawyer* (ABA) 1990, pp.899-917

The antitrust implications of airport lease restrictions. –
104 *Harvard LR* 1990, pp.548-567

PETKOFF, G.S. – Recent cases and developments in aviation law. X. Airports. –
56 *JALC* 1990, pp.491-556

HARDAWAY, R.M. – Airport regulation, law, and public policy: the management and growth of infrastructure. –
New York 1991

PENNINGTON, W. – Airport restrictions: a dilemma of federal preemption and proprietary control. –
56 *JALC* 1991, pp.805-845

DETTLING-OTT, R. – Zulassungszwang auf schweizerischen Flughäfen. –
ASDA Bulletin 1992-2, no. 113, [6]-50-[4] pp.

HOFFMAN, J.M. and HARRIS, P.S. – Recent developments in aviation case law. VI. Airports. –
58 *JALC* 1992, pp.47-57

HORN, W. – Sind Verkehrslandeplätze als öffentliche Einrichtungen des Kommunalrechts zu qualifizieren? –
Verwaltungsblatt für Baden-Württemberg 1992, no. 1, pp.5-9

APARICIO GALLEGO, J. – Aeropuertos españoles y navegación aérea: el nuevo ente público de la organización jurídico administrativa española. –
In: Aviación comercial, turismo, etc. Buenos Aires 1994, pp.195-199

GREINER, H.W. – Die Betriebspflicht von Flugplätzen. Rechtliche Grundlagen und 'Kleinflieger-Problematik'. –
Bayerische Verwaltungsblätter 1994, pp.449-457

RONELLENFITSCH, M. – Der Militärflugplatz. Merkmale und Kriterien. –
47 *Die öffentliche Verwaltung* 1994, no. 2, pp.45-52

YODICE, J. – Current issues in aviation involving airports. –
19 *Air and Space Law* 1994, pp.89-92

103. Duty to land on certain airports

BÖCKSTIEGEL, K.-H. and KRÄMER, P.M. – Die luftfahrtbehördliche Erlaubnis zu Aussenstarts und Aussenlandungen. –
42 *ZLW* 1993, pp.343-356

104. Concessions

FASSINA, G. – Riflessioni su problemi vecchi e nuovi dell'azienda aeroporto. –
13 *DPAC* 1989, pp.361-368

Schema di decreto legge concernente nuove attribuzioni delle società concessionarie delle gestioni aeroportuali e le modalità del loro esercizio. –
13 *DPAC* 1989, pp. 349-360

CARRÉ, A.-D. – Aéroports et stratégie d'entreprise. –
ITA, Paris 1990, xiv-350 pp.

QUERCI, F.A. – L'aeroporto come empresa. –
5/6 *Revista europea DNMA* 1990-91, pp.741-752

ASHFORD, N. and MOORE, C.A. – Airport finance. –
New York 1992, xi-240 pp.

FINNSON, G. – Move to privatization of airports requires careful consideration of numerous factors. –
48 *ICAO J*, Jan./Febr. 1993, pp.18-19

ENDLER, J. – Strip funding. –
Airfinance J, Nov. 1994, no. 167, pp.34-36

KIM, H.-R. – Das Planungsverfahren umweltrelevanter Grossvorhaben in der Bundesrepublik Deutschland und der Republik Korea am Beispiel der Flughafenplanung. –
Diss. Speyer, 1990, 349 pp.

105. Construction of airports

a. General

HOBMA, F.A.M. – Het beleidsconvenant plan van aanpak Schiphol en omgeving. –
28 *Bouwrecht* 1991, pp.829-836

HOOGEVEEN, J.P.; NOORDZIJ, A.S.; DE VOS, M. en VROLIJK, R. – Geluidshinder rondom Schiphol. –
's Gravenhage 1991, 108 pp.

TAN, T.G. e.a. – Het plan van aanpak Schiphol. –
Vereniging van Milieurecht 1991-92. Zwolle 1991, vi-80 pp.

HOBE, S. – Zur gerichtlichen Überprüfbarkeit behördlicher Planungsentscheidungen, dargestellt am Urteil BVerwGE 87,332 zum Flughafen München II. –
41 *ZLW* 1992, pp.248-254

ABEYRATNE, R.I.R. – The challenge of airports and planning laws. –
23 *Environmental Policy and Law*, April 1993, pp.79-86

ABEYRATNE, R.I.R. – Sydney's third runway. A global perspective. –
10 *Environmental and Planning LJ* 1993, pp.355-364

HOBE, S. – Zu den rechtlichen Grundlagen der Änderungen von Schutzauflagen im Planungsrecht und ihrer Relevanz für die Flughafenplanung. –
42 *ZLW* 1993, pp.258-262

KAISER, S.A. – Stolpersteine beim Flugplatzausbau in den neuen Bundesländern. –
42 *ZLW* 1993, pp.151-161

b. Airports and their neighbours

HERTZOG, R. – Le régime financier de la lutte contre le bruit autour des aéroports: condamnation provisoire ou disparition définitive? –
Revue juridique de l'environnement 1988, pp.117-142

ALLEN, E.A. – The Wright amendment: the constitutionality and propriety of the restrictions on Dallas Love Field. –
55 *JALC* 1990, pp.1011-1074

GRATJIOS, G. – Airport noise pollution: legal aspects. –
Diss. McGill. Montreal 1990

PETTITI, C. – Les riverains de l'aéroport d'Heathrow et la Convention Européenne des Droits de l'Homme. Affaire Powel et Rayner. –
44 *RFDAS* 1990, pp.395-404

VAN DALEN, J.A.W. – Geluidhinder en geluidzonering rond Schiphol. –
24 *Rooilijn* 1991, no. 4, pp.112-116

STEIN, P.B. – The price of success: mitigation and litigation in airport growth. –
57 *JALC* 1991, pp.513-556

MARCHESE, C.S. – The dormant commerce clause and airport noise: a case for narrow judicial review. –
44 *Baylor LR* (Waco TX) 1992, pp.645-709

STAFFELBACH, H.P. – L'attitude des aéroports face à la problématique de l'environnement. How airports are coping with environmental problems. –
ITA Études & documents/Studies & reports 92/2, vol. 26, pp.57-64

TSILAS, V. – An analysis of the phase-out provisions of the Airport Noise and Capacity Act of 1990. –
4 *Fordham Environmental Law Report*, fall 1992, pp.83-101

HILLESTAD, R. a.o. – Airport growth and safety: a study of the external risks of Schiphol Airport and possible safety-enhancement measures. –
Santa Monica 1993, Rand European-American Center for Policy Analysis, xxx-181 pp.

DE KRAMER, T. en VAN DEN BERG, C. – Rechtsbescherming en luchtvaartlawaai. Juridische instrumenten ter bescherming van de burger tegen luchtvaartlawaai, in het bijzonder tegen dat van militair vliegveld Soesterberg. –
Wetenschapswinkel Rechten Utrecht, mei 1993, 131 pp.

UYENO, D.; HAMILTON, W. and BIGGS, A.J.G. – Density of residential land use and the impact of airport noise. –
27 *J of Transport Economics and Policy* 1993, pp.3-18

Airports and environment. –
Chichester 1994, iv-176 pp.

Aviation noise policy and regulation. –
46 *Administrative LR* (Chicago IL) 1994, pp.413-427

HERMANN, M. – Schutz vor Fluglärm bei der Planung von Verkehrsflughäfen im Lichte des Verfassungsrechts: zur Auslegung des §9 Abs.2 LuftVG. –
Diss. Regensburg 1993. Berlin 1994, 378 pp.

ABEYRATNE, R.I.R. – Olympics 2000 and Sydney's airport policy: an environmental impact study. –
20 *AASL* 1995, vol. II, pp.1-45

d. Zoning laws

COLE, T.J. – Zoning control of airport expansion by host cities and the battle over Dallas/Fort Worth International Airport. –
59 *JALC* 1993, pp.193-237

HOBMA, F.A.M. – Het wetsvoorstel tot wijziging van de Luchtvaartwet. –
Ts voor Milieu en Recht 1993, no. 10, pp.542-549

WALDER, R. – Control of land use near airports is best means of reducing impact of aircraft noise. –
48 *ICAO J*, Jan./Febr. 1993, pp.8-11

HAMILTON, J.S. – Allocation of air space as a scarce national resource. –
22 *Transportation LJ* 1994, pp.251-290

HERMANN, M. – Schutz vor Fluglärm bei der Planung von Verkehrsflughäfen im Lichte des Verfassungsrechts: zur Auslegung des §9 Abs.2 LuftVG. –
Diss. Regensburg. Studien zum Umweltrecht Bd. 40. Berlin 1994, 378 pp.

107. Liability for the exploitation of airports. Birdstrikes

I riflessi sul trasporto aereo del processo di liberalizzazione del Mercato Comune Europeo: opportunità e prospettive. III. Le gestioni aeroportuali.

QUERCI, F.A.	L'aeroporto come empresa, pp.140-149
SALVI, B.	L'adeguamento delle infrastrutture aeroportuali in relazione all'aumento del traffico aereo in Europa, pp.150-155
CEMPELLA, D.	Lo snellimento delle procedure amministrative quale instrumento insostituibile dello sviluppo aeroportuale, pp.156-160
MARCHETTI, M.	Le formule organizzative dei principali aeroporti europei, pp.161-189
NICOLETTI, A.	La rete aeroportuale italiana e le esigenze dei principali centri nazionali, pp.190-195
CASANOVA, M.	Le competenze delle autorità regionali e locali in materia aeroportuale, pp.196-207
VERMIGLIO, G.	Aeroporti e interporti, pp.208-212

13 *DPAC* 1989, pp.139-221

BELLAN, P.G. – Responsabilità degli aeroporti in relazione ai servizi aeroportuali. –
14 *DPAC* 1990, pp.294-318

CAMPANA, C. – L'assicurazione dei rischi connessi all'esercizio delle attività aeroportuali.
14 *DPAC* 1990, pp.395-408

QUERCI, F.A. – L'azienda aeroportuale e di assistenza al volo e la loro responsabilità civile. –
14 *DPAC* 1990, pp.261-267

SANDULLI, M.A. – La disciplina della responsabilità nelle diverse realtà gestionali del sistema aeroportuale. –
14 *DPAC* 1990, pp.282-292

DE STEFANI, G. – La responsabilità civile del direttore dell'aeroporto. –
Trasporti 1990, no. 50-52, pp.159-168. 14 *DPAC* 1990, pp.270-280

QUERCI, F.A. – L'aeroporto come empresa. –
5/6 *Revista europea DNMA* 1990-91, pp.741-752

BONFANTONI, C. – Ancora sulla responsabilità dell'impresa aeroportuale. –
Diritto dei Trasporti 1991, pp.256-

CRAFT JR, R.R. – Aviation liability law developments in 1990. VII. Liability of airports. –
57 *JALC* 1991, pp.151-154

HORTON, N. – Ratschläge zur Vogelschlagverhütung auf Flughäfen: einige Erfordernisse und Missverständnisse. –
11 *Vogel und Luftverkehr* 1991, no. 1, pp.20-26

SINCLAIR, R.A. – Airport dominance and state action antitrust immunity for airport operators. –
96 *Dickinson LR* (Carlisle PA), fall 1991, pp.1-10

VUILLERMET, P. and BRIOT, J.L. – Französische Vorschriften für Massnahmen zur Vogelschlagverhütung auf Flughäfen. –
11 *Vogel und Luftverkehr* 1991, pp.27-33

DOGANIS, R. – The airport business. –
London 1992, xiii-226 pp.

GUERRERI, G. – The airport operator: air carrier's agent or independent contractor? –
17 *Air and Space Law* 1992, pp.231-234. Brussels symposium, April 1992, 10 pp.

RINALDI BACCELLI, G. – La responsabilità del gestore aeroportuale per la custodia delle merci dopo l'arrivo in aeroporto. –
DPAC 1993, no. 1, pp.111-132

STROUD, J.C. – Recent developments in aviation case law. VIII. Airports. –
59 *JALC* 1993, pp.60-64

TALICE, C. – Il direttore di aeroporto, organo amministrativo complesso. –
Rivista amministrativa (Roma) 1993, pp.1353-

YODICE, J.S. – Who pays the bill? –
36 *The AOPA Pilot*, July 1993, pp.119-120

ANDERSEN, D.R. – Recent cases and developments in aviation law. VI. Airports. –
60 *JALC* 1994, pp.120-123

KENNEY, S.C. – Recent developments in aviation law. VI. Airports and fixed base operators. –
61 *JALC* 1995, pp.99-118

108. Taxes

STIVEN, J.F. – Recent cases and developments in aviation law. V. Landing and terminal renting fees. –
55 *JALC* 1989, pp.49-51

FARIAS, H. DE CASTRO – As taxas aeronáuticas e aeroportuárias (user charges) na América Latina. –
RBDAE, May-June 1991, no. 54, pp.19-22

FOCKE, K. – Wem dient die Sicherheitsüberprüfung der Flugpassagiere? Einige Anmerkungen zur Zulässigkeit der Luftsicherheitsgebühr. –
41 *ZLW* 1992, pp.240-247

HUGHES, N. – Eurocontrol and airport liens and some other rights of detention/forfeiture of aircraft. –
17 *Air and Space Law* 1992, pp.137-146

RICHARDSON, J. – FAA passenger taxes assist airports, annoy airlines. –
56 *Tax Notes* (Arlington VA) 1992, pp.974-976

ABEYRATNE, R.I.R. – Air transport tax and its consequences on tourism. –
20 *Annals of Tourism Research* 1993, pp.450=460

HEINZE, C. – Benutzungs- und Entgeltordnungen für Flughäfen unter Berücksichtigung der Kartellrechtsnovelle von 1989-90. –
12 *Neue Zs für Verwaltungsrecht* 1993, pp.1145-1150

BAILEY, E.O. – Article 15 of the Chicago Convention: the duty of States to avoid discriminatory user charges: the US-UK London Heathrow user charges arbitration. –
19 *AASL* 1994, vol. II, pp.81-105

FINNSON, G. – Airports and route facilities: international cost recovery policies and their applicability in the framework of new forms of infrastructure provision. –
19 *AASL* 1994, vol. II, pp.283-309

MARGO, R.D. and MACCARY, W.T. – The Chicago Convention and the resolution of landing fee disputes. –
19 *AASL* 1994, vol. II, pp.501-521

PETERS, R.J. – Northwest Airlines v. County of Kent, Michigan: more than you ever wanted to know about airport rate setting. –
22 *Transportation LJ* 1994, pp.291-307

YODICE, J.S. – Current issues in aviation involving airports. –
19 *Air and Space Law* 1994, pp.89-92

United States-United Kingdom arbitration. Heathrow Airport user charges. –
88 *AJIL* 1994, pp.738-744

Airport charges: levelling the landing field. –
12 *The Avmark Aviation Economist*, June-July 1995, pp.6-7

IMES, S. – Airline passenger facility charges: what do they mean for an ailing industry? –
60 *JALC* 1995, pp.1039-1089

SKILBECK, J. – The US/UK arbitration concerning Heathrow airport user charges. –
44 *ICLQ* 1995, pp.171-179

109. Air Traffic Control

a. General

DE ROODE, A.A. – Luchtverkeersbeveiliging. De geschiedenis van de luchtverkeersbeveiliging in Nederland 1910-heden. –
Houten 1988, 160 pp.

I riflessi sul trasporto aereo del processo di liberalizzazione del Mercato Comune Europeo: opportunità e prospettive. IV. Assistenza al volo.

MAIONE, D.	Adeguamento dei servizi di assistenza al volo all'aumento del traffico aereo in Europa, pp.223-231
PUGLIESE, F.	Competenze civili e militari nell'esercizio dei servizi di assistenza al volo, pp.232-240
TURCO BULGHERINI, E.	Brevi considerazioni sull'attuale regime giuridico della gestione dei servizi di assistenza al volo in Europa e sull'unificazione internazionale della loro responsabilità, pp.249-256

13 *DPAC* 1989, pp.222-283

COURTOIS, K.N. – 'Standards and practices': the judiciary's role in promoting safety in the air traffic control system. –
55 *JALC* 1990, pp.1117-1157

GEUT, H. – The pilot and the air traffic controller. Division of responsibilities. –
IFALPA QR, March 1990. no. 17, pp.6-13

GRAUMANN, H. – Flugsicherung – Polizei oder Unternehmen? Ein Ansatz zu neuem Verständnis. –
39 *ZLW* 1990, pp.247-255

KEAN, A. – The language of air traffic control. –
J of Business Law (UK) 1990, pp.524-526

VILLIERS, J. – The 'capacity' barriers. –
ITA Magazine, Jan./Febr. 1990, no. 59, pp.14-21

KAISER, S.A. – Two recent cases of privatization: air traffic control and the space agency.
16 *Air Law* 1991, pp.125-132

RIEDEL, N.K. and SCHMIDT, A. – Die Nichtausfertigung des Gesetzes zur Privatisierung der Flugsicherung durch den Bundespräsidenten. –
44 *Die öffentliche Verwaltung* 1991, pp.371-375

VITT, E. – Rechtsfragen bei der Übermittlung von Radar-Daten durch die Bundesanstalt für Flugsicherung an einen Flughafen-Betreiber. –
40 *ZLW* 1991, pp.123-131

YODICE, J.S. – Who's in command, anyway? –
34 *The AOPA Pilot*, June 1991, pp.125-126

Air traffic control errors. –
36 *The Trial Lawyer's Guide* (Deerfield IL) 1992, pp.376-388

RINALDI BACCELLI, G. – Projet d'instrument international concernant la responsabilité des services de la circulation aérienne. –
ILA Report, Cairo 1992, pp.74-81

YODICE, J.S. – The pilot's emergency authority. –
35 *The AOPA Pilot*, Oct. 1992, pp.132 and 134

KUNZ, D. – Rechtliche Aspekte der neueren Luftraumorganisation und der internationalen Flugsicherungszusammenarbeit. –
ASDA Bulletin 1993-1, no. 114, pp.19-44

PASCALL, S.C. – The ATLAS study. –
35 *J of ATC* 1993, no. 3, pp.78, 80-82

RINALDI BACCELLI, G. – ILA. Conference 1992. Committee on the legal aspects of air traffic control. –
DPAC 1993, no. 1, pp.79-85

SCHUBERT, F. – Air traffic control – a time for change. –
18 *AASL* 1993, vol. I, pp.257-264 (in French: pp.265-273)

SCHUBERT, F. – Les effets de la délégation de compétences en matière de services de la circulation aérienne sur la souveraineté nationale. –
46 *RFDAS* 1993, pp.289-300

SCHUBERT, F. – Éléments en faveur d'une révision de la réglementation internationale en matière de contrôle de la circulation aérienne. –
18 *AASL* 1993, vol. I, pp.265-273 (in English: pp.257-264)

GETHIN, S. – Is privatisation the answer? –
3 *Air Traffic Management* 1994, no. 6, pp.7-9

HABIB, P.B. – ATC privatisation: how far can you go? –
11 *The Avmark Aviation Economist*, Nov. 1994, pp.11-14

MAJUMDAR, A. – Air traffic control problems in Europe: their consequences and proposed solutions. –
1 *J of Air Transport Management* 1994, no. 3, pp.165-177

MEREDITH, J. – Air traffic management in Europe – can it cope with future growth? –
1 *J of Air Transport Management* 1994, no. 3, pp.179-180

WHITTINGTON, H. – Canada is set to 'commercialize' ANS. –
75 *Business & Commercial Aviation* 1994, no. 5, pp.58-61

BRADLEY, P. – Free flight. –
76 *Business & Commercial Aviation* 1995, no. 6, pp.90-92, 94

Mensch und Maschine / L'homme et la machine / Man and machine. –
Swisscontrol, Berne 1995, 12 pp.

b. State liability

Finanziamento e responsabilità civile dei servizi di assistenza alla navigazione aerea. Riflessi di diritto interno ed internazionale. –
12 *DPAC* 1988, pp.5-104

KIM, D.-H. – Some considerations on the liability of Air Traffic Control agencies. –
1 *Korean JAL* 1989, pp.9-37 (in Korean) and 38-46 (English summary)

STIVEN, J.F. – Recent cases and developments in aviation law. III B. Air Traffic Control.
55 *JALC* 1989, pp.31-35

CONWAY, L.M. – Microbursts: will technology ever catch up? –
56 *JALC* 1990, pp.263-303

QUERCI, F.A. – L'azienda aeroportuale e di assistenza al volo e la loro responsabilità civile. –
14 *DPAC* 1990, pp.261-267

TURCO BULGHERINI, E. – L'esperienza giurisprudenziale della responsabilità degli enti di controllo della circolazione aerea ed il progetto di convenzione dell'International Law Association. –
14 *DPAC* 1990, pp.319-325

CRAFT JR, R.R. – Aviation liability law developments in 1990. III E. General liability of other operators and owners of aircraft. –
57 *JALC* 1991, pp.92-93

L'esercizio del diritto di sciopero nei servizi aerei, aeroportuali e di assistenza al volo, pp.1-31.
La tutela del servizio pubblico essenziale di trasporto aereo in Italia ed in Europa, pp.32-65. –
15 *DPAC* 1991, pp.1-65

JONES, R.H. – Reconsidering the FAA's dual role. –
33 *J of ATC* 1991, no. 2, pp.19-21

KIM, D.-H. – Liability of governmental bodies in international civil aviation. –
3 *Korean JAL* 1991, pp.7-23 (in Korean) and 24-49 (in English)

Air traffic control errors (Budden v. United States). –
36 *The Trial Lawyer's Guide* (Deerfield IL) 1992, pp.376-388

HOFFMAN, J.M. and HARRIS, Ph.S. – Recent developments in aviation case law. III B. Air Traffic Control. –
58 *JALC* 1992, pp.35-37

KOLCZYNSKI, Ph.J. a.o. – Aviation and space law: annual survey. III. Governmental liability – Air Traffic Control. –
27 *Tort & Insurance LJ* (ABA) 1992, pp.161-163

Alleged air traffic control negligence failure of proof (Sonnemaker v. United States). –
36 *The Trial Lawyer's Guide* (Deerfield IL) 1993, pp.595-604

DESBIENS, C. – Government liability for the control of air traffic as well as the inspection and certification of aircraft. –
Diss. McGill. Montreal 1993

FRANCHI, B. – Il problema della responsabilità dei servizi di assistenza al volo e della relativa limitazione. –
Responsabilità civile e della previdenza (Milano) 1993, pp.889-

HEESEN, D. – Luftsicherheit – eine neue Aufgabe des Bundesgrenzschutzes. –
Die Polizei 1993, pp.105-117

LA PENNA, V. – La responsabilità del controllore del traffico aereo e l'esigenza di unificazione internazionale delle regole in materia. –
Rivista della Corte di conti (Roma) 1993, no. 6, pp.302-

SCHUBERT, F. – La responsabilité des services de la circulation aérienne. –
ASDA Bulletin 1993-2, no. 115, pp.5-34

ANDERSEN, D.R. – Recent cases and developments in aviation law. V B. Air Traffic Control. –
60 *JALC* 1994, pp.110-119

SCHUBERT, F. – La responsabilité des agences du contrôle de la circulation aérienne. –
Diss. Genève. Opfikon (Suisse) 1994, xvi-282 pp.

KENNEY, S.C. – Recent developments in aviation law. V.B. Air Traffic Control negligence. –
61 *JALC* 1995, pp.92-96

d. Eurocontrol

BOTHE, M. ; HOHMANN, H. and SCHMIDT, Chr. – Möglichkeiten einer Reform der europäischen Flugsicherung? –
39 *ZLW* 1990, pp.40-55

BOTHE, M.; HOHMANN, H. and SCHMIDT, Chr. – Rechtliche Möglichkeit und drängende Notwendigkeit einer EG-Initiative zur Reform der europäischen Flugsicherung. –
36 *Recht der intern. Wirtschaft* 1990, pp.199-206

MOUSSÉ, J. – La coopération européenne en matière de circulation aérienne; aspects juridiques du rôle d'EUROCONTROL. –
44 *RFDAS* 1990, pp.257-287

MOXON, J. – Eurocontrol managing ATC unity. –
138 *Flight International*, 8-14 August 1990, pp.65-67

DAVIES, J.G. – Eurocontrol keeps its powers. –
Airline Business, Sept. 1991, p.110

KLETTE, L. – De crisis in het Europese luchtverkeer. De NAVO streeft naar samenwerking tussen de civiele en de militaire luchtvaart. –
39 *NAVO Kroniek*, Febr. 1991, pp.24-29

MACK, K.R. – An Eurocontrol point of view. –
In: Air transport law and policy in the 1990s, Dordrecht 1991, at pp.61-68

MAJID, A.A. – Legal capacity of Eurocontrol to ensure smooth aviation in Europe. –
16 *Air Law* 1991, pp.267-279

SAILLARD, S. – Les institutions et aspects juridiques relatifs au contrôle aérien en Europe: Eurocontrol. –
Diss. McGill. Montreal 1991, 120 pp.

CHRISTOPHERSON, T. and BAX, J.-H. – Eurocontrol: U.K. detention rights. –
17 *Air and Space Law* 1992, pp.2-8

HUGHES, N. – Eurocontrol and airport liens and some other rights of detention/forfeiture of aircraft. –
17 *Air and Space Law* 1992, pp.137-146

THAINE, C. – Aircraft detention – the draconian rights of airport operators and Eurocontrol. –
Legal aspects of aircraft finance, supplement of *Airfinance J*, Sept. 1992, pp.39-44

Aircraft detention: the draconian rights of airport operators and Eurocontrol. –
In: Aids for the aviation financier, Wilde Sapte, London 1993, pp.1-17

FREDIANI, R. – Il processo di integrazione e armonizzazione dei sistemi di assistenza al volo in Europa e gestione dello spazio aereo. –
Trasporti 1993, no. 59, pp.75-87

KUNZ, D. – Rechtliche Aspekte der neueren Luftraumorganisation und der internationalen Flugsicherungszusammenarbeit. –
ASDA Bulletin 1993-1, no. 114, pp.19-44

MACK, K. – The development of European cooperation. –
35 *J of ATC* 1993, no. 3, pp.48-50

MIRABELLI, Ph. and PHIPPARD, S. – Rights and remedies open to airlines and other operators for non-payment of route navigation charges, with particular reference to the position of Italy. –
18 *Air and Space Law* 1993, pp.141-147

SCHWENK, W. and R. – Flugsicherung in Europa. –
42 *ZLW* 1993, pp.121-143

MOUSSÉ, J. – Le régime juridique des redevances de route et la Cour de Justice des Communautés Européennes. –
47 *RFDAS* 1994, pp.7-41

LAMBERT, Y. – Eurocontrol et l'OACI. –
19 *AASL* 1994, vol. I, pp.349-369

MOXON, J. – European dilemma. –
145 *Flight International*, 9-15 Febr. 1994, pp.30-31

HERTWIG, A. – Eurocontrol's exercise of detention rights in the United Kingdom illegal? –
20 *Air and Space Law* 1995, pp.277-287

MOUSSÉ, J. – The recovery of route charges and the exercise of the right of detention in the United Kingdom. –
20 *Air and Space Law* 1995, pp.137-145

MOUSSÉ, J. – Les redevances de route: De l'absence de contradiction entre la jurisprudence du Conseil d'État et celle de la Cour de Justice des Communautés. –
48 *RFDAS* 1995, pp.29-38

e. ASECNA

FAUJAS, A. – A new start for air traffic control in Africa. Out of the red ASECNA style. –
ITA Magazine, Jan./March 1991, no. 65, pp.25-26

TAHOU, R.S. – Les aspects institutionnels et juridiques de restructuration de l'ASECNA. –
18 *AASL* 1993, vol. I, pp.315-329

110. Operations. Meteorology. Communications. Charts. FANS. CNS/ATM

MAJID, A. – An analytical study of the constitutional structure of SITA and its legal status in international aw. –
DCL diss. McGill. Montreal 1985

CHIAVARELLI, E. – Satelliti e sicurezza della navigazione aerea: aspetti giuridici e ipotesi di responsabilità. –
14 *DPAC* 1990, pp.383-394

BELAUSTEGUI GOITIA, C. – World Administrative Radio Conference ends favourably for air transport sector. –
47 *ICAO J*, June 1992, pp.21-24

VAN DAM, R.D. – ICAO. I. Legal aspects 10th Air Navigation Conference. II. Date and agenda Legal Committee. –
17 *Air and Space Law* 1992, pp.125-126

VAN DAM, R.D. – 28th Session of the Legal Committee. –
17 *Air and Space Law* 1992, pp.224-226

HUSAIN KHAN, A. – Aeronautical communication, navigation and surveillance by satellite – Towards a global framework for civil aviation? –
In: Essays in honour of Henri A. Wassenbergh, Dordrecht 1992, pp.43-51

KAISER, S.A. – A new aspect of future air navigation systems: how secondary surveillance radar mode S could protect civil aviation. –
41 *ZLW* 1992, pp.154-164

KAISER, S.A. – Will the WARC '92 threaten ICAO's Future Air Navigation Systems? –
17 *Air and Space Law* 1992, pp.17-19

STOFFEL, W. – Legal aspects of aeronautical mobile satellite services. –
Diss. McGill. Montreal 1992

GHONAIM, M. – The sharing concept and the new aviation CNS/ATM systems (Communication, Navigation, Surveillance, and Air Traffic Management systems). –
18 *AASL* 1993, vol.I, pp.113-124

GULDIMANN, W. – Die künftigen Luftfahrt-Navigationssysteme (FANS-ICAO CNS/ATM systems). –
ASDA Bulletin 1993-1, no. 114, pp.7-18

GULDIMANN, W. and KAISER, S. – Future air navigation systems. Legal and institutional aspects.
GULDIMANN, W. — The institutional and legal aspects of the future air navigation systems. Report to the Legal Committee of the ICAO, pp.1-137
KAISER, S.A. — Legal implications of satellite-based communication, navigation and surveillance systems for civil aviation, pp.139-279
Dordrecht 1993, viii-281 pp.

MOORMAN, R.W. – Delaying the GPS promise. –
30 *Air Transport World*, Sept. 1993, pp.36-38, 40-41, 43

SHIN, H.-K. and HONG, S.-K. – Legal aspects of space activities of ICAO in implementing FANS. –
In: Proceedings of the 36th Colloquium on the Law of Outer Space, Graz 1993, pp.98-115

STOFFEL, W. – Legal aspects of aeronautical mobile satellite services. The ICAO FANS concept. –
In: Proceedings of the 36th Colloquium on the Law of Outer Space, Graz 1993, pp.116-122

WARWICK, G. – Opening up GPS. –
144 *Flight International*, 1-7 Sept. 1993, pp.28-29

ABEYRATNE, R.I.R. – The evolution from FANS to CNS/ATM and products liability of technology providers in the United States. –
43 *ZLW* 1994, pp.156-186

ABEYRATNE, R.I.R. – General principles of liability of States as providers of space technology in the field of air navigation. –
29 *ETL* 1994, pp.553-569

Cuestiones técnicas y jurídicas sobre los nuevos sistemas de comunicaciones en la navegación aérea.
ALVAREZ MENDEZ, J. idem, pp.161-169
BISSO, N.A. a.o. idem, pp.171-191
GRUNAUER DE FALU, M.C. Algunos aspectos jurídicos de aplicaciones de sistemas satelitales a la navegación aérea, pp.193-196
PALMIERI, I.A. Relaciones jurídicas surgidas de la implementación de los sistemas satelitales de navegación aérea, pp.197-204
La aviación civil internacional, XVIII Jornadas latinoamericanas, Buenos Aires 1994

VAN DAM, R. – ICAO/OACI. GNSS, CNS/ATM. –
19 *AASL* 1994, vol. II, pp.654-663 and 668-673

VAN DAM, R. – Legal Committee – 29th session. –
19 *Air and Space Law* 1994, pp.235-237

HENAKU, B.D.K. – The ICAO CNS/ATM system: new king, new law? –
19 *Air and Space Law* 1994, pp.146-151

HONG, S.-K. and SHIN, H.-K. – The need to improve the role of ICAO in relation to the legal and other aspects of ICAO CNS/ATM system implementation for the 21st century. –
19 *AASL* 1994, vol. II, pp.399-427

HONG, S.-K. and SHIN, H.-K. – The role of ICAO in implementing FANS. –
6 *Korean JAL* 1994, pp.293-315 (in Korean) and 316-319 (English summary)

KOTAITE, A. – ICAO ushers in a revolution in global navigation technology. –
19 *AASL* 1994, vol. I, pp.337-347

SALIN, P.A. – Les systèmes de navigation aérienne par satellites et l'aviation civile. –
19 *AASL* 1994, vol. I, pp.453-476

ALIMONTI, F.P. – Death by misinformation? Governmental liability for faulty FAA weather information. –
60 *JALC* 1995, pp.961-996

EPSTEIN, J.M. – Global Positioning System (GPS): defining the legal issues of its expanding civil use. –
61 *JALC* 1995, pp.243-285

SALIN, P.A. – Regulatory aspects of Future Satellite Air Navigation Systems (FANS) on ICAO's 50th birthday. –
44 *ZLW* 1995, pp.172-196

111. Flight safety

PANDIANI VLACHOS, A. – Air navigation safety over prohibited or danger areas: international regulations and State practice. –
Diss. McGill. Montreal 1989

MAPELLI, E. – El sobrecargo y la seguridad aérea. –
Airline (Madrid), July-August 1990, no. 19-20, pp.4-10

CASSADY, J.H. – Aviation safety regulation and enforcement: a survey of recent decisions. –
6 *Air & Space Lawyer* (ABA) 1991, no. 2, pp.1, 12-13

LEARMOUNT, D. – Standardizing global safety. –
139 *Flight International*, 19-25 June 1991, pp.34-35

PANGIA, M.J. – The Civil Penalty Assessment Demonstration Program – a demonstration of conflict. –
6 *Air & Space Lawyer* (ABA) 1991, no. 2, pp.1, 13-14

OSTER JR, C.V.; STRONG, J.S. and ZORN, C.K. – Why airplanes crash: aviation safety in a changing world. –
New York 1992, xv-200 pp.

Systemfehler in der Luftfahrt. –
Schweizer Rück, Zürich 1992, 40 pp.

JENISON, M.B. – Bilateral transfers of safety oversight will prove beneficial for all States. 48 *ICAO J*, May 1993, pp.16-17

SWIECICKI, E.M. – Liability of the Canadian government for the negligent enforcement of aviation safety legislation. –
18 *AASL* 1993, vol. I, pp.275-313

SUCHARITKUL, S. – Procedure for the protection of civil aircraft in flight. –
16 *Loyola of LA Int. and Comparative LJ* 1994, pp.513-535

112. Facilitation

ARALOB, N. – The Convention on International Civil Aviation and the norms relative to the simplification of formalities in international air transport. – *Soviet Law* (Tallinn) 1983, no. 4, pp.274-281 (in Russian)

FARIAS, H. DE CASTRO – Facilitação. –
25 *RBDAE* 1987, no. 42, pp.106-107

ABEYRATNE, R.I.R. – Facilitation and the ICAO role – A prologue for the nineties. –
15 *AASL* 1990, pp.3-14

ROUAUD, H. – The end of Community controls in air transport. –
ITA Magazine, July/August 1991, no. 67, pp.9-15

ABEYRATNE, R.I.R. – The development of the machine readable passport and visa and the legal rights of the data subject. –
17 *AASL* 1992, vol. II, pp.1-31

ABEYRATNE, R.I.R. – The role of automation in facilitation of air transport into the 21st century. –
20 *AASL* 1995, vol. I, pp.259-282

114. Slots

KORAN, D. and OGUR, J.D. – Airport access problems: lessons learned from slot regulation by the FAA. –
Washington DC 19 , Bureau of Economics, Staff report to the Federal Trade Commission, v-73 pp.

GAEBEL, C. – Slots als Eigentum. Verfassungsrechtlicher Eigentumsschutz von Start- und Landezeiten. –
13 *Transportrecht* 1990, pp.407-413

STARKIE, D. – Slot trading at United States airports: a report for the Director General for Transport of the Commission of the European Communities. –
London 1990, 34-24 pp.

BORRMANN, J. – Zur Allokation von Start- und Landerechten: Eine Kritik an den Regulierungsvorschlägen der EG-Kommission. –
41 *Wirtschaft und Wettbewerb* 1991, pp.678-688

CAMERON, D. – Europe opens slot machine. –
Airline Business, Febr. 1991, p.16

CAMERON, D. – Slot machinery. –
Airline Business, July 1991, pp.38-39, 41

Crans, B.J.H. and Loozen, E.M.H. – EC aviation scene. 2. Slot allocation. –
16 *Air Law* 1991, pp.179-183

Daly, K. – Insider dealing. –
139 *Flight International*, 20-26 March 1991, pp.22 and 24

Hardaway, R. – Economics of airport regulation. –
20 *Transportation LJ* (Denver CO) 1991, pp.47-75, at pp.56-72

Hulet, J.; Lake, H. and Perry, G. – Study on airport slot allocation: a study commissioned by the Department of Transport. –
London, Department of Transport, 1991, 150-145 pp.

Kaiser, S.A. – Die Neuregelung der Slotvergabe. –
14 *Transportrecht* 1991, pp.266-276

Tschentscher, T. and Koenig, C. – Rechtsqualität, Vergabe und Übertragbarkeit sogenannter 'Slots' nach dem deutschen Verkehrsrecht. –
10 *Neue Zs für Verwaltungsrecht* 1991, pp.219-236

Dettling-Ott, R. – Zulassungszwang auf schweizerischen Flughäfen. –
ASDA Bulletin 1992-2, no. 113, [6]-50-[4] pp.

First experiences with the new rules on slots.
Giardina, A. — Competition in air transport and the problem of slot allocation at airports, pp.17-32
Wittek, H. — The view of the airlines, pp.33-40
4 EALA Conference Papers 1992

Giemulla, E. and Schmid, R. – Wem gehört die Zeit? Rechtsprobleme der Slot-Zuteilung. –
41 *ZLW* 1992, pp.51-62. In English: 17 *Air and Space Law* 1992, pp.9-16

Giemulla, E. and Schmid, R. – Who owns the time? Legal problems regarding slots. A German view. –
17 *Air and Space Law* 1992, pp.9-16. In German: 41 *ZLW* 1992, pp.51-62

Kawano, M. – Environment, congestion and the development of international civil aviation. –
In: The highways of air and outer space, 1992, pp.195-201

Krämer, P.M. – Airport and en-route slot allocation. Brussels, October 28, 1991. –
41 *ZLW* 1992, pp.86-88

Airport & en route slot allocation. Brussels, 28 October 1991.
van Miert, K. — Slot allocation as an instrument for optimising airport and en route capacity utilization, pp.13-18

BERNAUW, K.	Airport/airspace congestion and slot allocation, pp.19-59
NAVEAU, J.	Airport slots and traffic rights, pp.61-68
LEVINE, M.E.	The U.S. experience with slot allocation, pp.70-76
BOUCKAERT, B.	Airport and en route slot allocation. A property rights approach, pp.77-99
LUMSDEN, J.	Paper (ECAC), pp.101-104
VEENSTRA, K.	Paper (AEA), pp.105-106
MCDERMID, A.S.	Paper (AACI Europe), pp.107-111
KLETTE, L.	European airport traffic management. The NATO perspective, pp.113-117
LAROY, P.	SLAP: slot allocation procedure. The pilots' point of view, pp.119-120
LOGAN, M.	The environmental capacity of airports: a method assessment, pp.125-131

28 *ETL* (Belgium) 1993, no. 1, 144 pp.

BALFOUR, J. – The slot problem – can the competition rules help? –
5 EALA Conference Papers 1993, pp.45-56

GIRARDI, P. and COLETTA, C. – La nuova disciplina dell'assegnazione delle bande orarie negli aeroporti comunitari. –
Diritto dei Trasporti 1993, pp.705-

JANDA, R. – Auctioning airport slots: airline oligopoly, hubs and spokes, and traffic congestion. –
18 *AASL* 1993, vol. I, pp.153-200

KANDULSKI, G. – Slot allocation. –
In: The new legal framework for aviation in the European Community; ICC, Paris 1993, pp.63-68

BASS, T.C. – Infrastructure constraints and the EC. –
1 *J of Air Transport Management* 1994, no. 3, pp.145-150

GIRARDI, P. and COLETTA, C. – La nuova ed attuale disciplina dell'assegnazione delle bande orarie negli aeroporti comunitari. –
Trasporti 1994, no. 64, pp.43-135

HAANAPPEL, P.P.C. – Airport slots and market access: some basic notions and solutions. –
19 *Air and Space Law* 1994, pp.198-206

HAWES, M. – Slot allocation – assigning scarce resources. –
IATA Review, March/April 1994, pp.16-18

HOWES, C. – Slot allocation at London Heathrow airport: the legal framework. –
6 EALA Conference Papers 1994, pp.51-65

MAPELLI, E. – Las franjas horarias. –
6 *Airline Ninety Two* (Madrid), febrero 1994, no. 62, pp.14-21

BÖCKSTIEGEL, K.-H. and KRÄMER, P.M. – Völkerrechtliche Gestaltungsvorgaben für die Einführung einer wettbewerbsorientierten Allokation von Start- und Landeslots. –
44 *ZLW* 1995, pp.269-283 and 371-386

CHAPMAN, Ph. – Aviation: slot allocation – current issues. –
2 *Transport Law & Policy* (London) 1995, no. 8, pp.63-64

GIEMULLA, E. and SCHMID, R. – Nochmals – Wem gehört die Zeit? –
44 *ZLW* 1995, pp.259-268

115. Handling

BELLAN, P.G. – Responsabilità degli aeroporti in relazione ai servizi aeroportuali. –
14 *DPAC* 1990, pp.294-318-

VALBUSA, S. – Handling aeroportuale e regolamenti C.E.E. –
Diritto dei Trasporti 1992, pp.109-

ZAFRA RIASCOS, M. – La influencia de las normas comunitarias sobre competencias en los servicios de asistencia en tierra ('handling'). Sus repercusiones respecto a los servicios aéreos intra-extra comunitarios. –
8 *Revista europea DNMA* 1992, pp.1369-1378

ANN, Chr. – Deregulierung in der Luft, Monopole auf dem Boden. Zur kartellrechtlichen Situation und Problematik der Märkte für Bodendienste auf deutschen Verkehrsflughäfen.
48 *Betriebsberater* 1993, Beilage 16 zu Heft 23, 12 pp.

CAMERON, D. and ODELL, M. – Brussels enters handling debate. –
Airline Business, July 1993, pp.20-21

Commission asked to review ground handling monopolies. –
5 *Janes Airport Review*, Sept. 1993, p.3

GOLDA, C. – Verso la 'deregulation' anche nei servizi aeroportuali. –
95 *Il Diritto Marittimo* 1993, pp.1003-1007

CRANS, B. – EC aviation scene. 3. Draft legislation in respect of ground handling services. –
19 *Air and Space Law* 1994, pp.232-233

DUSSART-LEFRET, C. and FEDERLIN, C. – Ground handling services and EC competition rules. –
19 *Air and Space Law* 1994, pp.50-61

RITTNER, F. – Zur Neuordnung der Bodenverkehrsdienste (groundhandling) auf den Flughäfen der Europäischen Union. –
13 *Neue Zs für Verwaltungsrecht* 1994, pp.429-435

VON SCHULTHESS, H.C. – Rechtsfragen zur Abfertigung von Passagieren und ihrem Gepäck auf den Schweizer Flughäfen, insbesondere auf dem Flughafen Zürich. –
ASDA Bulletin 1994-1, no. 116, pp.4-16

MAPELLI LÓPEZ, E. – El 'handling' en la Unión Europea. –
Airline (Madrid), Nov. 1995, no. 83, pp.17-24

Chapter VIII. Air transport

121. The Warsaw Convention, 1929

DARÍO Y BASUALDO, R. – Régimen jurídico del transporte aéreo internacional. –
Managua 1960

CHENG, B. – Compensation for airline passenger death and injury. The future of the Warsaw Convention. –
71 *J of the Royal Aeronautical Society* (UK) 1967, pp.501-502

CHENG, B. – Sixty years of the Warsaw Convention: airline liability at the crossroads. –
38 *ZLW* 1989, pp.319-344 and 39 *ZLW* 1990, pp.3-39

LEE, T.-H. – The current status of the Warsaw Convention and subsequent protocols in leading Asian countries. –
1 *Korean JAL* 1989, pp.147-158 (in Korean) and pp.159-162 (English summary)

STIVEN, J.F. – Recent cases and developments in aviation law. VI. Warsaw Convention. –
55 *JALC* 1989, pp.58-83

CARTER JR, J.D. a.o. – Aviation and space law: annual survey. II. Warsaw Convention. –
25 *Tort & Insurance LJ* (ABA) 1990, pp.215-219

GIEMULLA, E. and SCHMID, R. – Ausgewählte internationale Rechtsprechung zum Warschauer Abkommen in den Jahren 1987-1989. –
39 *ZLW* 1990, pp.165-187

PETKOFF, G.S. – Recent cases and developments in aviation law. IV. Warsaw Convention. –
56 *JALC* 1990, pp.20-21 and 69-91

CARTER JR, J.D. a.o. – Aviation and space law: annual survey. II. Warsaw Convention. –
26 *Tort & Insurance LJ* 1991, pp.181-184

DONADÍO, M.I. – Convenio para la unificación de determinadas reglas relativas al transporte aéreo internacional. Varsovia, Polonia, 4 de octubre de 1929. –
RBDAE, Jan./Febr. 1991, no. 52, pp.29-35

GODFROID, M. – L'application en Belgique de la Convention de Varsovie et du Protocole de La Haye (1983-1988). –
44 *RFDAS* 1991, pp.209-238

VIDELA ESCALADA, F. – The Warsaw Convention within Argentine law. –
40 *ZLW* 1991, pp.339-362

BRISE, S.T. – Warsaw Convention and economic view. –
Brussels symposium, April 1992, 8 pp.

CHAMPION, T. – A trial lawyer's response. –
17 *AASL* 1992, vol. I, pp.67-70

CHAPMAN, F.B. – Exclusivity and the Warsaw Convention: In re air disaster at Lockerbie, Scotland. –
23 *Univ. of Miami Inter-American LR* 1992, pp.493-513

VAN DAM, R.D. – Air liability: ICAO policy. –
17 *AASL* 1992, vol. I, pp.85-95

GIEMULLA, E. and SCHMID, R. – Ausgewählte internationale Rechtsprechung zum Warschauer Abkommen in den Jahren 1989-1991. –
41 *ZLW* 1992, pp.123-126

HOFFMAN, J.M. and HARRIS, Ph.S. – Recent developments in aviation case law. VII. Warsaw Convention and air carrier liability. –
58 *JALC* 1992, pp.57-66

KIRBY, M. Civil aviation liabilities: Australian development in a global context. –
17 *AASL* 1992, vol. II, pp.255-281

KOOIJMANS, P.H. – State succession and the 1929 Warsaw Convention: a case study. –
In: Essays in honour of Henri A. Wassenbergh, Dordrecht 1992, pp.113-133

LANDRY, J.E. – Airline liability: the long overdue updating of the Warsaw regime in the United States. –
17 *AASL* 1992, vol. I, pp.49-65

MANNIN, C. – The Warsaw dilemma within the European Community. An E.E.C. air travel protection directive? –
Brussels symposium, April 1992, 12 pp.

MARTIN, P. – Open letter. –
17 *Air and Space Law* 1992, pp.147-152

NAVEAU, J. – The Single European Market and the air carriers' liability regime. –
Brussels symposium, April 1992, 6 pp.

ROMANELLI, G. – Uniform rules of air carriage. –
94 *Il Diritto Marittimo* 1992, pp.1036-1045

TRONCOSO, F.M. – A plaintiff's aviation trial lawyer's view. –
17 *AASL* 1992, vol. I, pp.71-78

VANDYK, A. – US decried on Warsaw system. –
29 *Air Transport World* 1992, no. 4, pp.92-93

WOOD, E. – Yet another look at the Warsaw Convention. –
In: Essays in honour of Henri A. Wassenbergh, Dordrecht 1992, pp.149-157

VAN BAREN, W.H. – Recent aviation case law from the Benelux. 1. Warsaw Convention. –
18 *Air and Space Law* 1993, pp.29-33

BUNJES, H.J. – Aansprakelijkheid vaststellen is lastig en moeizaam karwei. –
23 *Welwezen*, juli 1993, pp.12-17

CAPLAN, H. – Air passenger compensation: an evolving practice and philosophy. –
1 *International Insurance LR* (London) 1993, pp.327-330

Carriage by air: private rights and liabilities. –
Clyde & Co., London 1993, 34 pp.

CHOI, J.-S. and KANG, S.-H. – Recent developments in aviation case law. –
5 *Korean JAL* 1993, pp.119-167 (in Korean) and pp.168-169 (English summary)

DETTLING-OTT, R. – Internationales und schweizerisches Lufttransportrecht. –
Zürich 1993, xxxix-315 pp.

GIEMULLA, E. and SCHMID, R. – Ausgewählte internationale Rechtsprechung zum Warschauer Abkommen in den Jahren 1991-1993. –
42 *ZLW* 1993, pp.386-400

HETTIARACHCHI, L. – The profound subtleties of the Warsaw private international air law regime: then, now and tomorrow. –
Diss. McGill. Montreal 1993

HOLLOWELL, D. – 1991-92 survey of international law in the Second Circuit. I. Warsaw Convention. –
19 *Syracuse JILC* 1993, pp.98-106

KIM, D.-H. – An international air carrier's liability in a changing era. –
5 *Korean JAL* 1993, pp.13-30 (in Korean) and pp.31-52 (in English)

LÉGIER, G. – L'application de la Convention de Varsovie par les juridictions américaines: évolution de la jurisprudence. –
46 *RFDAS* 1993, pp.123-178

LEONEL DE REZENDE, F. – A Convenção de Varsóvia e a responsabilidade civil no transporte aéreo internacional. –
RBDAE, May-June 1993, no. 63, pp.18-28

SHIN, S.-H. – The Warsaw system: developing instruments. –
5 *Korean JAL* 1993, pp.265-299

STROUD, J.C. – Recent developments in aviation case law. II. Warsaw Convention. –
59 *JALC* 1993, pp.8-27

TOMPKINS, G.N. – Unlimited liability: Japan and beyond. –
1 *International Insurance LR* (London) 1993, pp.159-163

ANDERSEN, D.R. – Recent cases and developments in aviation law. III. Warsaw Convention and air carrier liability. –
60 *JALC* 1994, pp.51-80

CHENG, B. – Limit on air carriers' liability for passenger injury or death: the Rising Sun eclipses Guatemala City and Montreal – USA quo vadis? –
13 *Lloyd's Aviation Law*, 15 May 1994, pp.1-8

GIEMULLA, E. amd SCHMID, R. – Ausgewählte internationale Rechtsprechung zum Warschauer Abkommen in den Jahren 1993-1994. –
43 *ZLW* 1994, pp.388-394

HAANAPPEL, P.P.C. – Les activités de l'IATA (hiver 1994). 2. Révision de la Convention de Varsovie. –
47 *RFDAS* 1994, p.140

HADDON-CAVE, Ch. – The Warsaw limit: medieval, unbreakable and unconscionable. –
1 *J of Air Transport Management* 1994, pp.245-249

Litigation with a foreign flavor: a comparison of the Warsaw Convention with the Hamburg rules. –
59 *JALC* 1994, pp.907-942

RAS, L.F. – Warsaw's wingspan over state laws: towards a streamlined system of recovery. –
59 *JALC* 1994, pp.598-615

TAYLOR, N.P. – Limitation of liability of aircarriers to aircrash victims – Has the Warsaw system reached its retirement age? –
J of Personal Injury Litigation (UK) 1994, pp.118-130

WHALEN, Th. – US Commission breathes new life into liability debate. –
Airfinance J, Jan. 1994, no. 158, pp.41 and 43

BECHKY, P.S. – Mismanagement and misinterpretation: U.S. judicial implementation of the Warsaw Convention in air disaster litigation. –
60 *JALC* 1995, pp.455-531

BURCKHARDT, Th. – Aus der deutschen Rechtsprechung zum Warschauer Abkommen. –
ASDA Bulletin 1995-1, no. 118, pp.4-27

CHENG, B. – The Warsaw system: mess up, tear up, or shore up? –
In: The use of airspace and outer space, The Hague 1995, pp.105-130

DUERI D., E.M. – La conferencia de IATA sobre responsabilidad civil de las aerolíneas. Washington DC, junio 19-23, 1995. –
5 *AITAL Boletín*, mayo-junio 1995, no. 24, pp.14-19

DUERI D., E.M. – El sistema de Varsovia de responsabilidad civil en el transporte aéreo: hacia una reforma urgente. –
5 *AITAL Boletín*, marzo-abril 1995, no. 23, pp.25-31

The Japanese initiative: absolute unlimited liability in international air travel. –
60 *JALC* 1995, pp.819-865

KENNEY, S.C. – Recent developments in aviation law. III.A.2 Warsaw Convention. –
61 *JALC* 1995, pp.27-50

MACINTYRE, J.D. – Where are you going? Destination, jurisdiction, and the Warsaw Convention: does passenger intent enter the analysis? –
60 *JALC* 1995, pp.657-697

MORALES RODRÍGUEZ, J.R. – La conferencia sobre la responsabilidad civil de las compañías aéreas (Washington DC, 19-27 de junio de 1995). –
5 *AITAL Boletín*, julio-agosto 1995, no. 25, pp.22-29

SAVITT, L.J. and COLLERAN, M.J. – Recent developments in aviation and space law. IV. Warsaw Convention. –
30 *Tort & Insurance LJ* 1995, pp.258-260

SEKIGUCHI, M. – Why Japan was compelled to opt for unlimited liability. –
20 *AASL* 1995, vol. II, pp.337-355

TOSI, J.-P. – Transport aérien. –
Paris, Juris-classeur de droit commercial 3, 1995. Fascicules 920 et 925

TOMPKINS JR, G.N. – Notice of the Warsaw Convention limits of liability. –
1 *LR of the Int. Academy of Trial Lawyers* (Austin TX) 1995, pp.73-102

WEBER, L. – Legal activities of the International Air Transport Association (IATA) 1993-1994. 1. Warsaw system of liability. –
20 *Air and Space Law* 1995, p.32

124. The Guatemala Protocol, 1971

ZUMARÁN, C. – El Protocolo de Guatemala. –
XIX Jornadas iberoamericanas, Madrid 1989, pp.149-155

124A. The Montreal Protocols, 1975

AMABILE CIBILS, G.M. – Responsabilidad aeronáutica. Modificaciones al sistema Varsovia-La Haya. Protocolos de Guatemala de 1971 y de Montreal de 1975. –
XIX Jornadas iberoamericanas, Madrid 1989, pp.93-99

COSENTINO, E. – Enfoques sobre el Protocolo de Guatemala de 1971 y los Protocolos de Montreal de 1975. –
XIX Jornadas iberoamericanas, Madrid 1989, pp.73-92

LÓPEZ SAAVEDRA, D.M. – La responsabilidad del transportador aéreo ante la ratificación de los Protocolos de Montreal. –
La Ley 1989 C, pp.1095-1105

TOVAR J. and ZUMARÁN, C. – Los Protocolos de Montreal de 1975. –
XIX Jornadas iberoamericanas, Madrid 1989, pp.141-148

CAPLAN, H. – Is there an alternative to the Montreal Protocols and the United States' supplemental compensation plan? –
5 *Air and Space Lawyer* (ABA) 1990, no. 2, pp.1, 6-9

GERSON, S.M. and ALLEN, G.W. – The Montreal Protocols and the supplemental compensation plan: a necessary change. –
41 *ZLW* 1992, pp.137-141

HARAKAS, A.J. – The Montreal Protocols in the United States 17 years later. The road to ratification or final defeat? –
41 *ZLW* 1992, pp.354-359

MÜLLER-ROSTIN, W. – The American supplemental compensation plan: an undue burden on the passenger, –
41 *ZLW* 1992, pp.349-353

LA TORRE, U. – Il risarcimento complementare nel trasporto aereo internazionale di persone: il piano statunitense del 1990. –
Diritto dei Trasporti 1992, pp.71-

COTUGNO, E. – No rescue in sight for Warsaw plaintiffs from either courts or legislature – Montreal Protocol 3 drowns in committee. –
58 *JALC* 1993, pp.745-793

MERCER, A.G. – The Montreal Protocols and the Japanese initiative: can the Warsaw system survive? –
19 *Air and Space Law* 1994, pp.301-317

MÜLLER-ROSTIN, W. – Erfordernis der Novellierung der frachtrechtlichen Vorschriften des Warschauer Abkommens durch eine Ratifikation des Montrealer Protokolls Nr. 4. –
17 *Transportrecht* 1994, pp.321-326

WHALEN, Th. – US commission breathes new life into liability debate. –
Airfinance J, Jan. 1994, no. 158, pp.41 and 43

CHENG, B. – A fifth jurisdiction without Montreal Additional Protocol No. 3, and full compensation without the Supplemental Compensation Plan. –
20 *Air and Space Law* 1995, pp.118-124

125. The Guadalajara Convention, 1961

COMENALE PINTO, M.M. – Brevi cenni intorno al vettore aereo di fatto e alla colpa grave di pilotaggio. In margine ad un caso di disapplicazione del sistema di Varsavia. –
90 *Il Diritto Marittimo* 1988, pp.160-167

HERBER, W. – The notion of 'actual carrier' in the Guadalajara Convention and in the Hamburg Rules. –
91 *Il Diritto Marittimo* 1990, pp.511-515

SCHMID, R. – Das Zusatz-Abkommen von Guadalajara und seine Bedeutung für das deutsche Reisevertragsrecht. –
17 *Transportrecht* 1994, pp.420-425

126. IATA General Conditions of Transport

DESIDERIO, G. and COMENALE PINTO, M. – Condizioni generali di contratto e condizioni di trasporto. –
208 *Archivio giuridico 'Filippo Serafini'* 1988, pp.51-73

BUSTI, S. – Il trattamento del passeggero nelle condizioni generali del contratto aereo. –
DPAC 1993, no. 1, pp.41-69

MOELKER, C. – De invloed van afdeling 6.5.3 NBW op standaardvoorwaarden in het vervoer. –
Mededelingenblad van de Nederlandse Vereniging voor Zee- en Vervoersrecht, februari 1993, no. 8, pp.1-3

RINKES, J.G.J. en VERSTAPPEN, M.P. – Algemene voorwaarden in het luchtvervoer van personen. –
Den Haag 1993, SWOKA onderzoeksrapporten 144, iii-207-81 pp.

WEBER, L. – IATA. III. General conditions of carriage (passenger and baggage)/Conditions générales de transport (passagers et bagages). –
18 *AASL* 1993, vol. I, pp.438-439

127. Contract of carriage

a. General

SALAMONE, A.X. – Il contratto di trasporto stipulato a mezzo computer ed il suo valore probatorio. –
Trasporti 1989, no. 48-49, pp.121-134

SARMIENTO GARCÍA, M.G. – Régimen jurídico nacional e internacional del contrato de transporte aéreo. –
XIX Jornadas iberoamericanas, Madrid 1989, pp.123-140

FÜHRICH, E. – Reiserecht. Handbuch des Reisevertrags-, Reiseversicherungs- und Individualreiserechts. –
Heidelberg 1990, 616 pp.

CAVALIERI FILHO, S. – O contrato de trasporte – Início e fim. –
RBDAE, May-June 1991, no. 54, pp.30-31

DE FUENTES TALICE, A. – Contratos de fletamento y transporte aéreo, pp.7-18.
Condiciones generales del contrato de transporte aéreo, pp.19-26.
Contracts of charter and carriage by air, pp.53-63.
General conditions of contracts of carriage by air, pp.65-72.
Montevideo 1991, 93 pp.

YATES, D. a.o., ed.- Contracts for the carriage of goods by land, sea and air. –
Lloyd's of London Press 1993, loose-leaf

BALIAN, E.N. – Incumplimiento en el contrato de transporte aéreo. –
Aviación comercial, turismo, etc., Buenos Aires 1994, pp.201-204

BARTL, H. – Das neue Reisevertragsrecht. –
17 *Transportrecht* 1994, pp.409-420

PALMIERI, I.A. – El incumplimiento del contrato de transporte aéreo. –
Aviación comercial, turismo, etc., Buenos Aires 1994, pp.229-235

b. Tickets. Reservation systems/CRS

REZENDES, V.S. – Competition in the airline computerized reservation system industry. –
Washington DC 1988, US General Accounting Office, GAO/RCED-88-62, 25 pp.

RODRÍGUEZ JURADO, A. and CAPALDO DE NOLFI, G. – Reservas aerocomerciales por computación. –
13 *Revista del CIDA* 1988, pp.29-51

HIRST, R.B. – The CRS mess, 1984-1989: from display bias to travel agency franchises. –
4 *Air and Space Lawyer* (ABA) 1989, no. 3, pp.5-6

HUMPHREYS, B. – Airliner computer reservation systems. / Les systèmes informatisés de réservations dans les compagnies aériennes. –
Proceedings symposium Dubrovnik, 9-10 November 1989. ITA Études & documents/Studies & reports 89/5, vol. 17, pp.149-157

KENNY, D.A. – Los computadores al servicio del transporte aéreo. –
49 *Aeroespacio*, enero-febrero 1989, pp.30-32

BRADEN, K.A. – Frequent flyer coupon brokering: a valid trade? –
55 *JALC* 1990, pp.727-762

CLARK, R.M. – The United States Supreme Court shoots down notice requirements under the Warsaw Convention. Chan v. Korean Air Lines. –
3 *The Transnational Lawyer* (Sacramento CA) 1990, pp.363-392

EVANS, J. – Divestiture as a legislative solution to the anti-consumer effects of airline ownership of computer reservation systems. –
10 *Computer-Law J* (Manhattan Beach CA), winter 1990, pp.1-46

HUMPHREYS, B. – The CRSs (Computer Reservation Systems) / Les SIR (Systèmes Informatisés de Réservations). –
ITA Études & documents/Studies & reports 1990/1, vol. 18, vi-190 pp.

KAYSER, V. – Chan v. Korean Airlines. Lisi v. Alitalia undone? –
15 *AASL* 1990, pp.505-510

KOEZUKA, Y. – Liquidated damage clauses in computer reservations systems contracts: are they enforceable? –
55 *JALC* 1990, pp.803-837

LATHROP, B. – Design-induced errors in computer systems. –
10 *Computer-Law J* (Manhattan Beach CA) 1990, pp.87-126

The legal and regulatory implications of airline computer reservation systems. – 103 *Harvard LR* 1990, pp.1930-1950

MANKIEWICZ, R.H. – The U.S. Supreme Court finally overrules Lisi v. Alitalia. –
15 *Air Law* 1990, pp.45-47

MOORE, L. – Chan v. Korean Air Lines Ltd.: the United States Supreme Court eliminates the American rule to the Warsaw Convention. –
13 *Hastings Int. and Comparative LR* (San Francisco CA) 1990, pp.229-240

SCHWARTZ, I.A. – Chan v. Korean Air Lines, Ltd.: skirting the legislative history of the Warsaw Convention. –
11 *Northwestern J of Int. Law & Business* (Chicago IL) 1990, pp.140-158

THOMAS, T.A. – 007 – licensed to limit without notice: the case of Chan v. Korean Air Lines Ltd. –
13 *Loyola of LA Int. and Comp. LJ* 1990, pp.95-131

ADELSON, Th.A. – Torts. Liability limitations under the Warsaw Convention. Failure to provide adequate notice will not exclude an air carrier from the damages cap under the Warsaw Convention for passenger injury or death. The Supreme Court rejects the purpose-oriented approach to the Warsaw Convention in favor of effectuating its plain meaning. Chan v. Korean Air Lines, Ltd. –
56 *JALC* 1991, pp.939-967

Computer reservation systems regulation: CRS competition rules are needed, DoT insists. 8 *The Avmark Aviation Economist*, June 1991, pp.11-13

ELLIG, J. – Computer reservation systems, creative destruction, and consumer welfare: some unsettled issues. –
19 *Transportation LJ* 1991, pp.287-307

FOUILLOUX, G. – Les systèmes informatisés de réservation dans la Communauté Économique Européenne. –
In: L'Europe et le droit: mélanges en hommage à Jean Boulouis, Paris 1991, pp.265-284

PARKER, R. – Just the ticket. –
126 *Taxation* (UK), 17 Jan. 1991, pp.409-410

PARKHURST, B.S. – Airline computer reservation systems – a national and international view of current legal issues. –
4 *Software LJ* (Los Angeles CA) 1991, pp.231-246

WEISS, J. – Computer reservation systems. –
20 *Transportation LJ* 1991, pp.169-172

BOUDREAUX, D.J. and ELLIG, J. – Beneficient bias: the case against regulating airline computerized reservation systems. –
57 *JALC* 1992, pp.567-597

BUSTI, S. – I sistemi telematici di prenotazione per il trasporto aereo nella disciplina comunitaria. –
Diritto dei Trasporti 1992, pp.15-

FOLCHI, M.O. – El nuevo derecho aeronáutico (los sistemas computerizados de reservas). –
Buenos Aires 1992, xv-120 pp.

KLEIT, A.N. – Computer reservation systems: competition misunderstood. –
37 *Antitrust Bulletin* (NY) 1992, pp.833-861

L'OACI adopte le premier code de conduite mondial sur les systèmes informatisés de réservation. –
45 *RFDAS* 1992, pp.209-210

RUBIO SAN ROMÁN, J. and ZAMORA CABOT, F.J. – Los sistemas informatizados de reservas (computer reservation systems) en el contexto de las relaciones CE-EEUU. –
8 *Revista europea DNMA* 1992, pp.1277-1286

TOMPKINS JR, G.N. – The road from Lisi to Chan – Notice of the Warsaw Convention limits of liability. –
In: Essays in honour of Henri A. Wassenbergh, Dordrecht 1992, pp.135-147

HAWES, M. – Fraud – a danger to airline health. –
IATA Review, Dec. 92/Jan. 93, pp.18-19

DA FONSECA, R.G. – O regime jurídico dos sistemas computerizados de reservas ('CRS') no Brasil. –
RBDAE, March/April 1993, no. 62, pp.16-23

KILLICK, J. and SMITH, J.C. – Trade Descriptions Act 1968 – whether airline ticket likely to be taken as containing a statement of fact as to time of return for purposes of Section 14. –
Criminal LR 1993, pp.709-711

LEAMING, M.P. – Enlightened regulation of computerized reservations systems requires a conscious balance between consumer protection and profitable airline marketing. –
21 *Transportation LJ* 1993, pp.469-517

TEMPESTA, A. – Protezione giuridica del sistema computerizzato di prenotazione e del processo elettronico internazionale automatizzato trattamento dati. –
12 *ADMA* 1993, pp.421-442

US anti-trust action: the silent conversations issue: farce or tragedy? –
10 *The Avmark Aviation Economist*, May 1993, pp.2-4

BAUCHET, P. – The effect of computerisation on the pricing policies of public services. –
6 EALA Conference Papers 1994, pp.121-129

CAVANI, R. – Computerized reservation systems for air transport: remarks on the European Community legislation. –
17 *Fordham Int. LJ* (NY) 1994, pp.441-457

CRANS, B. – EC aviation scene. 2. New block exemption on CRS. –
19 *Air and Space Law* 1994, p.232

HUMPHREYS, B. – Do airlines still need to own CRSs? –
11 *The Avmark Aviation Economist*, April 1994, pp.12-20

HUMPHREYS, B. – Les nouveaux développements des SIR/New developments in CRSs. –
Paris, ITA Études & documents/Studies & reports 94/4, vol. 32, 220 pp.

SPAGNOLO, L. – Desarrollo de los sistemas de reservas: CRS y GDS. –
Aviación comercial, turismo, etc. Buenos Aires 1994, pp.175-179

VENIT, J.S. and KALLAUGHER, J.J. – Computerised reservation systems. –
6 EALA Conference Papers 1994, pp.69-87

ABEYRATNE, R.I.R. – Contractual liability arising out of computer reservations systems of air transport. –
11 *Tolley's Computer Law and Practice* 1995, no. 4, pp.97-105

ABEYRATNE, R.I.R. – Legal and regulatory issues of computer reservations systems and code sharing agreements in air transport. –
Gif/Yvette (France) 1995

ABEYRATNE, R.I.R. – Some issues of the Warsaw Convention. Still some debate left? 1. The passenger ticket. –
44 *ZLW* 1995, pp.396-398

BOLTON, Ch. – Embarking on the ticketless journey. –
Airlines International, May-June 1995, pp.33-36

CHOI, J.-S. – Documents of air carriage. –
7 *Korean JAL* 1995, pp.101-131 (in Korean) and pp.132-134 (English summary)

LEVERE, J.L. – Paperless journey: electronic ticketing. –
11 *Airline Business*, Jan. 1995, pp.18-21

MARTIN, P. – 'Phone in, turn up, take-off'. A look at the legal implications of self-service ticketing. –
20 *Air and Space Law* 1995, pp.189-195

MOMBERGER, M. – Speeding up air travel – on the ground. –
25 *Airport Forum*, June 1995, pp.32-34

PARK, Y.-K. – Some considerations on Article 3 of the Warsaw Convention. –
7 *Korean JAL* 1995, pp.63-83 (in Korean)

TOMPKINS JR, G.N. – Notice of the Warsaw Convention limits of liability. –
1 *LR of the Int. Academy of Trial Lawyers* (Austin TX) 1995, pp.73-102

c. Duty to transport. Immigration issues. Asylum

BERJIKIAN, V. – Airline liability for the involuntary violation of immigration laws. –
4 *Northrop Univ. LJ of Aerospace, Energy and the Environment* 1983, pp.71-82

BOLLAG, B. and CRISP, J. – Airlines on collision course. –
Refugee, July 1987, p.18

KJAERUM, M., ed. – The role of airline companies in the asylum procedure. –
Copenhagen 1988, Danish Refugee Council, 22 pp.

VEDSTED-HANSEN, J. – Völkerrechtliche Aspekte der Sichtvermerkskontrolle und der Sanktionen gegen Beförderungsunternehmen im Hinblick auf das Asylrecht. –
68 *Die Friedenswarte* 1988, pp.125-139

FELLER, E. – Carrier sanctions and international law. –
1 *Int. J of Refugee Law* 1989, pp.48-66

MIGNON, E. – Réfugiés et compagnies aériennes. –
Revue du droit des étrangers (Bruxelles) 1989, no. 56, pp.287-296

RUFF, A. – The Immigration (Carriers' Liability) Act 1987: its implications for refugees and airlines. –
1 *Int. J of Refugee Law* 1989, pp.481-500

CRUZ, A. – Carrier sanctions in four Community States. Compatibility with international civil aviation and human rights obligations. –
66 *Nederlands Juristenblad* 1991, pp.179-188

CRUZ, A. – Compatibility of carrier sanctions in four Community States with international civil aviation and human rights obligations. –
In: H. Meijers et al., eds, Schengen; Deventer 1991, pp.37-56

VAN BAREN, W.H. – Discriminatory refusal of carriage by air. –
17 *Air and Space Law* 1992, pp.164-165

KAISER, S.A. – Zur Schadensersatzpflicht einer Linienfluggesellschaft aus §325 BGB bei Verweigerung der Beförderung eines Passagiers mit IT-Flugticket. –
15 *Transportrecht* 1992, pp.367-369

WARNER, K. – You can't get there from here: travel restrictions and the airlines. –
58 *JALC* 1992, pp.345-409

ALLGAIER, E. – Ausschluss eines Fluggastes – Mangelndes Wohlverhalten an Bord eines Flugzeuges zahlt sich nicht aus. –
40 *Versicherungsrecht* 1989, pp.128-130

SCHMID, R. – Is a carrier responsible for passengers arriving without travel documents? –
16 *Air Law* 1991, pp.142-143

VANDYK, A. – No entry. –
29 *Air Transport World*, Oct. 1992, pp.46-49

Frontières du droit. Frontières des droits. L'introuvable statut de la 'zone internationale'. –
Paris 1993, 240 pp.

O'KEEFE, C. – Immigration issues and airlines. –
59 *JALC* 1994, pp.357-392

e. Stop-overs

HENRIQUES, J.S. – Stop-over. –
RBDAE, March/April 1993, no. 62, pp.9-11

FOLCHI, M.O. – La parada-estancia o 'stop-over', las conexiones aéreas y los derechos comerciales. –
Aviación comercial, turismo, etc. Buenos Aires 1994, pp.63-68

128. The air consignment note. The airway bill

BISOGNO, E. – Il diritto di contrordine nella disciplina legale e convenzionale del trasporto aereo. –
208 *Archivio giuridico 'Filippo Serafini'* 1988, pp.152-167

COMENALE PINTO, M. – La prenotazione elettronica di spazio aereo. –
208 *Archivio giuridico 'Filippo Serafini'* 1988, pp.137-151

FOGLIANI, E. – Il ruolo della lettera di trasporto aereo. –
208 *Archivio giuridico 'Filippo Serafini'* 1988, pp.117-136

ROMANELLI, G. – La lettera di trasporto aereo non negoziabile. –
Diritto dei Trasporti 1988, no. 2, p.1; Studi in onore di Lorenzo Spinelli, Modena 1989, vol. 4, pp.1553-1583; *Archivo giuridico* 1989, no. 3, p.3

BONFANTONI, C. – In tema di esercizio dei diritti incorporati nella lettera di trasporto aereo e di responsabilità dell'operatore di handling. –
Diritto dei Trasporti (Padova) 1989, pp.153-

MÜLLER-ROSTIN, W. – The incomplete air waybill. –
16 *Air Law* 1991, pp.280-283

MÜLLER-ROSTIN, W. – Der unvollständig ausgefüllte Luftfrachtbrief. –
14 *Transportrecht* 1991, pp.277-278

PANEBIANCO, R. – Lettera di trasporto aereo e problematiche relative alla legittimazione ad agire contro il vettore. –
Diritto dei Trasporti 1991, pp.279-

LEE, K.B. – The character and negotiability of the air waybill. –
4 *Korean JAL* 1992, pp.65-82 (in Korean) and pp.83-85 (English summary)

WEBER, L. – IATA. II. Airway bill conditions of contract/Conditions au contrat de fret aérien. –
18 *AASL* 1993, pp.436-437

BRASIL, S.M. – O conhecimento aéreo e a cláusula not negotiable. –
RBDAE, Jan.-April 1994, no. 65, pp.11-12

DE MONTLAUR-MARTIN, E. – États-Unis. –
47 *RFDAS* 1994, pp.44-48

129. Liability in air law

a. General

ZUNINO, J.O. – Responsabilidad por daños a personas y cosas en el contracto de transporte aéreo-marítimo-terrestre. –
Buenos Aires 1979

ZUMARÁN, C.E. – La evolución de la responsabilidad civil en el transporte aéreo internacional de personas y cosas. –
Diss. Pontífica Universidad Católica de Perú 1987

BELCHIOR, S.B. – A responsabilidade civil no transporte aéreo. –
RBDAE 1990, no. 48, pp.10-12

CHENG, B. – Sixty years of the Warsaw Convention: airline liability at the crossroads. –
38 *ZLW* 1989, pp.319-344 and 39 *ZLW* 1990, pp.3-39

DEAN JR, W.L. – Airline liability in international air transportation: time for a change. –
4 *Air and Space Lawyer* (ABA) 1989, no. 2, pp.1, 8-11

WANG, S. – International air transportation and the question of compensation liability. –
Taipei 1990 (in Chinese)

BIANCA, C.M. – La responsabilità aeronautica: convergenze e divergenze rispetto ai principi civilistici. –
Diritto dei Trasporti 1992, pp.1-

CRAFT JR, R.R. – Aviation liability law developments in 1990. II. Liability of air carriers in Warsâw Convention carriage. –
57 *JALC* 1991, pp.50-68

GULDIMANN, W. – A future system of liability in air carriage. –
16 *AASL* 1991, pp.93-106

KIM, D.-H. – Liability of governmental bodies in international civil aviation. –
3 *Korean JAL* 1991, pp.7-23 (in Korean) and 24-49 (in English)

WEBB, R. – Étendue de la responsabilité de l'exploitation vis-à-vis du personnel de bord, des passagers et des tiers. –
In: Colloque 'L'avion spatial et le droit'; 44 *RFDAS* 1991, pp.535-540

HARBISON, P. – 'What a piece of work is Warsaw': the need for a pragmatic approach to air carrier liability. –
In: The highways of air and outer space, 1992, pp.165-175

MILDE, M. – Air transport, regulation of liability. –
In: Encyclopedia of Public International Law, Amsterdam 1992, vol. I, pp.78-82

SCHÖNWERTH, E. – Zur luftfahrttypischen Kausalität als Voraussetzung der Anwendung der Haftungsregeln von WA/HP und LuftVG. –
15 *Transportrecht* 1992, pp.11-13

CLETON, R. – Aansprakelijkheid en schadevergoeding als nasleep van luchtvaartongevallen. –
68 *Nederlands Juristenblad* 1993, pp.621-629

MENDES DE LEON, P. and MIRMINA, S. – The international and American law implications of the Bijlmer air disaster. –
6 *Leiden JIL* 1993, pp.111-122

DE MONTLAUR-MARTIN, E. – L'interprétation de l'article 17 de la Convention de Varsovie dans la jurisprudence américaine récente. –
46 *RFDAE* 1993, pp.33-35

PASTOR, M.V. – Absolute liability under Article 17 of the Warsaw Convention: where does it stop? –
26 *George Washington JILE* (Washington DC) 1993, pp.575-596

BROWN III, W.C. – Problems arising from the intersection of traditional maritime law and aviation death and personal injury liability. –
68 *Tulane LR* (New Orleans LA) 1994, pp.577-594

MAPELLI, E. – Urgente revisión del sistema de responsabilidad en el transporte aéreo. –
RBDAE, May-Sept. 1994, no. 66, pp.31-32

PINTO DE CARVALHO, L.C. – Observações em torno da responsabilidade civil no transporte aéreo. –
RBDAE, Jan.-April 1994, no. 65, pp.41-44

c. Wilful misconduct

STIVEN, J.F. – Recent cases and developments in aviation law. X. Negligence. –
55 *JALC* 1989, pp.107-115

PETKOFF, G.S. – Recent cases and developments in aviation law. VII. Negligence. –
56 *JALC* 1990, pp.511-515

FREITAS, P.R. DE AZEVEDO – Culpa grave no direito aeronáutico. –
RBDAE, May-June 1991, no. 54, pp.23-27

MCQUEEN, P. – Qantas Airways Ltd. v. S.S. Pharmaceutical Co. Ltd. –
Lloyd's MCLQ 1991, pp.165-169

REYNOLDS, D. – Cargo damage – Article 25 Warsaw Hague Convention. –
16 *Air Law* 1991, pp.19-21

HOFFMAN, J.M. and HARRIS, Ph.S. – Recent developments in aviation case law. XIII. Negligence. –
58 *JALC* 1992, pp.92-97

KILBRIDE, D.A. – Article 25 revisited. –
17 *Air and Space Law* 1992, pp.237-238

KIRBY, M. – Civil aviation liabilities: Australian developments in a global context. –
17 *AASL* 1992, vol. II, pp.255-281

CHOI, J.-S. – The concept of 'wilful misconduct' in the Warsaw Convention. –
6 *Korean JAL* 1994, pp.191-213 (in Korean) and 214-215 (English summary)

Court upholds liability of Pan American World Airways on basis of its wilful misconduct in regard to the bombing of flight 103 over Lockerbie, Scotland. –
38 *Trial Lawyer's Guide* (Deerfield IL) 1994, pp.226-261

HARRIS, R. – Article 25 of the Warsaw Convention in Canada. –
23 *Canadian Business LJ* 1994, pp.279-282

VEAUX, D. and VEAUX-FOURNERIE, P. – La pénétration en droit français de la théorie de la faute inexcusable en matière aérienne et maritime sous l'influence des conventions internationales. –
In: L'internationalisation du droit: Mélanges en l'honneur de Yvon Loussouarn, Paris 1994, pp.391-403

ABEYRATNE, R.I.R. – Some issue sof the Warsaw Convention. Still some debate left? 4. Wilful misconduct. –
44 *ZLW* 1995, pp.404-410

SCHILLER, K. – Das Warschauer Abkommen beim Wort genommen – zur Auslegung von Art. 25 WA/HP. –
ASDA Bulletin 1995-2, no. 119, pp.3-47

d. Time-limits

SANDERS, Ph. – Just when is a carrier liable for its passengers? –
39 *Insurance Intern.* (London), winter 1991/92, pp.41-42

HARRIS, R. – Warsaw Convention: 'disembarking in the United Kingdom'. –
42 *ZLW* 1993, pp.148-150

KEAN, A. – The Warsaw Convention: when do we disembark? –
J of Business Law (UK) 1993, pp.396-397

PASTOR, M.V. – Absolute liability under Article 17 of the Warsaw Convention: where does it stop? –
26 *George Washington JILE* (Washington DC) 1993, pp.575-596

MAPELLI, E. – Responsabilidad del transportista aéreo durante las operaciones de embarque y desembarque. –
Anuario de la Facultad de Derecho de Alcalá de Henares 1993-94, vol. III, pp.201-213

ABEYRATNE, R.I.R. – Some issues of the Warsaw Convention. Still some debate left? 2. Accident. –
44 *ZLW* 1995, pp.399-402

e. Punitive damages

BUONO, B.J. – The recoverability of punitive damages under the Warsaw Convention in cases of wilful misconduct: is the sky the limit? –
13 *Fordham ILJ* (NY) 1990, pp.570-603

PAULSEN, S.R. – Choice of the punitive damage law in airline accidents: the Chicago rule comes crashing down. –
15 *J of Corporation Law* (Iowa City IA) 1990, pp.803-847

BUHLER, G.W. – Punitive damages in aviation tort litigation. –
6 *Air and Space Lawyer* (ABA) 1991, no. 1, pp.1, 9-11

DUBUC, C.E. – Les dommages et intérêts punitifs et la Convention de Varsovie ou l'alchimie judiciaire. –
45 *RFDAS* 1991, pp.45-55

DUBUC, C.E. – More judicial alchemy: punitive damages under the Warsaw Convention. –
58 *Defense Counsel J* (Chicago IL), Jan. 1991, pp.39-46

Federal preemption in the airline industry: is there room for a common law breach of contract claim? West v. Northwest Airlines Inc. –
8 *Cooley LR* (Lansing MI) 1991, pp.679-702

GREMS, K.C. – Punitive damages under the Warsaw Convention: revisiting the drafters' intent. –
41 *American Univ. LR* (Washington DC), fall 1991, pp.141-182

OLIN, M.S. and PERWIN, J.S. – Punitive damages under the Warsaw Convention (trains, planes, and automobiles). –
27 *Trial* (Washington DC), Febr. 1991, pp.40-43

SIEGMUND, J. – Rechtsunsicherheit in den Vereinigten Staaten hinsichtlich der Einklagbarkeit von 'Punitive Damages' im Rahmen des Warschauer Abkommens. –
14 *Transportrecht* 1991, pp.278-281

Warsaw Convention damages curtailed by two courts (mental damages and punitive damages). –
58 *Defense Counsel J* (Chicago IL), Sept.-Oct. 1991, pp.305-306

WILKINSON, R. – Recovery of punitive damages under the Warsaw Convention. A hotly contested issue in the USA. –
16 *Air Law* 1991, pp.25-30

CRAFT JR, R.R. – Survol rapide des récentes décisions américaines relatives aux préjudices indemnisables sous l'empire de la Convention de Varsovie. –
45 *RFDAS* 1992, pp.223-227

BARLOW, P. – Punitive damages under the Warsaw Convention: mixing apples with oranges. –
17 *AASL* 1992, vol. II, pp.71-122

EDELMAN, H.T. – Punitive damages crash in the Second Circuit. –
58 *Brooklyn LR* 1992, pp.497-552

HOFFMAN, J.M. and HARRIS, Ph.S. – Recent developments in aviation case law. IX-A. Punitive damages. –
58 *JALC* 1992, pp.68-72

KATZ, D.M. – Tort law. International aviation. Punitive damages not recoverable under Warsaw Convention regardless of carrier's willful misconduct. In re Air disaster at Lockerbie, Scotland on December 21, 1988. –
16 *Suffolk Transnational LJ* (Boston MA) 1992, pp.366-377

MOORE, L. – The Lockerbie air disaster: punitive damages in international aviation under the Warsaw Convention. –
15 *Houston JIL*, fall 1992, pp.67-89

O'BRIEN, T.P. – Flying the Warsaw Convention's not-so-friendly skies: should air carriers' wilful misconduct go unpunished? –
29 *San Diego LR* 1992, pp.335-360

ROAZEN, M. – International law: punitive damages unavailable in cases of willful misconduct under the Warsaw Convention. Korean Air Lines disaster at September 1, 1993. –
65 *Temple LR* (Philadelphia PA) 1992, pp.1103-1118

KENNEY, S.C. – Recent developments in aviation law. VIII. Punitive damages. –
61 *JALC* 1995, pp.138-139

f. Mental damages. Psychic injuries

JOHNSON, L. – Warsaw Convention. A new cause of action for emotional distress under old section 17: a look at Floyd v. Eastern Airlines. –
20 *Georgia J of Int. and Comp. Law* 1990, pp.619-643

RIVERS JR, R.J. – Torts – Intentional infliction of emotional distress – Recovery for mental injuries unaccompanied by physical injury permitted under Warsaw Convention, Floyd v. Eastern Air Lines. –
14 *Suffolk Transnational LJ* 1990, pp.353-365

SISK, G.C. – Recovery for emotional distress under the Warsaw Convention: the elusive search for the French legal meaning of lésion corporelle. –
25 *Texas ILJ* 1990, pp.127-162

SYDNOR II, Th.D. – Damages for a decedent's pre-impact fear: an element of damages under Alaska's survivorship statute. –
7 *Alaska LR* 1990, pp.351-379

FROMM, L.M. – Eastern Airlines v. Floyd: airline passengers denied recovery for emotional distress under the Warsaw Convention. –
25 *Akron LR* (Akron OH) 1991, pp.425-437

HARAKAS, A.J. – Warsaw Convention: mental injury unaccompanied by physical injury. –
40 *ZLW* 1991, pp.363-365

Warsaw Convention damages curtailed by two courts (mental damages and punitive damages). –
58 *Defense Counsel J* (Chicago IL), Sept.-Oct. 1991, pp.305-306

CRAFT JR, R.R. – Survol rapide des récentes décisions américaines relatives aux préjudices indemnisables sous l'empire de la Convention de Varsovie. –
45 *RFDAS* 1992, pp.223-227

CUNNINGHAM III, E.A. – Negligent infliction of emotional distress in air crash cases: a new flight path? –
70 *Washington Univ. LQ* (St Louis MO) 1992, pp.935-957

DESBIENS, C. – Air carriers' liability for emotional distress under Article 17 of the Warsaw Convention: can it still be invoked? –
17 *AASL* 1992, vol. II, pp.153-193

DE MONTLAUR-MARTIN, E. – L'affaire 'Floyd v. Eastern Airlines'. –
45 *RFDAS* 1992, pp.337-338

YORAN, D. – Recovery of emotional distress damages under Article 17 of the Warsaw Convention: the American versus the Israeli approach. –
18 *Brooklyn JIL* 1992, pp.811-844

EATON, D.M. – Recovery for purely emotional distress under the Warsaw Convention: narrow construction of lésion corporelle. –
Wisconsin LR 1993, pp.563-587

FISHER, R. – Recovery for negligent infliction of emotional distress. –
36 *Trial Lawyer's Guide* (Deerfield IL) 1993, pp.590-594

HOLMES, S.W. – Recovery for purely mental injuries under the Warsaw Convention. Eastern Airlines, Inc. v. Floyd. –
58 *JALC* 1993, pp.1205-1222

COLLINS, L.A. – Pre- and post-impact pain and suffering and mental anguish in aviation accidents. –
59 *JALC* 1994, pp.403-447

ABEYRATNE, R.I.R. – Some issues of the Warsaw Convention. Still some debate left? 3. Mental injury. –
44 *ZLW* 1995, pp.402-404

130. Liability for

a. persons

SARMIENTO GARCÍA, M.G. – La responsabilidad en el transporte aéreo de personas. –
Diss. Universidad externada de Colombia. Bogotá 1978

NATOV, N.S. – La responsabilité contractuelle du transporteur en transport aérien des passagers entre les pays socialistes. –
78 *Annuaire de l'Université de Sofia* 1985, pp.306- (in Bulgarian)

ASSIS DE ALMEIDA, J.G. – A responsabilidade da empresa de transporte aéreo pelo transporte de passageiro sem documentação. –
25 *RBDAE* 1987, no. 42, pp.27-28

CHOI, W.-S. – The liability of air carriers for injuries to passengers resulting from international aviation terrorism. –
34 *Korean JIL* 1989, pp.117-137 (in Korean)

Airports and the disabled passenger. –
20 *Airport Forum*, August 1990, pp.8-12

ANTONINI, A. – La tutela assicurativa del passeggero nel trasporto aereo di persone. –
14 *DPAC* 1990, pp.328-335

HELFREY, D.B.B. and PIRAINO, R.W. – Equal access to air transportation – the only way to fly. –
8 *Law & Inequality* (Minneapolis MN) 1990, pp.469-483

NATHER, D. – Flying the unfriendly skies. –
Business and Society Review (Boston MA), spring 1990, pp.44-50

PETKOFF, G.S. – Recent cases and developments in aviation law. XII. Passenger actions against air carriers. –
56 *JALC* 1990, pp.542-546

The struggle for equal access includes commercial air transportation: the need for a private right of action for disabled persons to enforce the Air Carrier Access Act of 1986.
30 *Santa Clara LR* (Santa Clara CA) 1990, pp.1007-1042

ABEYRATNE, R.I.R. – Mobility laws in the international transportation by air of the elderly and disabled – A legal dilemma for the airlines? –
16 *Air Law* 1991, pp.155-166

ASSIMOTOS, J.E. – To warn or not to warn?: the airlines' duty to disclose terrorist threats to passengers. –
56 *JALC* 1991, pp.1095-1133

BARKSDALE, B.C. – Child safety restraints: a controversy over safe infant air travel. –
57 *JALC* 1991, pp.201-255

DEMPSEY, P.S. – The civil rights of the handicapped in transportation: the Americans with Disabilities Act and related legislation. –
19 *Transportation LJ* 1991, pp.309-333

JIANDUAN, W. – Some thoughts on compensation for passengers in China in a recent air crash. –
16 *Air Law* 1991, pp.76-81

MARGADANT S., G.F. – La fórmula japonesa para la indemnización de víctimas de accidentes aéreos. –
Estudios jurídicos en memoria de Alfonso Noriega Cantú, Ciudad de México 1991, pp.147-154

SUGIE, T. – An introduction to the law which applies to the international transport by air of passengers. –
32 *Seikei Hogaku* 1991, no. 1, pp.1-68 (in Japanese)

AWFORD, I. – Handling the legal consequences of aviation disasters passenger compensation. –
41 *ZLW* 1992, pp.17-40

EISENHAUER, N. – Implied causes of action under federal statutes: the Air Carriers Access Act of 1986. –
59 *Univ. of Chicago LR* 1992, pp.1183-1207

HEGEDUS, L.E. – Shinault v. American Airlines, Inc. (936 F.2d 796): compensatory and emotional distress damages under the Air Carrier Access Act. –
66 *Tulane LR* (New Orleans LA) 1992, pp.1564-1574

JENSEN, V. – Statutory sources of protection for the handicapped traveler. –
57 *JALC* 1992, pp.907-936

MAPELLI, E. – Comer volando. –
Elites (Madrid) 1992, no. 108, pp.12-14

MÜLLER-ROSTIN, W. – Haftungsgrenzen für Personenschäden im internationalen Luftverkehr und die Notwendigkeit ihrer Revision. –
4 *Europ. Zs für Wirtschaftsrecht* 1992, pp.121-126

CHENG, B. – Air carriers' liability for passenger injury or death: the Japanese initiative and response to the recent EC Consultation Paper. –
18 *Air and Space Law* 1993, pp.109-122 and 182

ICC. Commission on Transport. 18 June 1993 – Public statement on the attempts to preserve and update the Warsaw system on passenger liability in international air transport. –
42 *ZLW* 1993, pp.295-297

MAPELLI LÓPEZ, E. – Los derechos del pasajero por aire. –
Revista General de Derecho (Valencia), junio 1993, no. 585, pp.6021-6031

MURPHY, B.S. – How the ADA affects airlines and railroads (Americans with Disabilities Act of 1990). –
18 *ALI-ABA Course Materials J* (American Law Institute, Philadelphia), August 1993, pp.35-50

PARKE, R.B. – Realities of the new Disability Law. –
73 *Business & Commercial Aviation*, August 1993, pp.74-75, 77

ABEYRATNE, R.I.R. – Proposals and guidelines for the carriage of elderly and disabled by air. –
33 *J of Travel Research 1994,* no. 3, pp.52-59

SCHOCH, F. – Haftungsfragen bei der Fluggastbeförderung im nationalen Binnenluftverkehr. –
49 *Betriebs-Berater* 1994, pp.1513-1516

BEZDICHEK, K.B. – Liability of air carrier for injury to passenger caused by fall of object from overhead baggage compartment. –
32 ALR 5th, 1995, pp.1-29

CHRYSTAL, Ph. – Airline passenger liability. Part I 1929-1989. Evolution & disillusion. –
ASDA Bulletin 1995-2, no. 119, pp.58-65

FEARON, S.J. – Recoverable damages in wrongful death actions governed by the Warsaw Convention. –
62 *Defense Counsel J* (Chicago IL) 1995, pp.367-377

OKABE, S. – Aviation personal injury claim settlement practice in Japan. –
In: The use of airspace and outer space, The Hague 1995, pp.319-328

SAKAMOTO, T. – The fate of passenger liability limitation in the Warsaw system. –
In: The use of airspace and outer space, The Hague 1995, pp.131-139

b. Baggage

MEDINA, C. Ancora sul concorso o meno di responsabilità contrattuale e extracontrattuale del vettore aereo e sulla decadenza dell'azione di responsabilità. –
91 *Il Diritto Marittimo* 1989, pp.1138-

FULTON, S.C. – Airline baggage claims: a tour through the legal minefield. –
5 *Florida ILJ* (Gainesville FL) 1990, pp.349-379

THOMAS, T.A. – 007 – licensed to limit without notice: the case of Chan v. Korean Air Lines, Ltd. –
13 *Loyola of Los Angeles ICLJ* 1990, pp.95-131

SCHMID, R. – Security checks of carry-on baggage examined in the light of the Warsaw Convention. –
18 *Air and Space Law* 1993, pp.292-295

SCHÖNWERTH, E. – and MÜLLER-ROSTIN, W. – Unmittelbare Ansprüche des Eigentümers von Gepäck und Fracht gegen den Luftfrachtführer. –
42 *ZLW* 1993, pp.21-28

BEZDICHEK, K.B. – Liability of air carrier for injury to passenger caused by fall of object from overhead baggage compartment. –
32 ALR 5th, 1995, pp.1-29

HOFF, J.S. and YOUNG, Th.J. – Crashing carry-on: a look at falling luggage liability. –
74 *Michigan Bar J*, March 1995, pp.303-503

c. cargo, freight

FOGLIANI, E. and BISOGNO, E. – Il fenomeno della consolidazione nel trasporto aereo. –
208 *Archivio giuridico 'Filippo Serafini'* 1988, pp.97-116

PAPACHRONOPOULOS, N. – Civil liability for the international transport of goods by air in the Warsaw system. –
Athens 1988, xiv-196 pp. (in Greek)

ROMANELLI, G. – Aspetti di trasporto aereo di merci: quadro normativo. –
208 *Archivio giuridico 'Filippo Serafini'* 1988, pp.41-73

ESPINOSA PÉREZ, C.A. – La responsabilidad en el transporte aéreo de mercancías. –
3 *Revista de Derecho Privado*, Univ. de los Andes, Facultad de Derecho, 1989, no. 6, pp.93-

ESTEBAN CHAMI, D. – La protesta aeronáutica. Teoría y práctica. –
Buenos Aires 1989, 116 pp.

LEE, K.-B. – Legal aspects of the contract of international carriage of goods by air. –
1 *Korean JAL* 1989, pp.193-219 (in Korean) and 220-222 (English summary)

SILINGARDI, G. – Trasporto aereo di opere d'arte: rischio di empresa e profili risarcitori. –
Diritto dei Trasporti 1989, no. 2, pp.103-

CHOI, J.-S. – Compensation for damage to cargo occurred during international carriage by air. –
2 *Korean JAL* 1990, pp.189-209 (in Korean)

OTT, G. – Die Luftfrachtbeförderung im nationalen und internationalen Bereich: anwendbares Recht, Vertrag, Versicherung. –
Diss. München. Rechtswissenschaftliche Forschung und Entwicklung, Band 258. München 1990, 182 pp.

LEE, K.-B. – A study of the contract of carriage of goods by air. –
2 *Korean JAL* 1990, pp.69-84 (in Korean)

STORM VAN 'SGRAVESANDE, J.W.E. – Luchtvracht: enkele juridische beschouwingen. –
26 *Ts voor Vervoerswetenschap* 1990, pp.309-324

TOSI, J.-P. – Transport of perishables by air. –
ITA Magazine, Sept.-Oct. 1990, no. 63, pp.6-7

CAPUTO, A. – Régimen jurídico de la carga aérea de acuerdo con el convenio de Varsovia. –
15 *Revista del CIDA* (Montevideo) 1991, pp.59-63

MÜLLER-ROSTIN, W. – Keine Ausdehnung der Haftung des Luftfrachtführers bei Lagerung von Frachtsendungen ausserhalb des Flughafens. –
40 *ZLW* 1991, pp.137-143

MÜLLER -ROSTIN, W. – Recent developments in German aviation law. –
16 *Air Law* 1991, pp.13-18

POLLAK VARELA, J.P. – Carga aérea y su problemática jurídica. –
RBDAE, July-Dec. 1991, no. 55, pp.27-34

REYNOLDS, D. – Cargo damage – Article 25 Warsaw Hague Convention. –
16 *Air Law* 1991, pp.19-21

SCHMID, R. – Legal consequences of the Chan v. Korean Airlines judgment for cargo cases. –
16 *Air Law* 1991, pp.22-24

SCHMID, R. – Trucking air cargo- which liability regime is applicable? –
16 *Air Law* 1991, pp.31-33

COMENALE PINTO, M.M. – Trasporto aereo e consegna della merce a persona diversa dal destinatario., –
Diritto dei Trasporti 1992, pp.166-

KUZNICKI, Th. – Terrorismus und luftspezifische Gefahr in bezug auf eine Haftung des Luftfrachtführers gemäss Artikel 17 des Warschauer Abkommens. –
41 *ZLW* 1992, pp.360-376

MÜLLER-ROSTIN, W. – Air carrier's liability for surface transportation. –
17 *Air and Space Law* 1992, pp.291-296

ZAMPONE, A. – In tema di colpa temeraria e consapevole del vettore aereo di merci. –
Diritto dei Trasporti 1992, pp.564-

BENDER, J. – Maritime Insurance Co. Ltd. v. Emery Air Freight Corp. –
18 *North Carolina J of Int. Law and Commercial Regulation* 1993, pp.663-684

BRIANT, A.M. – International carriage of cargo: a comparative study of the liability of the carrier in maritime and air transport law. –
18 *AASL* 1993, vol. I, pp.45-77

DOMBROFF, M.A. – New precedents make claims processing easy. –
83 *Air Cargo World*, April 1993, pp.38-39

RINALDI BACCELLI, G. – La responsabilità del gestore aeroportuale per la custodia delle merci dopo l'arrivo in aeroporto. –
DPAC 1993, no. 1, pp.111-132

SCHOBEL, B. – Die Haftungsbegrenzung des Luftfrachtführers nach dem Warschauer Abkommen: Bestandsaufnahme und Ansätze für eine Neuregelung. –
Diss. Erlangen-Nürnberg 1992. Frankfurt am Main 1993, 182 pp.

SCHÖNWERTH, E. and MÜLLER-ROSTIN, W. – Unmittelbare Ansprüche des Eigentümers von Gepäck und Fracht gegen den Luftfrachtführer. –
42 *ZLW* 1993, pp.21-28

YATES, D., ed. – Contracts for the carriage of goods by land, sea and air. – Lloyd's of London Press 1993, loose-leaf

GARDINER, R. – Treaty interpretation in English courts. Antwerp United Diamond v. Air Europe. –
Lloyd's MCLQ 1994, pp.184-189

PESCE, A. – Merkmale und Grundlagen für den Ausschluss der Höchstentschädigungspflicht des internationalen Frachtführers. –
17 *Transportrecht* 1994, pp.227-232

MÜLLER-ROSTIN, W. – Die Anspruchsberechtigung für Güterschäden nach dem Warschauer Abkommen. –
18 *Transportrecht* 1995, pp.89-94

SCHÖNWERTH, E. – Unmittelbare Ansprüche des Eigentümers von Gepäck und Fracht gegen den Luftfrachtführer. –
44 *ZLW* 1995, pp.168-171

VERGANI, E. – Alcune questioni relative alla responsabilità del vettore aereo. –
97 *Il Diritto Marittimo* 1995, pp.198-209

d. non-paying passengers

GODFROID, M. – Les transports à titre onéreux et gratuit dans la Convention de Varsovie et en droit belge. –
In: Mélanges offerts à Robert Pirson, Brussels 1989, pp.131-141

g. air mail

BERNAUW, K.C. – Air courier services and the debate on the postal monopoly. –
16 *AASL* 1991, pp.11-30

CHUN, S.-H. – Die Haftung des Luftfrachtführers bei der Beförderung von Luftpost. –
7 *Korean JAL* 1995, pp.177-201 (in Korean) and pp.202-203 (German summary)

131. Liability of the

b. carrier

DONATO, A.M. – Perspectivas del sistema de responsabilidad del transportador aéreo. –
XIX Jornadas iberoamericanas, Madrid 1989, pp.109-115

LÓPEZ SAAVEDRA, D.M. – La responsabilidad del transportador aéreo ante la ratificación de los Protocolos de Montreal. –
La Ley (Argentine) 1989 C, pp.1095-1105

DOKAS, C. – The duty to warn in civil aviation: a new tort theory in the aftermath of Pan American flight 103. –
8 *NY Law School J of Human Rights*, fall 1990, pp.227-256

DE FEO, A. – L'esperienza del vettore aereo nei più recenti processi di risarcimento. –
14 *DPAC* 1990, pp.253-258

RINALDI BACCELLI, G. – Responsabilità del vettore aereo. –
14 *DPAC* 1990, pp.225-229

SONN, J.-C. – Liability of the air carrier under West German air law and the limits of liability in different countries. –
2 *Korean JAL* 1990, pp.7-29 (in Korean)

FOLLIOT, M.G. – Les grandes tendances du transport aérien en France. Ouverture du ciel et évolution de la responsabilité du transporteur. –
46 *RFDAS* 1993, pp.7-14

GUERRERI, G. – Does the hospitalisation and the taking care of an injured passenger of an aircrash amount to an admission of liability by the air carrier? –
19 *Air and Space Law* 1994, pp.189-190

BEZDICHEK, K.B. – Liability of air carrier for injury to passenger caused by fall of object from overhead baggage compartment. –
32 ALR 5th, 1995, pp.1-29

GONZALEZ LEBRERO, R.A. – Accidentes de aviación, una gran fuente de variadas responsabilidades. –
30 *ETL* 1995, pp.429-447

KENNEY, S.C. – Recent developments in aviation law. III. Air carrier liability and defenses. –
61 *JALC* 1995, pp.11-80

KIM, D.H. – The liability of international air carriers in a changing era. –
In: The use of airspace and outer space, The Hague 1995, pp.89-104

c. crew, ground personnel

GIEMULLA, E. and SCHMID, R. – Rechtsprobleme beim Flugzeugschlepp nach dem PTS-Verfahren. –
40 *ZLW* 1991, pp.269-275

d. passengers, shippers of cargo

SCHMID, R. – Must a passenger refund the costs for an emergency landing due to medical reasons? –
17 *Air and Space Law* 1992, p.310

da. shippers of dangerous goods

COHAN, P. – Proceed with caution. –
80 *Air Cargo World*, Nov. 1990, pp.31-34

PETKOFF, G.S. – Recent cases and developments in aviation law. XV b. Hazardous materials aboard aircraft. –
56 *JALC* 1990, pp.555-556

SCHNITKER, R.M. – Transport of dangerous goods by air. –
Year Book and List of Members for the International Association of Airport & Seaport Police 1990, pp.14-18

MATTE, N.M. – International regulation of responsibilities in aerospace transport of dangerous goods. –
26 *ETL* 1991, pp.273-307

MATTE, N.M. – La réglementation internationale sur les responsabilités en matière de transport aérien des marchandises dangereuses. –
16 *AASL* 1991, pp.125-159

DIEDERIKS-VERSCHOOR, I.H.Ph. – Responsibility for transportation by the passenger of dangerous materials by air. –
In: Essays in honour of Henri A. Wassenbergh, Dordrecht 1992, pp.101-112

e. handling, warehouses

BONFANTONI, C. – In tema di esercizio dei diritti incorporati nella lettera di trasporto aereo e di responsabilità dell'operatore di handling. –
Diritto dei Trasporti 1989, 1, pp.153-

RINALDI BACCELLI, G. – L'exploitant de l'assistance aéroportuaire comme préposé du transporteur aérien. –
15 *AASL* 1990, pp.17-33

DU CHEYRON, A. – Transports aériens. Marchandises. Convention de Varsovie. Transporteur. Qualité de guardien des marchandises. Constatations suffisantes. –
11 *ADMA* 1991, pp.355-361

COLETTA, C. – In tema di responsabilità dell'operatore di handling per la custodia delle cose trasportate dal vettore (handling aeroportuale). –
Diritto dei Trasporti 1992, pp.176-

GUERRERI, G. – The airport operator: air carrier's agent or independent contractor? –
17 *Air and Space Law* 1992, pp.231-234

HOWES, K.A. – International law – Warsaw Convention – Warsaw Convention inapplicable to goods lost in shipper's warehouse outside airport boundaries. Victoria Sales Corp. v. Emery Air Freight. –
15 *Suffolk Transnational LJ* 1992, pp.846-857

RINALDI BACCELLI, G. – La responsabilità del gestore aeroportuale per la custodia delle merci dopo l'arrivo in aeroporto. –
DPAC 1993, no. 1, pp.111-132

HARRIS, R. – Article 25 of the Warsaw Convention in Canada. –
23 *Canadian Business LJ* 1994, pp.279-282

h. customs

WOLD, S.A. – International travelers and shippers beware: is anyone liable when customs agents damage property? –
59 *JALC* 1994, pp.493-547

132. Liability in case of

a. international transport

BOOYSEN, H. – When is a domestic carrier legally involved in international carriage in terms of the Warsaw Convention? –
39 *ZLW* 1990, pp.329-344

b. domestic transport

NELSON-JONES, R. – Injuries and deaths on domestic flights. –
140 *New LJ* (UK), 23 November 1990, p.1652

CRAFT JR, R.R. – Aviation liability law developments in 1990. III. Liability of operators of aircraft in non-Warsaw carriage. –
57 *JALC* 1991, pp.68-93

VAN BAREN, W.H. – Recent aviation case law from The Netherlands. 2. Non-Warsaw carriage. –
18 *Air and Space Law* 1993, pp.33-34

SCHOCH, F. – Haftungsfragen bei der Fluggastbeförderung im nationalen Binnenluftverkehr. –
49 *Betriebs-Berater* 1994, pp.1513-1516

133. Liability

a. Limited

GUIMARÃES, F.C. – Evolução do conceito da limitação da responsabilidade do transportador aéreo. –
25 *RBDAE* 1987, no. 42, pp.39-41

POLLAK VARELA, J.P. – La limitación de la responsabilidad del transportista en caso de daños intencionales. –
XIX Jornadas iberoamericanas, Madrid 1989, pp.117-121

RINALDI BACCELLI, G. – Imputazione obiettiva e limite di risarcimento del danno nel trasporto aereo internazionale. –
Rivista di Diritto Civile 1989 II, pp.391-

SILINGARDI, D. – L'istituto del limite risarcitorio nella disciplina uniforme sul trasporto di cose aereo, su strada e per ferrovia. –
Diritto dei Trasporti 9189, 1, pp.45-

SILINGARDI, G. – Limite di risarcimento nei trasporti aerei internazionali di persone. –
12 *Le nuove leggi civili commentate* (Padova) 1989, pp.773-

ZUMARÁN Z., C.E. – La limitación limitativa de responsabilidad en el sistema Varsoviana. –
Tesis de post-grado, Universidad Nacional Mayor de San Marcos, Lima 1989

GUIMARÃES, F.C. – A limitação de responsabilidade do transportador aéreo. –
RBDAE 1990, no. 51, pp.35-36

LOPEZ, C. – La riforma legislativa italiana della responsabilità del vettore aereo nel trasporto interno ed internazionale. –
14 *DPAC* 1990, pp.239-248

ROMANELLI, G. – Giurisprudenza costituzionale. –
14 *DPAC* 1990, pp.234-238

SOON, J.-C. – Liability of the air carrier under West German air law and the limits of liability in different countries. –
2 *Korean JAL* 1990, pp.7-29 (in Korean)

CAPLAN, H. – The passenger's choice: neglected jewels in the Warsaw Convention's crown. –
93 *Il Diritto Marittimo* 1991, pp.533-544

HIRT, M. – The constitutions of Italy, the Federal Republic of Germany and the United States in relation to Article 22 of the Warsaw Convention. –
Diss. McGill, Montreal 1991

MURTAS, L. – Ius superveniens e limitazione del debito del vettore aereo. – *Diritto dei Trasporti* 1991, pp.189-

OLIN, M.S. – [The legal and regulatory environment: safety and labor.] – 20 *Transportation LJ* 1991, pp.114-118

JOS, F. – Le régime de responsabilité du transporteur aérien international envers les passagers et les marchandises: mécanismes et évolution de la limitation. – Diss. McGill, Montreal 1993

MILDE, M. – Warsaw system and limits of liability – yet another crossroad? – 18 *AASL* 1993, pp.201-239

OH, S.-G. – A historical analysis of the limitation of carriers' liability. – 5 *Korean JAL* 1993, pp.171-203 (in Korean) and 204-205 (English summary)

ŻYLICZ, M. – Increasing air passenger compensation within or around the Warsaw system. – 20 *Polish Yb of IL* 1993, pp.195-208

HADDON-CAVE, Ch. – The Warsaw limit: medieval, unbreakable and unconscionable. – 1 *J of Air Transport Management* 1994, pp.245-249

MILDE, M. – Warsaw system and limits of liability – yet another crossroad. – 6 *Korean JAL* 1994, pp.43-81

KNIBB, D. – Pushing the limits. – 11 *Airline Business*, June 1995, pp.86-87, 89

Passenger liability deal may force up the insurance rates. – *Airfinance J*, July-Aug. 1995, no. 175, p.12

STEEL, D. – Ships are different: the case for limitation of liability. – *Lloyd's MCLQ* 1995, pp.77-87

TOMPKINS JR, G.N. – Notice of the Warsaw Convention limits of liability. – 1 *LR of the Int. Academy of Trial Lawyers* (Austin TX) 1995, pp.73-102

WEBER, L. – IATA. I. Warsaw system of liability. – 19 *AASL* 1994, vol. II, pp.674-677

ABEYRATNE, R.I.R. – Some issues of the Warsaw Convention. Still some debate left? 5. Liability limitation v. strict liability? – 44 *ZLW* 1995, pp.411-412

Passenger liability deal may force up insurance rates. – *Airfinance J*, July-Aug. 1995, no. 175, p.12

b. Unlimited

NATOV, N.S. – The falling away of the limits of liability of the air carrier. –
2 *Durzhava i Pravo* 1989, no.8-9, pp.135- (in Bulgarian)

KHAN KHURESHI, A. – Air carrier's unlimited liability under the Warsaw Convention. –
Diss. McGill, Montreal 1990

MARTIN, P. – Japanese Airlines – Looking forward rather than backward. –
11 *Lloyd's Aviation Law* 1992, no. 22, pp.2-5

CHENG, B. – Air carriers' liability for passenger injury or death: the Japanese initiative and response to the recent EC Consultation Paper. –
18 *Air and Space Law* 1993, pp.109-122 and 182

HAYASHIDA, K. – Waiver of Warsaw Convention and Hague Protocol limits of liability on injury or death of passenger by Japanese carriers. –
42 *ZLW* 1993, pp.144-147

ABE, K. – The so-called 'Japanese initiative'. Japanese airlines' abolition of liability limits for personal injury or death in international carriage by air. –
6 *Korean JAL* 1994, pp.149-164

MCKAY, J.S. – Unlimited liability of the air carrier. –
6 *Korean JAL* 1994, pp.137-147

CHENG, B. – A fifth jurisdiction without Montreal Additional Protocol No. 3, and full compensation without the Supplemental Compensation Plan. –
20 *Air and Space Law* 1995, pp.118-124

The Japanese initiative: absolute unlimited liability in international air travel. –
60 *JALC* 1995, pp.819-865

SEKIGUCHI, M. – Why Japan was compelled to opt for unlimited liability. –
20 *AASL* 1995, vol. II, pp.337-355

c. Contractual

PACHECO, J. da SILVA – Da responsabilidade contratual no Código Brasileiro de Aeronáutica. –
25 *RBDAE* 1987, no. 42, pp.42-58

e. Strict, absolute

CHUN, S.-H. – Die verschuldungsunabhängige Haftung im Luftverkehr. –
4 *Korean JAL* 1992, pp.107-132 (in Korean) and 133-137 (German summary)

HOFFMAN, J.M. and HARRIS, Ph.S. – Recent developments in aviation case law. XII. Strict liability. –
58 *JALC* 1992, pp.89-92

WELLS, M.A. and MAYHAN, D.G. – Federal preemption of strict liability claims in aviation litigation: a fresh look. –
27 *Tort & Insurance LJ* (ABA) 1992, pp.693-708

134. Liability

a. Delay

BRASIL, S.M. – O atraso no transporte de passageiros de acordo com o Código Brasileiro de Aeronáutica. –
RBDAE, March-April 1991, no. 53, p.44

SCHMID, R. – Loss of cargo as a result of war during a delay – what is the right legal basis for a claim? –
19 *Air and Space Law* 1994, p.40

b. Overbooking

GIRARDI, P. – Riflessi giuridici dell'overbooking nel trasporto aereo di linea. –
Diritto dei Trasporti 1988, no. 2, pp.169-

CRAFT JR, R.R. – Aviation liability law developments in 1990. III B. Denied boarding, exclusion, or removal from aircraft. –
57 *JALC* 1991, pp.80-84

CRANS, B.J.H. and LOOZEN, E.M.H. – EC aviation scene. 4. Denied boarding compensation. –
16 *Air Law* 1991, pp.185-186

MAPELLI, E. – Regulación de sobreventa (overbooking) en la Comunidad Económica Europea. –
RBDAE, May-June 1991, no. 54, pp.32-38

Overboeking op lijndienstvluchten. –
19 *Consumenten-reisgids*, mei 1991, pp.14-15

SCHMID, R. – Die Entschädigung von Fluggästen bei Nichtbeförderung wegen Überbuchung. –
14 *Transportrecht* 1991, pp.128-131

FULLEN, C.M. – Constitutional law – federal preemption – the Federal Aviation Law does not preempt state claim against an airline for breach of the covenant of good faith and fair dealing arising from overbooking. West v. Northwest Airlines. –
23 *Rutgers LJ* (Newark NJ) 1992, pp.427-439

GIRARDI, P. – Recenti sviluppi della regolamentazione dell'overbooking ed applicazione degli schemi di indennizo per mancato imbarco. –
Diritto dei Trasporti 1992, pp.413-

CAVALLI, M. – Rifiuto all'imbarco e overbooking: problemi di diritto interno e di diritto comunitario. –
32 *Diritto Comunitario e degli Scambi Internazionali* 1993, pp.377-379

NICOL, D.E. and HERD, R.A.J. – The practice of overbooking – a brief outline. –
21 *Scots Law Times* (Edinburgh) 1993, pp.207-210

ABEYRATNE, R.I.R. – Airline liability for denied boarding of passengers. –
Bar Association LJ 1994, vol. IV, part II, pp.27-32

c. Smoking, drinking

RANSOM, D. – Flight attendants appeal dismissal of passive smoking suit. Broin v. Philip Morris Cos. –
28 *Trial* (Washington DC), Sept. 1992, p.98(2)

ABEYRATNE, R.I.R. – Tobacco smoking in aircraft – A fog of legal rhetoric? –
18 *Air and Space Law* 1993, pp.50-60

YOH, Y.-M. – World trends and prospects of the ban on smoking in civil aircraft. –
6 *Korean JAL* 1994, pp.85-96 (in Korean)

ALLEN, K. and HOFF, J.S. – Food and drinking injuries aboard airlines. –
3 *Nevada Lawyer*, August 1995, pp.20-22

135. Use of aircraft

a. General

GRIGOLI, M. – L'esercizio dell'aeromobile. –
Milano 1988, xi-700 pp.

VON ERLACH, B. – Public aspects of lease, charter and interchange of aircraft in international operations. –
Diss. McGill, Montreal 1990

PFAFF, M.J. – Die Beschaffung von Verkehrsflugzeugen. Nationale Vorbehalte und wirtschaftliche Determinanten auf offenen Verkehrsmärkten. –
Diss. Erlangen-Nürnberg 1991. R.v.Deckers rechts- und sozialwissenschaftliche Abhandlungen, Bd 56; Abteilung Verkehrsrecht und Verkehrspolitik, Bd 5. Heidelberg 1992, xvi-299 pp.

ROMANELLI, G. – I contratti di utilizzazione della nave e dell'aeromobile nel Codice della Navigazione italiano. –
12 *ADMA* 1993, pp.59-70

STORM VAN 'SGRAVESANDE, J.W.E. – Wie vliegt? –
Ts voor Vervoerswetenschap 1993, pp.303-314

BALIAN, E.N. – Modos de adquisición de aeronaves. –
La aviación civil internacional, XVIII Jornadas latinoamericanas, Buenos Aires 1994, pp.151-158

PERUCCHI, H.A. – Modos de adquisición de aeronaves por las líneas aéreas. –
La aviación civil internacional, XVIII Jornadas latinoamericanas, Buenos Aires 1994, pp.135-150

b. Hire

DONSIMONI, P. – TVA intracommunautaire. Acquisition des aéronefs neufs et location d'aéronefs en provenance d'un autre État membre de l'Union européenne par des assujetis établis en France. –
47 *RFDAS* 1994, pp.127-138

c. Charter

DE FUENTES TALICE, A. – Contratos de fletamento y transporte aéreo, pp.7-18.
Condiciones generales del contrato de transporte aéreo, pp.19-26.
Contracts of charter and carriage by air, pp.53-63.
General conditions of contracts of carriage by air, pp.65-72.
Montevideo 1991, 93 pp.

e. Pools

ZITTERSTEYN, J. – Airline pooling arrangements. –
Term paper McGill, Montreal 1979, 70-x pp.

f. Leasing

BUNKER, D.H. – The intricacies of Canadian leasing regulations. –
Airfinance J, Sept. 1990, no. 118, pp.84 and 86

FORTIER, J.M. – Leasing of aircraft in the province of Quebec. –
15 *AASL* 1990, pp.61-72

HANCOCK, R. – Charting the minefield. –
Airfinance J, Nov. 1990, no. 120, pp.38 and 40

PEASE, A. and PETERSON, J. – Maintaining flexibility for aircraft leasing. – *Airfinance J*, April 1990, no. 113, pp.64-65

PILARSKI, A.M. – Where the planes fly full: aircraft leasing in Asia. – 12 *East Asian Executive Reports* (Washington DC), 15 Nov. 1990, p.21(3)

RICHARDS, W. – Perspectives on air finance securisation programmes. – *Airfinance J*, March 1990, no. 112, pp.32-33, 35

STRAUSS, R.D. – Sale-leasebacks retain US Bankruptcy Code protection. – *Airfinance J*, May 1990, no. 114, pp.31-32

VIDELA ESCALADA, F.N. – L'article 83bis de la Convention de Chicago. Importance de sa ratification. – 15 *AASL* 1990, pp.221-245

CAHILLANE, J., ed. – Cross-border aircraft leasing. – London 1991, 200 pp.

CHIPKIN, S. – Cross-border US aircraft deals – an Australian perspective. – Legal aspects of aircraft finance, supplement to *Airfinance J*, May 1991, no. 126, pp.8-11

FRENCH, T. – Seeking cover. – *Airline Business*, April 1991, pp.52-53

GDANSKI, M. – The French tax lease. – *Airfinance J*, July 1991, no. 128, pp.30-32

GERSTELL, J. and GRUSHKIN, J. – Familiarity breeds respect for the FSC. – *Airfinance J*, April 1991, no. 125, pp.50-52, 54, 56

KAHN, G. – Looking after lessors' rights: making more of operating leases. – Legal aspects of aircraft finance, supplement to *Airfinance J*, May 1991, no. 126, pp.25-27

MACGUINESS, J.D. – Need for flexibility. – *Airfinance J*, Jan. 1991, no. 122, pp.36-37

VERCHÈRE, I. – Leased aircraft need new service law. – 46 *Interavia Aerospace Review*, March 1991, pp.41-44

WENZLER, Th. – Die Registrierung von Luftfahrzeugen in der Luftfahrzeugrolle nach dem 'Leasingerlass' des Bundesministers für Verkehr vom 12. Februar 1991. – 40 *ZLW* 1991, pp.276-277

WISSUM, C. and ASKERUD, T. – Tax leasing favours the few. – *Airfinance J*, May 1991, no. 126, pp.33-34

BOIDMAN, N. – Proposed exemption for U.S. and other foreign aircraft lessors. –
21 *Tax Management Int. J* (Washington DC), 14 Febr. 1992, pp.88-91

Cross-border aircraft leasing. –
Clifford Chance, Lloyd's of London Press Industry Report 1992, 216 pp.

SABINO, A.M. – Flying the unfriendly skies: a year of reorganizing airlines, aircraft lessors, and the Bankruptcy Code. –
57 *JALC* 1992, pp.841-903

BALDWIN, M. and CONLON, M. – Lessors face VAT penalty. –
Airfinance J, March 1993, no. 148, p.43

CRANS, B.J.H. – The third EC aviation package: its impact on the leasing industry. –
18 *Air and Space Law* 1993, pp.102-108

JERRIS, S.I. – The airline industry and the double dip. –
19 *The Intern. Tax J* (NY), winter 1993, pp.82-86

MORILLAS JARILLO, M.-J. – Algunos aspectos del leasing de aeronaves en España. –
Revista de Derecho Mercantil 1993, no. 208, pp.471-586

RICKETTS, R. and BALFOUR, J. – Aircraft use, registration and leasing in the EC. –
18 *Air and Space Law* 1993, pp.25-28

SCHIESSL, M. and WEHLAU, A. – Die Auswirkungen von Flugzeugleasing und Übernahmeangeboten auf Fluglinien in deregulierten Märkten. –
39 *Recht der internationalen Wirtschaft* 1993, pp.709-716

SIDDELL, I.R. – Aircraft operating leases: the lessee's perspective. –
8 *Butterworths J of Int. Banking & Financial Law* 1993, pp.369-371

VAN DAM, R.D. – Lease, charter and interchange of aircraft and the Chicago Convention – some observations. –
19 *Air and Space Law* 1994, pp.124-130

GRITTA, R.D.; LIPPMAN, E. and CHOW, G. – Lease capitalization and the effect on the debt ratios of the major US airlines. –
22 *Transportation LJ* 1994, pp.1-14

MURIEL, A. and CLARK , D. – Security assignments and the lessee. –
Airfinance J, March 1994, no. 160, pp.40-41

BUDGETT, T., ed. – Cross-border aircraft leasing. –
Clifford Chance, Lloyd's of London Press, London 1995, xi-406 pp., 2nd ed.

CANNING, R. – Climbing steppes. –
Airfinance J, July-Aug. 1995, no. 175, pp.14-16 and 18-19

CRANS, B.J.H., ed. –	Aircraft finance. Recent developments and prospects.
CRANS, B.J.H.	Selected pitfalls and booby-traps in aircraft finance, pp.1-21
WALTON, S.M.	Review of important funding sources, pp.23-31
GÜNTHER, K. and ERBACHER, P.	Aspects of aircraft leasing in Germany, pp.33-51
SMIT, H.G.	Prospects for the aviation industry: has the recession ended?, pp.53-69
VAN MIERLO, T.I.M.	Security rights in aircraft and engines under Netherlands law, pp.71-82
FALCÓN RAVELO, J.F.	An overview on aircraft leasing in Spain, pp.83-94
HOFLAND, D.A.	Recent developments in tax law, pp.95-101
EKBOM, P.G.	Legal status of aircraft finance in Sweden, pp.103-108
LE GALL, J.-P. and REEB, S.	Highlighting various tax and security law aspects of aircraft financing – France, pp.109-115
CRANS, B.J.H.	The third EC aviation package: its impact on the leasing industry, pp.117-125
GORIS, W.	Security rights in aircraft under Belgian law, pp.127-138
CLUMPKENS, R.	The role of the notary under the law of the Netherlands with respect to the transfer of title and encumbrance of registered aircraft, pp.139-147

PIJNACKER HORDIJK, E.H. Relevant EC-law topics, pp.149-154
The Hague 1995, viii-154 pp.

GARABGA, T. – Air finance for Africa, legal issues. The airline perspective. –
20 *Air and Space Law* 1995, pp.18-21

KJELGAARD, C. – Buddy, can you spare the time. –
Airfinance J, Febr. 1995, no. 170, pp.34-35

WOOL, J. – Unidroit's proposed convention on security interests in, and leasing of, mobile equipment: recommendations of an aviation working group. –
Airfinance J, July-Aug. 1995, no. 175, pp.32-35

136. Successive transports

PECEGUEIRO DO AMARAL, N. – Transporte successivo no direito aeronáutico. –
RBDAE, May-June 1991, no. 54, pp.28-29

137. Multimodal transport

DONATO, A.M. – Implicancias del transporte multimodal de mercaderías en el transporte de carga aérea. –
XIV Jornadas iberoamericanas, Lima 1984, pp.165-189

PELLÓN RIVERO, R. – El transporte multimodal internacional de mercancías. – XIV Jornadas iberoamericanas, Lima 1984, pp.55-95

GAGGERO, E.D.; ALGORTA, O. and MILLER , A. – Comentarios al proyecto de ley-tipo de transporte multimodal de mercancías. –
15 *Revista del CIDA-E* (Montevideo) 1991, pp.45-58

VARLET, J. – L'interconnexion des réseaux de transport en Europe. Éléments de géographie prospective. / Interconnection of transport networks in Europe. Elements for a prospective geography. –
ITA, Études & documents/Studies & reports 1991/3, Paris 1991, vol. 24, 200 pp.

VERMILYE, J. – Intermodal travel systems. –
IATA review, Oct.-Nov. 1992, pp.19-20

LEE, K.-B. – Revised standard conditions governing the FIATA Multimodal Transport Bill of Lading. –
6 *Korean JAL* 1994, pp.165-190

138. Agents

a. Booking agents. Freight forwarders

FOGLIANI, E. – Il ruolo del spedizioniere agente merci nel trasporto aereo. –
208 *Archivio giuridico 'Filippo Serafini'* 1988, pp.74-96

COLETTA, C. – Sulla nozione di preposto del vettore aereo, agente nell'esercizio delle proprie funzioni. –
Diritto dei Trasporti 1989, 1, pp.238-

MÜLLER-ROSTIN, W. – Recent developments in German aviation law. –
16 *Air Law* 1991, pp.13-18

b. Travel agencies. Tour operators

FISCHER, P. – Haftung des Reiseveranstalters bei Flugbeförderung. –
Schriftenreihe Aktuelles Reiserecht, Bd 2. Wiesbaden 1990, 143 pp.

PEDRINO, E. – La proposta direttiva CEE in materia di 'viaggi organizzati': responsabilità oggettiva del tour operator e risarcimento dei danni da parte del vettore aereo. Le prospettive politiche. –
14 *DPAC* 1990, pp.250-251

Los intermediarios en el transporte aéreo.

FOSMAN, J.	Las compañías aéreas como 'organizadores' según las directivas del Mercado Común Europeo y sus responsabilidades, pp.1297-1302

MAPELLI, E. Las agencias de viajes y el transporte aéreo, pp.1317-1323

COSENTINO, E.T. La intermediación del transitario en el ámbito del transporte aéreo, pp.1325-1329

DE MARZI DE VERA, G. and PERUCCHI, H.A. Naturaleza jurídica del agente de viajes, pp.1331-1336

RIVERA CESTERO, G. Las agencias de viajes en el derecho norteamericano, pp.1337-1347

KEMPNER, J.E. Las intermediaciones en el transporte aéreo (agencias de viajes y agencias de cargas), pp.1349-1354

RIVERA CESTERO, G. Actuaciones de las líneas internacionales estatales de sus agentes que producen la pérdida de inmunidad del soberano en los Estados Unidos y Puerto Rico, pp.1355-1359

XXI Jornadas iberoamericanas, Lisboa 1991. 8 *Revista europea DNMA* 1992, pp.1279-1359

PENGILEY, W. – Singapore Airlines did not misuse its market power in changing arrangements with a tour wholesaler: it all depends on the definition of the market. –
20 *Australian Business LR* 1992, pp.351-356

BARTL, H. – Das neue Reisevertragsrecht. –
17 *Transportrecht* 1994, pp.409-420

SCHMID, R. – Rechtsprobleme bei der Beförderung im Rahmen von Flugpauschalreisen. –
38 *Neue Juristische Wochenschrift* 1994, pp.2451-2456

139. Claims

a. General. Cause of action

STIVEN, J.F. – Recent cases and developments in aviation law. IV. Contribution and indemnity. –
55 *JALC* 1989, pp.39-41

Class actions not applicable to aviation claims. –
34 *Trial Lawyer's Guide* (Deerfield IL) 1990, pp.500-503

FELDMAN, J. – See you in court! –
29 *Air Transport World* 1992, no. 4, pp.44-49

FREEMAN, A.D. and FARRIS, J.E. – Grassroots impact litigation: mass filing of small claims. –
26 *Univ. of San Francisco LR* 1992, pp.261-281

WELLS, M.A. and MAYHAN, D.G. – Federal preemption of strict liability claims in aviation litigation: a fresh look. –
27 *Tort & Insurance LJ* (ABA) 1992, pp.693-708

SOIRET, J.E. – The foreign defendant: overview of principles governing jurisdiction, venue, extraterritorial service of process and extraterritorial discovery in U.S. courts. –
28 *Tort & Insurance LJ* (ABA) 1993, pp.533-574

ANDERSEN, D.R. – Recent cases and developments in aviation law. VII. Practice and procedure. –
60 *JALC* 1994, pp.123-143

PANGIA, M.J. – Aircraft accident litigation in a litigation environment. –
39 *Trial Lawyer's Guide* (Deerfield IL) 1995, pp.205-229

b. Terms

ESTEBAN CHAMI, D. – La protesta aeronáutica. Teoría y práctica. –
Buenos Aires 1989, 115 pp.

STIVEN, J.F. – Recent cases and developments in aviation law. VII. Limitations of actions. –
55 *JALC* 1989, pp.83-85

HOFFMAN, J.M. and HARRIS, Ph.S. – Recent developments in aviation case law. VIII. Limitations of actions. –
59 *JALC* 1992, pp.66-68

c. Forums

FRIENDLY, H.J. – Indiscretion about discretion. –
31 *Emory LJ* (Atlanta GA) 1982, pp.747-784

STIVEN, J.F. – Recent cases and developments in aviation law. I. Jurisdiction. –
55 *JALC* 1989, pp.2-9

WASHINGTON, J.S. – The impact of Piper Aircraft Co. v. Reyno on the foreign plaintiff in the forum non conveniens analysis. –
55 *JALC* 1989, pp.303-347

CARTER JR, W.D. a.o. – Aviation and space law: annual survey. I.A. Forum non conveniens. –
25 *Tort & Insurance LJ* (ABA) 1990, pp.209-212

CARTER JR, W.D. a.o. – Aviation and space law: annual survey. I. Jurisdiction. –
25 *Tort & Insurance LJ* (ABA) 1992, pp.209-215

NOMURA, Y. – Jurisdiction and forum non conveniens in airplane crash cases: a U.S.-Japan comparison. –
156 *Handai Hogaku* 1990, pp.341-385 (in Japanese)

PETKOFF, G.S. – Recent cases and developments in aviation law. I.C. Forum non conveniens. –
56 *JALC* 1990, pp.21-25

PETKOFF, G.S. – Recent cases and developments in aviation law. I. Jurisdiction. –
56 *JALC* 1990, pp.2-37

SHARP, R.M. – In re Aircrash Disaster, New Orleans: a new view of forum non conveniens. –
25 *Tort & Insurance LJ* (ABA) 1990, pp.892-899

WENZLER, Th. – Art. 28 Abs. 1 Warschauer Abkommen in der Rechtsprechung US-amerikanischer Gerichte. –
13 *Transportrecht* 1990, pp.414-418

CARTER JR, W.D. a.o. – Aviation and space law: annual survey. I. Jurisdiction. –
26 *Tort & Insurance LJ* (ABA) 1991, pp.177-180

SASAMORI, N.C. – Forum non conveniens: foreign plaintiffs and United States aviation litigation. –
Diss. McGill, Montreal 1991

ASSELTA, J.J. – Products liability: new ball games in the United States and Europe. A United States view. –
Brussels symposium, April 1992, 18 pp.

BRACKIN, K. – Salvaging the wreckage: multidistrict litigation and aviation. –
57 *JALC* 1992, pp.655-714

BRYMER, T.R. – Le 'forum shopping' ou la course à la compétence: la réponse des tribunaux anglais. –
45 *RFDAS* 1992, pp.9-23

CLEMEN, J.D. and ROSENZWEIG, J.S. – Federal preemption in the area of airline services and forum-shopping. The air carrier's dilemma. –
20 *Transportation LJ* (Denver CO) 1992, pp.339-352

HOFFMAN, J.M. and HARRIS, Ph.S. – Recent developments in aviation case law. I. Jurisdiction. –
58 *JALC* 1992, pp.3-18

KENNELLY, J.J. – Choice of forums for aviation claims: pro and con. Plaintiff's viewpoint. –
Brussels symposium, April 1992, 92-9 pp.

KOLCZYNSKI, Ph.J. – Aviation and space law: annual survey. IV. Jurisdiction and Warsaw Convention center. –
27 *Tort & Insurance LJ* (ABA) 1992, pp.165-168

SOIRET, J. – Choice of forum: have United States courts closed the door? –
6 *Air and Space Lawyer* (ABA) 1992, no. 3, pp.3-5

DRAKE, M.H. – The D.C. Circuit's dubious approval of U.S. long-arm jurisdiction over extraterritorial crimes. United States v. Yunis. –
87 *Northwestern Univ. LR* (Chicago IL) 1993, pp.697-734

HAYASHIDA, K. – Jurisdiction in aviation cases in Japan. –
42 *ZLW* 1993, pp.250-257

PITKO, S.L. – Aviation law: preemption of state law tort claims by the Federal Aviation Act – do state law tort claims survive the attack? –
33 *Washburn LJ* (Topeka KA) 1993, pp.234-246

SPEER, Chr. – The continued use of forum non conveniens: is it justified? –
58 *JALC* 1993, pp.845-884

STARRY, S.J. – Federal preemption in commercial aviation: tort litigation under 49 U.S.C. §1305. –
58 *JALC* 1993, pp.657-701

TOMPKINS, G.N. – Multidistrict litigation proceedings. –
37 *Trial Lawyer's Guide* 1993, pp.24-

ANDERSEN, D.R. – Recent cases and developments in aviation law. I. Jurisdiction. –
60 *JALC* 1994, pp.5-14

LIN, A. – Jurisdictional splashdown: should aviation torts find solace in admiralty? –
60 *JALC* 1994, pp.409-452

MUNRO, M.P. – Subject matter jurisdiction in Warsaw Convention cases after Malik v. Butta. –
7 *NY Intern. LR* 1994, pp.171-188

CHENG, B. – A fifth jurisdiction without Montreal Additional Protocol No. 3, and full compensation without the Supplemental Compensation Plan. –
20 *Air and Space Law* 1995, pp.118-124

KENNEY, S.C. – Recent developments in aviation law. II. Jurisdiction. –
61 *JALC* 1995, pp.6-11

MACINTYRE, J.D. – Where are you going? Destination, jurisdiction, and the Warsaw Convention: does passenger intent enter into the analysis? –
60 *JALC* 1995, pp.657-697

d. Law of evidence

KRUK, Th.L. – Res ipsa loquitur in aviation accidents. –
25 ALR 4th., 1983, pp.1237-1307

CARTER JR, W.D. a.o. – Aviation and space law: annual survey. VI. Evidence and practical developments. –
25 *Tort & Insurance LJ* (ABA) 1990, pp.225-227

PETKOFF, G.S. – Recent cases and developments in aviation law. VIII. Evidence. –
56 *JALC* 1990, pp.516-522

SHAPIRO, S.H. – The Supreme Court's broad interpretation of Federal Rule of Evidence 803(8)(C) makes waves in the admiralty community. Beech Aircraft Corp. v. Rainey. –
14 *Tulane Maritime LJ* 1990, pp.405-414

CARTER JR, W.D. a.o. – Aviation and space law: annual survey. VII. Evidence and practical developments. –
26 *Tort & Insurance LJ* 1991, pp.193-195

ASSELTA, J.J. – Products liability: new ball games in the United States and Europe. A United States view. –
Brussels symposium, April 1992, 18 pp.

KOLCZYNSKI, Ph.J. a.o. – Aviation and space law: annual survey. VI. Discovery, evidence, amd practice developments. –
27 *Tort & Insurance LJ* 1992, pp.170-172

BURD, W.G. and LOZANO, M.S. – Experts: is the end near for their use? –
59 *JALC* 1993, pp.77-111

GOODRICH, M.H. and CORDES, R. – Discovering and preserving evidence in aviation cases. –
29 *Trial* (Washington DC), Febr. 1993, pp.40-44

O'REILLY, T. – Ethics and experts. –
59 *JALC* 1993, pp.113-130

WELLS, M.A. – Pillage and plunder in aircraft accidents: potential for spoliation. –
60 *Defense Counsel J* (Chicago IL) 1993, pp.280-286

KENNEY, S.C. – Recent developments in aviation law. VII.C. Evidence and trial practice. 61 *JALC* 1995, pp.122-133

SAVITT, L.J. and COLLERAN, M.J. – Recent developments in aviation and space law. II. Evidence. –
30 *Tort & Insurance LJ* 1995, pp.254-256

e. Who can sue?

HARRIS, M.W. – The propriety of class actions in mass aviation disaster litigation. –
56 *JALC* 1990, pp.559-587

JACQUOT, J.-C. – Les spécificités de l'indemnisation des familles et des ayants-droits en Afrique Centrale. –
44 *RFDAS* 1990, pp.417-419

SASSOON, D.M. – Air carrier may be sued by owner of goods though unnamed in airway bill. (Israel) –
J of Business Law (UK) 1991, pp.500-501

WILKINSON, R. – The cargo owner's right to sue under the Warsaw Convention. –
17 *AASL* 1992, vol. II, pp.441-479

SCHÖNWERTH, E. and MÜLLER-ROSTIN, W. – Unmittelbare Ansprüche des Eigentümers von Gepäck und Fracht gegen den Luftfrachtführer. –
42 *ZLW* 1993, pp.21-28

MÜLLER-ROSTIN, W. – Die Anspruchsberechtigung für Güterschäden nach dem Warschauer Abkommen. –
18 *Transportrecht* 1995, pp.89-94

SCHÖNWERTH, E. – Unmittelbare Ansprüche des Eigentümers von Gepäck und Fracht gegen den Luftfrachtführer. –
44 *ZLW* 1995, pp.168-171

f. Choice of law

CARSON, L.D. – Choice of law issues in mass tort litigation. –
56 *JALC* 1990, pp.199-262

CRAFT JR, R.R. – Aviation liability law developments in 1990. I.D. Choice of law. –
57 *JALC* 1991, pp.25-36

HARRINGTON, M.J. – A review of state, diversity jurisdiction, and FTCA decisions concerning choice of law rules in the United States. –
5 *Air and Space Lawyer* (ABA) 1991, no. 4, pp.3-11

LAGERBERG, E.M. – Conflicts of laws in private international air law. –
Diss. McGill, Montreal 1991

REAVLEY, Th.M. and WESEVICH, J.W. – An old rule for new reasons: place of injury as a federal solution to choice of law in single-accident mass-tort cases. –
71 *Texas LR*, Nov. 1992, pp.1-50

SEIDELSON, D.E. – The Foreign Sovereign Immunities Act: Whose conflicts law? Whose local law? –
58 *Brooklyn LR* 1992, pp.427-454

MARGO, R.D. – Conflicts of laws in aviation insurance. –
19 *Air and Space Law* 1994, pp.2-7

NAFZIGER, J.A.R. – Choice of law in air disaster cases: complex litigation rules and the common law. –
54 *Louisiana LR* 1994, pp.1001-1084

WITTE, R.J. – ... or would you rather have what's behind door number two? Uniform choice of law proposals: big deal of the day or just another zonk? –
59 *JALC* 1994, pp.617-659

VAN COUTER, Y. – Barkanic: the New York choice-of-law method and recovery for air crashes abroad. –
60 *JALC* 1995, pp.759-815

KENNEY, S.C. – Recent developments in aviation law. VII.B. Conflicts of law. –
61 *JALC* 1995, pp.120-122

MARGO, R.D. – Conflict of laws in aviation insurance. –
In: The use of airspace and outer space, The Hague 1995, pp.309-318

h. Award. Interest

WEINER, M. – Zicherman v. Korean Air Lines. –
6 *NY Intern. LR* 1993, pp.130-

ANDERSEN, D.R. – Recent cases and developments in aviation law. –
60 *JALC* 1994, pp.143-150

i. FSIA

RIVERA CESTERO, G. – Los derechos y defensas de las compañías aéreas estatales en los Estados Unidos y Puerto Rico bajo la Ley de Inmunidades de Soberanos Extranjeros (the Foreign Sovereign Immunities Act). –
XIX Jornadas iberoamericanas, Madrid 1989, pp.197-233

STIVEN, J.F. – Recent cases and developments in aviation law. I.B. Foreign Sovereign Immunities Act. –
55 *JALC* 1989, pp.5-7

CARTER JR, W.D. a.o. – Aviation and space law: annual survey. I.B. Sovereign Immunities Act. –
25 *Tort & Insurance LJ* 1990, pp.212-214

PETKOFF, G.S. – Recent cases and developments in aviation law. III. Foreign Sovereign Immunities Act. –
56 *JALC* 1990, pp.13-17 and 49-69

CARTER Jr, W.D. a.o. – Aviation and space law: annual survey. IV. Governmental immunity. –
26 *Tort & Insurance LJ* 1991, pp.187-191

CRAFT JR, R.R. – Aviation liability law developments in 1990. VI. Liability of foreign States: the Foreign Sovereign Immunities Act. –
57 *JALC* 1991, pp.140-151

HO, P.-K. – International law. Actions against sovereign or instrumentality. Foreign Sovereign Immunities Act of 1976 provides the sole basis for obtaining jurisdiction over foreign States in United States courts. Argentine Republic v. Amerada Hess Shipping Corp. –
56 *JALC* 1991, pp.1187-1209

HOFFMAN, J.M. and HARRIS, Ph.S. – Recent developments in aviation case law. I.B. Foreign Sovereign Immunities Act (FSIA). –
58 *JALC* 1992, pp.4-7

RIVERA CESTERO, G. – Actuaciones de las líneas aéreas internacionales estatales a través de sus agentes que producen la pérdida de inmunidad del soberano en los Estados Unidos y Puerto Rico. –
8 *Revista europea DNMA* 1992, pp.1355-1359

SEIDELSON, D.E. – The Foreign Sovereign Immunities Act: Whose conlicts law? Whose local law? –
58 *Brooklyn LR* 1992, pp.427-454

STROUD, J.C. – Recent developments in aviation case law. I. Foreign Sovereign Immunities Act. –
59 *JALC* 1993, pp.2-8

THORNTON, J.T. and ARES, A.A. – The Foreign Sovereign Immunities Act of 1976: misjoinder, nonjoinder, and collusive joinder. –
58 *JALC* 1993, pp.703-742

ANDERSEN, D.R. – Recent cases and developments in aviation law. I.B. Foreign Sovereign Immunities Act. –
60 *JALC* 1994, pp.7-8

KENNEY, S.C. – Recent developments in aviation law. II.B. Foreign Sovereign Immunities Act (FSIA). –
61 *JALC* 1995, pp.7-9

k. Amount of compensation

CARTER JR, W.D. a.o. – Aviation and space law: annual survey. V. Damages. –
25 *Tort & Insurance LJ* 1990, pp.223-225

CARTER JR, W.D. a.o. – Aviation and space law: annual survey. V. Damages. –
26 *Tort & Insurance LJ* 1991, pp.191-193

HOFFMAN, J.M. and HARRIS, Ph.S. – Recent developments in aviation case law. IX. Damages. –
58 *JALC* 1992, pp.68-75

KOLCZYNSKI, Ph.J. – Aviation and space law: annual survey. V. Noteworthy damage and liability decisions. –
27 *Tort & Insurance LJ* 1992, pp.168-170

140.b. Special drawing rights

DONADÍO, M.I. and PEREA DE TADDEI, E.M.L. – Derechos especiales de giro. Su virtualidad previa. La vigencia de los Protocolos de Montreal de 1975. –
XIX Jornadas iberoamericanas, Madrid 1989, pp.101-107

BERLINGIERI, F. – 'Ragionevolezza' della conversione del franco Poincaré in diritto speciale di prilievo. –
92 *Il Diritto Marittimo* 1990, pp.47-

PEREIRA DA SILVA, L. – O franco ouro Poincaré e o direito especial de saque no direito aeronáutico. –
RBDAE 1990, no. 51, pp.12-14

Chapter IX. Damage to third parties

142. Rights in airspace of underlying property

BARRIENTOS PARRA, J.D. – O direito aeronáutico em face dos direitos de superfície. O problema dos danos causados pelos ruidos das aeronaves. – 16 *Revista do curso de direito da Univ. Federal de Uberlandia* 1987, no. 1-2, pp.101-

CAHOON, C. – Low altitude airspace: a property rights no-man's land. – 56 *JALC* 1990, pp.157-198

GORDON, E.A. – The sky's the limit: the apportionment of overflights and property taxation after Alaska Airlines v. Department of Revenue. – 26 *Willamette LR* (Salem OR) 1990, pp.711-748

GRAY, K.J. – Property in thin air. – 50 *Cambridge LJ* 1991, pp.251-302

GRINLINTON, D.P. – Who owns the air space above a unit title? – *New Zealand LJ* 1991, pp.428-430

MAPELLI, E. – Limitación de propiedad por la navegación aérea, según el derecho español. – *Boletín del Ilustre Colegio de Abogados de Madrid*, mayo-junio de 1992, no. 3, pp.43-55

MCGILL, D. – Building works intruding into air space. – 24 *Queensland Law Society J* 1994, pp.159-163

143. Damage by overflying aircraft

EBOE-OSUJI, Ch. – Aviation incidents and the earth-based victims: a review of Anglo-American tort law. – Diss. McGill, Montreal 1991, xxv-203 pp.

144. Damage by aircraft in agriculture

CHAPPUIS JR, R.D. – The flight of toxic tort – Aerial application of insecticides and herbicides: from drift liability to toxic tort. – 58 *JALC* 1992, pp.411-453

145. Noise – Sonic boom

BARRIENTOS PARRA, J.D. – O direito aeronáutico em face dos direitos de superfície – O problema dos danos causados pelos ruidos das aeronaves. –

16 *Revista do curso de direito da Univ. Federal de Uberlandia* 1987, no. 1-2, pp.101-

WALKER, S. – Noise legislation: implications for European airlines. –
The Avmark Aviation Economist, August 1988, pp.9-13

STIVEN, J.F. – Recent cases and developments in aviation cases. V.G. Noise abatement. –
55 *JALC* 1989, pp.51-53

CZYBULKA, D. and WANDRES, Th. – Rechtsschutz gegen zivilen Fluglärm bei der Festlegung von 'Flugrouten'. –
43 *Die öffentliche Verwaltung* 1990, pp.1033-1040

LYLE, C. – The noise issue. –
45 *The ICAO J*, Nov. 1990, pp.7-8

The search continues for aircraft-noise agreement. –
45 *The ICAO Bulletin*, March 1990, pp.23-24

COLLOGAN, D. – The national noise policy. –
69 *Business & Commercial Aviation*, Dec. 1991, p.94

Luchtvaartlawaai. Verslag symposium 20 maart 1991. –
Nederlandse Stichting Geluidshinder, Delft 1991, 57 pp.

QUAAS, M. – Der Schutz vor unzumutbarem Fluglärm in der Planfeststellung. Rechtliche Anwendungsprobleme nach dem Luftverkehrsgesetz. –
11 *Neue Zs für Verwaltungsrecht* 1991, pp.16-22

Rumore degli aerei e tutela dell'ambiente.
I. Il quadro normativo internazionale, pp.67-118
II. La situazione italiana ed il quadro normativo, pp.119-147
15 *DPAC* 1991, pp.67-147

ROBERTS, M.J. – Transfers of 'base level' rights for state 2 aircraft. –
59 *Transportation Practitioners J* (Washington DC) 1992, pp.403-405

VALLET, M. – Les nuisances sonores engendrées par le trafic aérien. Noise annoyance caused by air traffic. –
ITA, Études & documents / Studies & reports 1992/2, vol. 26, pp.1-37

DAVIES, P. and GOH, J. – Air transport and the environment: regulating aircraft noise. –
18 *Air and Space Law* 1993, pp.123-135

DAVIES, P. and GOH, J. – EC law on aircraft noise: recent developments. –
2 *European Environmental LR* 1993, pp.229-232, 241-242

RAYMOND, Chr. – Analysis and developemnts of the EC aircraft noise directives. –
18 *Air and Space Law* 1993, pp.2-15

VON ZEBINSKY, A.M. – Les nuisances sonores des avions subsoniques. –
28 *ETL* 1993, pp.807-872

ABEYRATNE, R.I.R. – Aircraft engine emissions and noise. –
24 *Environmental Policy and Law* 1994, pp.238-250

Aviation noise policy and regulation. –
46 *Administrative LR* (ABA) 1994, pp.413-427

JENKINS JR, J.J. – The Aircraft Noise and Capacity Act of 1990: has Congress finally solved the aircraft noise problem? –
59 *JALC* 1994, pp.1023-1055

GOH, J. – Problems of transnational regulation: a case study of aircraft noise regulation in the European Community. –
23 *Transportation LJ* 1995, pp.277-300

KJELGAARD, Chr. – Justified and ancient. –
Airfinance J, June 1955, pp.26-28

SULLIVAN, A. – Sounding out Stage 4. –
Airfinance J, Oct. 1995, no. 177, pp.18-23

147. Rome Convention, 1952

JAKUBOVICZ, I. – A Convenção de Roma sobre danos causados a terceiros na superfície por aeronaves estrangeiras e seus protocolos. –
25 *RBDAE* 1987, no. 42, pp.86-98

PARK, H.-M. – A study of the liability of the air carrier for damages to third parties. –
1 *Korean JAL* 1989, pp.163-189 (in Korean) and 190-191 (English summary)

148. Environment. De-icing

ROSENTHAL, G. – Umweltschutz im internationalen Luftrecht. Völkerrechtliche Lösungsansätze für die umweltrelevanten Auswirkungen des zwischenstaatlichen zivilen Luftverkehrs. –
Diss. Köln, Köln 1989, lxxiii-233 pp.

CRAYSTON, J. – ICAO's environmental programme under review. –
46 *ICAO J*, Febr. 1991, p.5

VAN RIJN, Th. – EG-Kommission. Flugzeuglärm. –
2 *Europäische Zs für Wirtschaftsrecht* 1991, p.418

Rumore degli aerei e tutela dell'ambiente.
I. Il quadro normativo internazionale, pp.67-118
II. La situazione italiana ed il quadro normativo, pp.119-147
15 *DPAC* 1991, pp.67-147

Air transport and the environment. –
IATA Review, June-July 1992, pp.10-14

Air transport & the environment. –
IATA, Geneva 1992, 24 pp.

STAFFELBACH, H.P. – L'attitude des aéroports face à la problématique de l'environnement. How airports are coping with environmental problems. –
ITA Études & documents/Studies & reports 1992/2, vol. 26, pp.57-64

CHASE, R. – The environment: our common concern. –
IATA Review, Dec. 1992 / Jan. 1993, pp.15-17

HUGHES, N. – Eighth Annual Aviation Law Operations and Claims Conference. Aviation and the protection of the environment. –
17 *Air and Space Law* 1992, pp.23-24

KAWANO, M. – Environment, congestion, and the development of international civil aviation. –
In: The highways of air and outer space, 1992, pp.195-201

LONGROY, S.A. – The regulation of storm water runoff and its impact on aviation. –
58 *JALC* 1992, pp.555-604

NEUHOFF JR, T. – Obstacles to increasing airspace: jumping through environmental law hoops. –
58 *JALC* 1992, pp.221-266

ORT, P.D. – The narrowing of the scope of NEPA's alternative analysis. –
6 *Tulane Environmental LJ* (New Orleans LA) 1992, pp.179-186

DAVIES, P. and GOH, J. – Air transport and the environment: regulating aircraft noise. –
18 *Air and Space Law* 1993, pp.123-135

LOGAN, M. – The environmental capacity of airports: a method of assessment. –
28 *ETL* 1993, pp.125-131

ZAFRA RIASCOS, M. – Una estrategia global para un desarrollo del transporte aéreo respetuoso con el medio ambiente. –
9 *Revista europea DNMA* 1993, pp.1515-1533

ABEYRATNE, R.I.R. – Aircraft engine emissions and noise. –
24 *Environmental Policy and Law* 1994, pp.238-250

La actividad aeronáutica y la protección del medio ambiente.
MOYANO BONILLA, C., pp.207-250
AMABILE CIBILS, G.M., pp.253-272
BALIAN, E.N., pp.273-300
GIORDANO ECHEVERRÍA, M.E. and CHARPANTIE PRIETO, M.C., pp.301-318
DELUCA, H.O. and ROMERO DELUCA, E.M., pp.319-326
DUHALDE, J., pp.327-340
LIZARRAGA LACALLE, M.D., pp.341-357
MAPELLI, E., pp.359-377
XXIV Jornadas iberoamericanas, Salamanca 1994, pp.207-377

HARTMANN, C. – NEPA: business as usual: the weaknesses of the National Environmental Policy Act. –
59 *JALC* 1994, pp.709-761

MAPELLI Y LÓPEZ, E. – Notas sobre aeroecología. –
RIDAT (Lima) 1994, no. 52, pp.50-55. XXIV Jornadas iberoamericanas, Salamanca 1994, pp.359-377

PAYLOR, A. and GOULD, R., eds – Airports and the environment. –
MDIS Reports, Chichester 1994, iv-175 pp.

STEPPICK, D.C. – Military mess: CERCLA liability and the Base Closure and Realignment Act. –
59 *JALC* 1994, pp.449-491

VAN DER WAL, J.M. – The legal regulation of the disposal of aircraft de-icing fluids on airports: a comparative study. –
19 *Air and Space Law* 1994, pp.211-231

ABEYRATNE, R.I.R. – Olympics 2000 and Sydney's airport policy: an environmental impact study. –
20 *AASL* 1995, vol. II, pp.1-45

EPPERSON, L.A.K. – The South Coast basin: the long-awaited FIP and the aviation industry. –
60 *JALC* 1995, pp.917-957

Chapter X. Accidents – Towage and Salvage

151. Aircraft accidents

BALLARINO, T. – Questions de droit international privé et dommages catastrophiques. Chapitre II. La réglementation internationale du risque. Section I. Les accidents aériens. –
RdC 1990-I, vol. 220, pp.328-335

PARK, W.-H. – Use of the terms 'accident' and 'incident' in air law. –
15 *Air Law* 1990, pp.193-204

MAPELLI, E. – Consideraciones jurídicas sobre el accidente aéreo. –
Revista General de Derecho (Valencia), mayo 1994, no. 596, pp.5291-5308

GONZALEZ LEBRERO, R.A. – Accidentes de aviación, una gran fuente de variadas responsabilidades. –
30 *ETL* 1995, pp.429-447

152. Collisions

SCHÖNWERTH, E. – Die mitwirkende Betriebsgefahr des bei einer Kollision auf der Rollbahn beschädigten Luftfahrzeugs. –
42 *ZLW* 1993, pp.424-429

KENNELLY, J.J. – Midair collisions. –
38 *Trial Lawyer's Guide* (Deerfield IL) 1995, pp.492-500

154. Investigation

a. Procedure

BOURGEOIS, M. – Une étude des enquêtes sur les accidents d'aviation en Canada. –
Diss. McGill, Montreal 1981, iii-120 pp.

BITTENCOURT, J.C. – Investigação de acidentes aeronáuticos. –
25 *RBDAE* 1987, no. 42, p.75

KANE, R.F. – Accident investigation and the public interest. –
IFALPA QR , Dec. 1989, no. 16, p.20

STIVEN, J.F. – Recent cases and developments in aviation law. II.E. NTSB accident investigation. –
55 *JALC* 1989, pp.27-28

FADELY, K.G. – Use of computer-generated visual evidence in aviation litigation: interactive video comes to court. –
55 *JALC* 1990, pp.839-901

DE MONTLAUR-MARTIN, E. – Réglementation des enquêtes-accidents en Grande-Bretagne. 44 *RFDAS* 1990, pp.123-125

PRECELLA, K.S. – Freedom of the press: does the media have a special right of access to air crash sites? –
56 *JALC* 1990, pp.641-687

SCHNITKER, R.M. – Overheidsoptreden bij luchtvaartongevallen in wetstechnisch perspectief. –
Handboek ongevallen- en rampenbestrijding, aanvulling 38, sept. 1990, pp.A1550-1 – A1550-33

ANTONINI A. – Le inchieste sugli accidenti aerei. –
93 *Il Diritto Marittimo* 1991, pp.133-142

CLEMEN, J.D.; LONG, S.R. and SHANLEY & FISHER – Representing potential litigants as parties to NTSB public hearings: some problems in search of solutions. –
56 *JALC* 1991, pp.969-998

RAGSDALE, T.B. – The Constitutional right to privacy and the psychotherapist-patient privilege as limitations on the National Transportation Safety Board's right to investigate air traffic accidents. –
57 *JALC* 1991, pp.469-512

VAN DAM, R.D. – Accident Investigation Divisional meeting. –
17 *Air and Space Law* 1992, p.226

GEUT, H. – IFALPA, Legal Committee meeting, San Diego, 30-31 October 1991. Investigation of accidents. –
17 *Air and Space Law* 1992, pp.166-168

HENDRICKS, W.R. – International aircraft accident investigation. –
6 *Air & Space Lawyer* (ABA) 1992, no. 4, pp.3-6

KEAN, A. – Self-incrimination and accident investigation. –
J of Business L (UK) 1992, pp.319-321

ANTONINI, A. – I sinistri aeronautici. –
Trasporti 1993, no. 61, pp.51-70

GEUT, H. – IFALPA, Legal Committee meeting, Cape Town, South Africa, 19-20 October 1992. Independence. –
18 *Air and Space Law* 1993, p.96

FIORITA, D.M. – The international framework of aircraft accident investigation. Contemporary issues. –
19 *AASL* 1994, vol. I, pp.161-210

MARTIN, P. – Aircraft accident investigation and airworthiness – A practical example of the interaction of two disciplines with some reflections on possible legal consequences. –
19 *Air and Space Law* 1994, pp.158-163

TOMPKINS JR, G.N. and HARAKAS, A.J. – ICAO and aviation accident investigation – Lessons to be learned from the Korean Air Lines 007 investigation. –
19 *AASL* 1994, vol. II, pp.375-398

GRIEF, N. – New E.C. directive on the investigation of air accidents and incidents. –
J of Business L (UK) 1995, pp.422-429

CRANS, B.J.H. – EC aviation scene. –
20 *Air and Space Law* 1995, pp.206-213, at p.213

LANG, K.R.; CLANCY, P. and FLESHER, M.D. – Spoliation of evidence: the continuing search for a remedy and implications for aviation accident investigation. –
60 *JALC* 1995, pp.997-1035

MAPELLI, E. – El incidente aeronáutico en la Unión Europea. –
XX Jornadas latinoamericanas, Buenos Aires 1995, 13 pp.

PANGIA, M.J. – Aircraft accident investigation in a litigation environment. –
39 *Trial Lawyer's Guide* (Deerfield IL) 1995, pp.205-229

RIJSDIJK, O. – European guidelines for aircraft accident and incident investigations. –
20 *Air and Space Law* 1995, pp.196-200

b. Use of investigation documents in court

GULDIMANN, W. – Some legal aspects of aircraft accident investigation. –
15 *AASL* 1990, pp.99-107

SMITH, W.J. – A practical approach to Rule 26(c) protective orders in aviation litigation. –
56 *JALC* 1991, pp.765-801

VAN BAREN, W.H. – Recent aviation case law from the Benelux. 4. Aviation accident reports. –
18 *Air and Space Law* 1993, pp.34-35

WHITE, L.A. – NTSB reports. The war over admissibility. A strict reading of 49 U.S.C. §1441(e) prohibits admission of NTSB accident reports in multi-district litigation arising out of a civilian air crash. In re Air crash disaster at Sioux City, Iowa, on July 19, 1989. –
58 *JALC* 1993, pp.887-908

c. Aviation accident boards

GRAVER, H.P. – Flyhavarikommisjonen for sivil luftfart – oppgaver og saksbehandling. –
103 *Tidsskrift for Rettsvitenskap* (Norway) 1990, pp.592-624

RICHARD, G. – The Civil Aviation Board of Canada after five years. –
16 *AASL* 1991, pp.179-194

DE CASTRO FARIAS, H. – Tribunal aeronáutico, uma lacuna a ser preenchida. –
RBDAE, July-Dec. 1993, no. 64, pp.7-8

155. General average. Abandonment

MAPELLI, E. – El abandono del aeronave y la responsabilidad del comandante. –
Airline (Madrid), June 1991, no. 30, pp.4-7

157. Towage and salvage

VOLLI, E. – Assistenza, salvataggio e recupero. –
89 *Il Diritto Marittimo* 1987, pp.644-653

Chapter XI. Insurance

161. General

BAUZÁ ARAÚJO, A. – El seguro en el derecho aéreo. –
25 *RBDA* 1987, no. 42, pp.17-26

STIVEN, J.F. – Recent cases and developments in aviation law. VIII. Insurance coverage. –
55 *JALC* 1989, pp.85-101

ANTONINI, A. – La tutela assicurativa del passeggero nel trasporto aereo di persone. –
14 *DPAC* 1990, pp.328-335

BUCKINGHAM, L. and FRENCH, T. – Insurance survey: for whom does the bell toll? –
Airline Business, April 1990, pp.49-52, 55-56, 58-59, 62-64, 67

CAMPANA, C. – L'assicurazione dei rischi connessi all'esercizio delle attività aeroportuali.
14 *DPAC* 1990, pp.395-408

FRANZ, P. – Appunti e proposte in materia di assicurazione nel settore aeronautico. –
14 *DPAC* 1990, pp.351-355

HARAKAS, A. – Aviation insurance: a New York perspective. –
Diss. McGill, Montreal 1990

KNOTTNERUS, J.W. – Aviation insurance: requiring a causal connection between the loss and an unambiguous exclusion. –
40 *Federation of Insurance & Corporate Counsel Quarterly* (Marblehead MA) 1990, pp.302-324

PETKOFF, G.S. – Recent cases and developments in aviation law. IX. Insurance. –
56 *JALC* 1990, pp.522-526

AWFORD, I. – Leading developments in international aviation insurance. –
Lloyd's of London Press 1991, xiv-94 pp.

CLERC, A. – Couverture des responsabilités par les assurances. –
44 *RFDAS* 1991, pp.549-557

CRAFT JR, R.R. – Aviation liability law developments in 1990. VIII. Liability of insurers.
57 *JALC* 1991, pp.154-164

FRENCH, T. – Seeking cover. –
Airline Business, April 1991, pp.52-53

SPURWAY, M.J. – Aviation insurance. The market and underwriting practice. – London 1991, vi-85 pp.

BARRETT, J. – Aviation insurers at war. –
Brussels symposium, April 1992, 22 pp.

BARRETT, J. and PILKINGTON, M. – CAAC Guangzhou hi-jacking – Insurance issues. –
17 *Air and Space Law* 1992, pp.133-136

BRENNER, D.I. – Recent aviation developments in Canada. –
17 *Air and Space Law* 1992, pp.227-230

FIORITA, D. – Coronation Ins. Co. v. Taku Air Transport Ltd. –
17 *AASL* 1992, vol. II, pp.528-541

HETHERINGTON, S. – Non-disclosure in marine insurance of aircraft. –
Lloyd's MCLQ 1992, pp.21-25

HOFFMAN, J.M. and HARRIS, Ph.S. – Recent developments in aviation case law. X. Insurance coverage. –
58 *JALC* 1992, pp.75-83

KOLCZYNSKI, Ph.J. a.o. – Aviation and space law: annual survey. II. Aviation insurance. –
27 *Tort & Insurance LJ* (ABA) 1992, pp.158-161

LEE, T.H. – Legal and insurance developments in aviation in Korea. –
4 *Korean JAL* 1992, pp.52-63

MARGO, R.D. – Insurance considerations for airline operations in the Asia Pacific region. In: The highways of air and outer space, 1992, pp.149-162

MARGO, R.D. – Risk management and insurance. –
17 *AASL* 1992, vol. I, pp.79-84

WILKINSON, R. – Aviation insurance: some developments. –
17 *Air and Space Law* 1992, pp.206-216

BRINDLEY, J. – Airlines and insurance. –
IATA Review, Febr.-March 1993, pp.16-17

STROUD, J.S. – Recent developments in aviation case law. IV. Insurance. –
59 *JALC* 1993, pp.36-46

ANDERSEN, D.R. – Recent cases and developments in aviation law. IX. Insurance coverage. –
60 *JALC* 1994, pp.150-165

MCQUILLEN, M.G. – The deception about the inception rule: coverage for VFR pilots in IFR conditions. –
60 *JALC* 1994, pp.179-235

MARGO, R.D. – Conflicts of laws in aviation insurance. –
19 *Air and Space Law* 1994, pp.2-7

RABY, W.L. – Air transportation tax as liability insurance premium. –
62 *Tax Notes* (Arlington VA), 31 Jan. 1994, pp.606-609

WOO, H.-K. – A study on aviation insurance. –
6 *Korean JAL* 1994, pp.15-42 (in Korean)

HARRIS, R. – Aviation insurance in Canada: current regulatory issues. –
44 *ZLW* 1995, pp.197-202

KENNEY, S.C. – Recent developments in aviation law. IX. Insurance coverage. –
61 *JALC* 1995, pp.139-142

LOBBY, J.B. – War risk aviation exclusions. –
60 *JALC* 1995, pp.609-656

MARGO, R.D. – Conflict of laws in aviation insurance. –
In: The use of airspace and outer space, The Hague 1995, pp.309-318

Passenger liability deal may force up insurance rates. –
Airfinance J, July-Aug. 1995, no. 175, p.12

162. Voluntary or obligatory

SCHÖNWERTH, E. – Zur Versicherungspflicht des Luftfahrzeughalters. –
39 *ZLW* 1990, pp.77-78

UWECHIA, C. – Aviation insurance: a case for compulsory air insurance law. –
16 *Air Law* 1991, pp.284-286

KADLETZ, A. – Zur Versicherungspflicht bei internationalen Luftbeförderungen. –
44 *ZLW* 1995, pp.284-290

Chapter XII. Criminal law

171. General

ARAUJO, L.I. DE AMORIM – Direito penal aeronáutico. –
RBDA 1989, no. 46, pp.10-11

ENROTH, K.B. – United States v. Georgescu: special aircraft jurisdiction in the United States. –
18 *Brooklyn JIL* 1992, pp.225-249

HAILBRONNER, K. – Civil aviation, unlawful interference with –
In: Encyclopedia of Public Int. Law, Amsterdam 1992, vol. I, pp.583-586

THAKER, J.S. – Model clause on aviation security for bilateral air transport agreements. –
17 *AASL* 1992, vol. II, pp.403-440

ABEYRATNE, R.I.R. – Legal aspects of unlawful interference with international civil aviation. –
18 *Air and Space Law* 1993, pp.262-274

WEBER, L. – IATA. IV. Unlawful acts committed on board aircraft not covered by existing conventions. –
19 *AASL* 1994, vol. II, pp.680-681

ABEYRATNE, R.I.R. – The effect of unlawful interference with civil aviation on world peace and the social order. –
22 *Transportation LJ* (Denver CO) 1995, pp.449-494

ARANGO, A.J. – El uso deliberado de aeronaves civiles con fines ilícitos: un delito contra la paz y el derecho internacional. –
11 *Revista europea DNMA* 1995, pp.1643-1654

WEBER, L. – Legal activities of the International Air Transport Association (IATA) 1993-1994. 4. Unlawful acts committed on board aircraft not covered by existing conventions. –
20 *Air and Space Law* 1995, pp.33-34

172. Tokyo Convention, 1963

SCHEDLBERGER, R. – Die Bestimmungen über Anwendungsbereich und Gerichtstbarkeit des Tokioter Abkommens. –
30 *Zs für Rechtsvergleichung* (Austria) 1989, pp.268-291

MAPELLI, E. – El sexo, la aviación y el derecho aeronáutico. –
Airline Ninety Two (Madrid), dic. 92/enero 93, nos. 48-49, pp.38-43

KANE, R. – Time to put teeth into Tokyo? –
43 *ZLW* 1994, pp.187-198

173. Hijacking

a. General

HUNG, H.-C. – A study of aircraft hijacking in international law. –
Taipei 1987, 160 pp. (in Chinese)

ALEXANDER, Y. and SOCHOR, E., eds – Aerial piracy and aviation security. –
Dordrecht 1990, xi-210 pp.

TAYLOR, L. – Aerial piracy – a pilot viewpoint. –
In: Aerial piracy and aviation security, 1990, pp.33-53

HELTON, A.C. – The case of Zhang Zhenhai: reconciling the international responsibilities of punishing air hijacking and protecting refugees. –
13 *Loyola of Los Angeles Int. and Comp. LJ* 1991, pp.841-849

FALLER, E. – Aviation security: the role of ICAO in safeguarding international civil aviation against acts of unlawful interference. –
17 *AASL* 1992, vol. I, pp.369-381

TOURET, C. – La piraterie au vingtième siècle. Piraterie maritime et aérienne. –
Paris 1992, xiv-306 pp.

b. The Hague Convention, 1970

KIM, S.-S. – A study of the International Convention for the Prevention of Aircraft Crimes. –
35 *Korean JIL* 1990, pp.135-162 (in Korean)

YASUTOMI, K. – Political offenses and extradition with the Japanese law for the extradition of fugitives from justice. –
34 *Japanese Annual of Int. Law* 1991, pp.69-81

LEVINE, M.W. – Cuban hijackers and the United States: the need for a modified Aut Dedere Aut Judicare rule. –
32 *Columbia JTL* 1994, pp.133-153

VENNELL, M.A. McGregor – Acts of interference with civil aviation in Australia and New Zealand. –
20 *Air and Space Law* 1995, pp.208-210

d. Search and seizure

ABEYRATNE, R.I.R. – Freedom of arrest and detention in Sri Lanka. The Veeradas case. –
43 *ICLQ* 1994, pp.635-645

MILLER, J.L. – Search and seizure of air passengers and pilots: the Fourth Amendment takes flight. –
22 *Transportation LJ* 1994, pp.199-223

MILLER, J.L. – Searches and seizures of air passengers and pilots. –
22 *Search and Seizure Law Report* (NY), March 1995, pp.105-112

e. Liability

ASANO, Y. – The convention on aviation terrorism and the airline: the airline's liability for damage to passengers. –
33 *Toyo Hogaku* 1989, no. 1, pp.33-85 (in Japanese)

CHOI, W.-S. – Air carrier's liability for injuries to passengers resulting from international aviation terrorism. –
1 *Korean JAL* 1989, pp.47-83 (in Korean) and 83-85 (English summary)

MAGDELÉNAT, J.-L. – Liability for damages resulting from air terrorism. –
In: Aerial piracy and aviation security, 1990, pp.55-75

DUNCAN, J.C. – Battling aerial terrorism and compensating the victims. –
39 *Naval LR* (Newport RI) 1990, pp.241-268

LOWENFELD, A.F. – Liability of airlines for injury caused by terrorism. –
In: Essays in honour of Henri A. Wassenbergh, 1992, pp.83-91

174. Sabotage

a. General

JHE, S.-H. – Sabotage of the Korean Airliner 858 in international legal perspective. –
2 *Korean JAL* 1990, pp.85-136 (in Korean)

COLEMAN, K. – Terror takes to the sky: the bombing of Pan Am flight 103. –
7 *Adelphia LJ* (Chicago IL) 1991, pp.109-123

b. Montreal Convention, 1971

BEVERIDGE, F. – The Lockerbie affair. –
41 *ICLQ* 1992, pp.907-920

CHAPPEZ, J. – Questions d'interprétation et d'application de la Convention de Montréal de 1971 résultant de l'incident aérien de Lockerbie (Jamahiriya Arabe Libyenne c. Royaume-Uni). Mesures conservatoires, ordonnance du 14 avril 1992. –
38 *AFDI* 1992, pp.468-479

VISHESH, A. – The Lockerbie case and the New World Order. –
17 *AASL* 1992, vol. II, pp.519-527

EVANS, S.S. – The Lockerbie incident cases: Libyan-sponsored terrorism, judicial review and the political question doctrine. –
18 *Maryland J of Int. Law & Trade* (Baltimore MD) 1994, pp.21-76

176. National control of aviation

a. General

STIVEN, J.F. – Recent cases and developments in aviation law. IX. FAA enforcement/Local regulations/Administrative law. –
55 *JALC* 1989, pp.101-107

MECHLEM, H.P. – Rechtsgrundlagen für Sicherungsmassnahmen von Luftfahrtbehörden und Luftfahrtunternehmen gegen Angriffe auf den Luftverkehr. –
Diss. Augsburg, Augsburg 1991, 176 pp.

HOFFMAN, J.M. and HARRIS, Ph.S. – Recent developments in aviation case law. XI. FAA enforcement/Local regulation. –
58 *JALC* 1992, pp.83-89

b. Aviation police

VAN DEN BERG, J. – De derde dimensie van de politie. –
8 *Maandblad Luchtvaart*, juni 1991, pp.180-183

ROODZANT, R.W. – Het complexe politiebestel op Schiphol. –
53 *Het Ts voor de Politie* 1991, pp.255-260

VAN WIJNGAARDEN, P. – Veertig jaar luchtvaartpolitie. –
9 *Vliegwereld* 1993, no. 2, pp.8-9 en 12-13

177. Airport security. Montreal Protocol, 1988

GALANTINI, N. – Tutela penale della sicurezza della navigazione aerea e diritto internazionale. –
Studi Parmensi 1988, pp.27-

LABAYLE, H. – Sécurité dans les aéroports et progrès de la collaboration internationale contre le terrorisme. –
35 *AFDI* 1989, pp.711-723

POURCELET, M. – Le Protocole du 24 février 1988 pour la répression des actes illicites de violence dans les aéroports servant à l'aviation civile internationale. –
44 *RFDAS* 1990, pp.289-295

DE LA VERPILLIÈRE, Ch. – La loi du 10 juillet 1989. –
44 *RFDAS* 1990, pp.323-328

ZUZAK, C.A. – Liability for breaches of aviation security obligations: a Canadian perspective. –
Diss. McGill, Montreal 1990

PHIPPS, D. – The management of aviation security. –
London 1991, xii-367 pp.

PLANT, G. – The Aviation and Maritime Security Act 1990. –
Lloyd's MCLQ 1991, pp.44-51

SCHNITKER, R.M. – Lacunes in verdragen ter bescherming van de luchtvaart. –
140 *Algemeen Politieblad* 1991, no. 4, pp.13-14

SCHWEINSBERG, R. – Ensuring aviation security in the Federal Republic of Germany. –
RBDAE, March-April 1991, no. 53, pp.15-17

SHAVIT, U. – The Montreal Protocol of February 24th, 1988 – a critical evaluation. –
Diss. McGill, Montreal 1991

WELLS, A.T. – Commercial aviation safety. –
Blue Ridge Summit PA 1991, xi-340 pp.

WALLIS, R. – Government responsibility and aviation security. –
In: The highways of air and outer space, 1992, pp.123-137

CHOI, W.-S. – Some new problems of international aviation security – considerations focused on its legal aspects. –
5 *Korean JAL* 1993, pp.53-72 (in Korean) and 73-75 (English summary)

DOW, S.L. – Airport security, terrorism, and the Fourth Amendment: a look back and a step forward. –
58 *JALC* 1993, pp.1149-1201

ROKITA, Th.E. – Why U.S.-enforced international flight suspension due to deficient foreign airport security should be a no-go. –
5 *Indiana Int. & Comp. LR* (Indianapolis IN) 1994, pp.205-236

CZAJA, F. – Eigensicherungspflichten von Verkehrsflughäfen. Die Beteiligung von Verkehrsflughäfen an der Abwehr äusserer Gefahren für die Sicherheit des Luftverkehrs. –
Schriften zum Luft- und Weltraumrecht, Bd. 13. Köln 1995, xviii-191 pp.

FIORITA, D.M. – Aviation security: have all the questions been answered? –
20 *AASL* 1995, vol. II, pp.69-93

178. Terrorism. Explosives

CHOI, W.-S. – The liability of air carriers for injuries to passengers resulting from international aviation terrorism. –
34 *Korean JIL* 1989, pp.117-137 (in Korean)

ALEXANDER, Y. and SOCHOR, E., eds – Aerial piracy and aviation security. –
Dordrecht 1990, xi-210 pp.

BAUZÁ ARAÚJO, A. – El terrorismo aeronáutico, en base a los convenios de Tokio, la Haya y Montreal. –
Montevideo 1990, 78 pp.

DUNCAN, J.C. – Battling aerial terrorism and compensating the victims. –
39 *Naval LR* (Newport RI) 1990, pp.241-268

KRIEG, J. – Security fee in the Federal Republic of Germany. –
15 *AASL* 1990, pp.145-151

MEYER, H. – 'Building together'. ECAC symposium on civil aviation security. (Paris, 6-8 November 1990) –
ITA Magazine, Dec. 1990, no. 64, pp.18-20

MILDE, M. – Draft convention on the marking of explosives. –
15 *AASL* 1990, pp.155-179

POURCELET, M. – Le projet de convention de l'OACI sur le marquage de certains explosifs. –
44 *RFDAS* 1990, pp.385-394

STRANTZ, N.J. – Aviation security and Pan Am Flight 103: what have we learned? –
56 *JALC* 1990, pp.413-489

VAN DAM, R.D. – Defusing the crisis. –
46 *ICAO J,* June 1991, pp.7-8

VAN DAM, R.D. – A new Convention on the marking of plastic explosives for the purpose of detection. –
16 *Air Law* 1991, pp.167-177

GRAUMANN, H. – 'Übereinkommen über die Kennzeichnung von Plastiksprengstoffen zum Zweck der Entdeckbarkeit' vom 1. März 1991. –
40 *ZLW* 1991, pp.250-268

International Conference on Air Law, Montreal, 12 February-1 March 1991. –
16 *Air Law* 1991, pp.93-101

JACKSON, N. – The aviation industry's response to terrorism and 'the war on drugs'. –
RBDAE, March-April 1991, no. 53, pp.18-20

JHE, S.-H. – The prevention and suppression of aircraft terrorism. –
3 *Korean JAL* 1991, pp.207-231 (in Korean)

NORTON, G. – The terrorist and the traveller: a Gulf aftermath assessment. –
47 *The World Today* (UK) 1991, pp.80-81

AUGUSTIN, J.V. – The role of ICAO in relation to the Convention on the marking of plastic explosives for the purpose of detection. –
17 *AASL* 1992, vol. II, pp.33-69

FOCKE, K. – Wem dient die Sicherheitsüberprüfung der Flugpassagiere? Einige Anmerkungen zur Zulässigkeit der Luftsicherungsgebühr. –
41 *ZLW* 1992, pp.240-247

GIEBLER, W. – Reclaiming the skies from terrorism: the Aviation Security Improvement Act of 1990. –
16 *Seton Hall Legislative J* (Newark NJ) 1992, pp.757-813

KUZNICKI, Th. – Terrorismus und luftspezifische Gefahr in bezug auf eine Haftung des Luftfrachtführers gemäss Artikel 17 des Warschauer Abkommens. –
41 *ZLW* 1992, pp.360-376

LOWENFELD, A.F. – Airline liability and terrorism. –
In: The highways of air and outer space, 1992, pp.139-147

MILDE, M. – Law and aviation security. –
In: Essays in honour of Henri A. Wassenbergh, 1992, pp.93-98

DE MONTLAUR-MARTIN, E. – Récentes mesures prises aux États-Unis et en Grande-Bretagne contre le terrorisme aérien. –
46 *RFDAS* 1992, pp.81-83

TSWANYA, L. – Analysis of the Convention on the Marking of Plastic explosives for the purpose of detection. –
Diss. McGill, Montreal 1992

DOW, S.L. – Airport security, terrorism, and the Fourth Amendment: a look back and a step forward. –
58 *JALC* 1993, pp.1149-1201

KASH, D. – Abductions of terrorists in international airspace and on the high seas. –
8 *Florida JIL* 1993, pp.65-96

CHOI, J.-T. – Aviation terrorism. –
New York 1994, xiii-255 pp.

JAKUBOVICZ, I. and RODRIGUES PEREIRA, G. – Conferéncia internacional de direito aéreo. Convenção sobre a marcação de explosivos plásticos para fins de detecção. –
RBDAE, Jan.-April 1994, no. 65, pp.13-26

MILLER, J.L. – Search and seizure of air passengers and pilots: the Fourth Amendment takes flight. –
22 *Transportation LJ* 1994, pp.199-223

MILDE, M. – The international fight against terrorism in the air. –
In: The use of airspace and outer space, The Hague 1995, pp.141-158

179. Drugs

BUNKER, D.H. – Aircraft financing and drugs. –
16 *AASL* 1991, pp.31-40

CRAFT JR, R.R. – Aviation liability law developments in 1990. IX.B. Drug and alcohol testing. –
57 *JALC* 1991, pp.169-170

HANCHETT, K.M. – The role of the Federal Aviation Administration in the control of aviation drug-trafficking. –
56 *JALC* 1991, pp.999-1025

JACKSON, N. – The aviation industry's response to terrorism and 'the war on drugs'. –
RBDAE, March-April 1991, no. 53, pp.18-20

PARK, K.-G. – Misuse of civil aviation – especially about illicit traffic in narcotic drugs and psychotropic substances. –
3 *Korean JAL* 1991, pp.191-206 (in Korean)

STACK, R.A. – Airport drug searches: giving content to the concept of free and voluntary consent. –
77 *Virginia LR* 1991, pp.183-209

STIKDYK, S.B. – Airborne drug trafficking deterrence: can a shoot-down policy fly? –
38 *UCLA LR* (Los Angeles CA) 1991, pp.1287-1324

DUBUC, C.E. and BROWN, J.F. – Drug testing in aviation: the double standard continues. –
21 *Transportation LJ* 1992, pp.43-90

WILCOX, L.A. – Random drug testing in the aviation industry. –
26 *Univ. of San Francisco LR* 1992, pp.559-587

MILLER, J.L. – Search and seizure of air passengers and pilots: the Fourth Amendment takes flight. –
22 *Transportation LJ* 1994, pp.199-223

Chapter XIII. Acts on board aircraft

183. Marriages

MAPELLI, E. – El matrimonio a bordo de aeronaves. – Centenario del Código Civil, Alicante 1989, vol. 2, pp.299-323

184. Deaths. Wills

REZENDE DE FARIA, F.E. – Testamento aeronáutico. – *RBDAE* 1990, no. 51, pp.37-38

Chapter XIV. Solution of disputes

191. General

ATHERTON, T.C. and T.-A. – The resolution of civil aviation disputes. –
9 *J of Intern. Arbitration* (Geneva) 1992, pp.105-122

MANIATIS, D. – Conflict in the skies: the settlement of international aviation disputes – from the law of the jungle to the rule of law. –
20 *AASL* 1995, vol. II, pp.167-239

MENDES DE LEON, P. – Settlement of disputes in air and space law. –
In: The use of airspace and outer space, The Hague 1995, pp.329-339, at pp.329-335

192. Interpretation of treaties

GARDINER, R. – Treaty interpretation in English courts. Antwerp United Diamonds v. Air Europe. –
Lloyd's MCLQ 1994, pp.184-189

GARDINER, R. – Treaty interpretation in the English courts since Fothergill v. Monarch Airlines (1980). –
44 *ICLQ* 1994, pp.620-628

193. Function of the ICAO Council

JHE, S.-H. – Dispute settlement by ICAO. –
34 *Korean JIL* 1989, pp.191-214 (in Korean)

UCHIGASAKI, Y. – Rethinking the ICAO case. –
98 *Hogaku Shimpo* 1991, no. 3-4, pp.121-154 (in Japanese)

194. The institution of an international court for aviation disputes

BOURÉLY, M. – La création d'une cour internationale d'arbitrage aérien et spatial. –
43 *ZLW* 1994, pp.401-410

BECHKY, P.S. – Mismanagement and misinterpretation: U.S. judicial implementation of the Warsaw Convention in air disaster litigation. –
60 *JALC* 1995, pp.455-531

195. Arbitration

Arbitration in the airlines. –
42 National Academy of Arbitrators. Proceedings of the Annual Meeting 1990, pp.189-203

HOFFMAN, L.M. and HARRIS, Ph.S. – Recent developments in aviation case law. V.D. Arbitration. –
58 *JALC* 1992, pp.46-47

BOURÉLY, M.G. – Creating an international space and aviation arbitration court. –
In: Proceedings of the 36th Colloquium on the Law of Outer Space, Graz 1993, pp.144-149

BAILEY, E.O. – Article 15 of the Chicago Convention and the duty of States to avoid discriminatory user charges: the US-UK London Heathrow Airport user charges arbitration. –
19 *AASL* 1994, vol. II, pp.81-105

BOURÉLY, M. – La création d'une cour internationale d'arbitrage aérien et spatial. –
43 *ZLW* 1994, pp.401-410

United States-United Kingdom arbitration. Heathrow Airport user charges. –
88 *AJIL* 1994, pp.738-744

BÖCKSTIEGEL, K.-H. – France-United States air transport arbitration (1963). –
In: Encyclopedia of Public Int. Law, Amsterdam 1995, vol. II, pp.459-461

BÖCKSTIEGEL, K.-H. – Italy-United States air transport arbitration (1965). –
In: Encyclopedia of Public Int. Law, Amsterdam 1995, vol. II, pp.1508-1510

Cour internationale d'arbitrage aérien et spatial, pp.7-32
International court of aviation and space arbitration, pp.33-54
Corte internacional de arbitraje aéreo y espacial, pp.55-81
Corte internazionale di arbitro aereo e spaziale, pp.83-108
Internationaler Schiedsgerichtshof für Luft- und Raumfahrt, pp.109-136
48 *RFDAS* 1995, no. 2

VAN HAERSOLTE-VAN HOF, J.J. – US/UK arbitration concerning Heathrow Airport user charges. Some procedural aspects. –
8 *Leiden JIL* 1995, pp.203-216

OELLERS-FRAHM, K. – France-United States air transport arbitration (1978). –
In: Encyclopedia of Public Int. Law, Amsterdam 1995, vol. II, pp.461-463

SKILBECK, J. – The US/UK arbitration concerning Heathrow Airport user charges. –
44 *ICLQ* 1995, pp.171-179

WITTEN, S.M. – The U.S.-U.K. arbitration concerning Heathrow Airport user charges. –
89 *AJIL* 1995, pp.174-192

196. Sanctions. Reprisals

DAVIDSON, G.E. – United States' use of economic sanctions, treaty bending, and treaty breaking in international aviation. –
59 *JALC* 1994, pp.291-356

MUKAI, M. – The use of force against civil aircraft: the legal aspects of joint international action. –
19 *AASL* 1994, vol. II, pp.567-587

Chapter XV.

Military aviation. The laws of war and neutrality

201. Military aviation

ALY, S.F. – A claims officer's guide to aviation claims. –
33 *The Air Force LR* (Washington DC) 1990, pp.113-136

RONELLENFITSCH, M. – Der Militärflugplatz. Merkmale und Kriterien. –
47 *Die öffentliche Verwaltung* 1994, no. 2, pp.45-52

STEPPICK, D.C. – Military mess: CERCLA liability and the Base Closure and Realignment Act. –
59 *JALC* 1994, pp.449-491

LIBBY, J.B. – War risk aviation exclusions. –
60 *JALC* 1995, pp.609-656

202. Military aircraft in peacetime

a. Legal status

APARICIO GALLEGO, J. – Comandante de aeronave militar: comandante militar de aeronave. Su concepto en el derecho español. –
In: El comandante de aeronave, Madrid 1993, pp.105-134

b. Liability for transport

GROSS, R.J. – Special considerations in military flying club litigation. –
59 *JALC* 1994, pp.561-586

c. Liability to third parties. Noise

MEYER, J.-Cl. – L'incident entre la Belgique et le Grand-Duché de Luxembourg de 1981. Les principes de réparation dans la Convention de Londres du 19 juin 1951 sur le Statut des Forces. –
23 *Revue belge de Droit international* 1990, pp.496-509

SORENSON, R.B. – Use of the FTCA discretionary function exception in sonic boom and low overflight litigation. –
33 *The Air Force LR* (Washington DC) 1990, pp.137-146

GUILLERM, J. – Problèmes liés à la circulation des aéronefs militaires. La réparation des dommages causés par les aéronefs militaires. –
44 *RFDAS* 1991, pp.34-39

LEFFERTS, A. – De stand van zaken rond de militaire luchtvaartterreinen. – 16 *Geluid*, juni 1993, pp.60-63

GROSS, R.J. – Special considerations in military flying club litigation. – 59 *JALC* 1994, pp.561-586

d. Accidents

SALMON, J. – Chute sur le territoire belge d'un avion militaire soviétique le 4 juillet 1989. Problèmes de responsabilité. –
23 *Revue belge de Droit international* 1990, pp.510-516

e. Liability of manufacturer

STIVEN, J.F. – Recent cases and developments in aviation law. II.B. Government contractor defense. –
55 *JALC* 1989, pp.10-15

CARTER JR, W.D. a.o. – Aviation and space law: annual survey. III. Government contractor defense. –
25 *Tort & Insurance LJ* (ABA) 1990, pp.219-223

CARTER JR, W.D. a.o. – Aviation and space law: annual survey. III. Government contractor defense. –
26 *Tort & Insurance LJ* (ABA) 1991, pp.184-187

CRAFT JR, R.R. – Aviation liability law developments in 1990. IV.D. Government contractor defense. –
57 *JALC* 1991, pp.110-122

HOFFMAN, J.M. and HARRIS, Ph.S. – Recent developments in aviation case law. II.B. Government contractor defense. –
58 *JALC* 1992, pp.22-24

STEWART, E. – The Government made me do it!: has Boyle v. United Technologies extended the government contractor defense too far? –
57 *JALC* 1992, pp.981-1016

STROUD, J.C. – Recent developments in aviation case law. V.C. Government contractor defense. –
59 *JALC* 1993, pp.51-52

ANDERSEN, D.R. – Recent cases and developments in aviation law. IV.C. Government contractor defense. –
60 *JALC* 1994, pp.87-99

CAHOON, C.P. – Boyle under siege. –
59 *JALC* 1994, pp.815-866

KENNEY, S.C. – Recent developments in aviation law. IV.B. Government contractor defense. –
61 *JALC* 1995, pp.82-84

SAVITT, L.J. and COLLERAN, M.J. – Recent developments in aviation and space law. I.B. Government contractor defense. –
30 *Tort & Insurance LJ* 1995, pp.252-253

204. Red Cross conventions

HAECK, L. – Le droit du milieu aérospatial et les militaires. –
15 *AASL* 1990, pp.109-143

DOSWALD-BECK, L. – Vessels, aircraft and persons entitled to protection during armed conflicts at sea. –
65 *British Year Book of International Law* 1994, pp.211-301, at pp.262-269 and 292-294

205. The laws of war

a. General

ANDRÉS VÁZQUEZ, E. – Derecho internacional aéreo. –
San Javier 1957, 60 pp.

PARKS, W.H. – Air law and the law of war. –
32 *Air Force LR* (Washington DC), winter 1990, pp.1-225

HANKE, H.M. – Luftkrieg und Zivilbevölkerung. –
Frankfurt am Main 1991, xiv-310 pp.

VON DER HEYDTE, F.A. Freiherr – Air warfare. –
In: Encyclopedia of Public Int. Law, Amsterdam 1992, vol. I, pp.82-86

SHOTWELL, C.B. – Economy and humanity in the use of force: a look at the aerial rules of engagement in the 1991 Gulf War. –
4 *US Air Force Academy J of Legal Studies* 1993, pp.15-57

MCILMAIL, T.P. – No-fly zones: the imposition and enforcement of air exclusion regimes over Bosnia and Iraq. –
17 *Loyola of Los Angeles Int. & Comp. LJ* 1994, pp.35-83

ROUCOUNAS, E. – Some issues relating to war crimes in air and sea warfare. –
24 *Israel Yb of Human Rights* 1994, pp.223-240

b. The Hague Rules, 1923

WAALWIJK, H.P. – Whitehall en Plein. VII. Naar beheersing van de gevaren uit de lucht. –
Diss. Utrecht. Terneuzen 1985, pp.95-135

HANKE, H.M. – Les Règles de La Haye de 1923 concernant la guerre aérienne. –
75 *Revue int. de la Croix-Rouge* (Genève) 1993, no. 799, pp.13-49

c. Bombardments

FORMAN JR, W.H. – Smart bombs and the law of air war; the beginning of a new era in the Persian Gulf war. –
39 *Federal Bar News & J* 1992, pp.152-157

ELLIOTT, H.W. – Open cities and (un)defended places. –
The Army Lawyer (Washington DC), April 1995, pp.39-50

206. Blockades by aircraft

SCHMITT, M.N. – Aerial blockades in historical, legal, and practical perspective. –
2 *J of Legal Studies* (Tuscaloosa AL) 1991, pp.21-86

208. Position of civil aircraft during a war

EWING, D.A. – The downing of Iran Air flight 655: highlighting the need for international adjudication of damages. –
13 *Suffolk Transnational LJ* (Boston MA) 1990, pp.656-685

PARK, K.-G. – The aerial incident of 3 July 1988 and international law. –
35 *Korean JIL* 1990, pp.185-200 (in Korean)

LINNAN, D.K. – Iran Air flight 655 and beyond: free passage, mistaken identity, and State responsibility. –
16 *Yale JIL* 1991, pp.245-389

JABBARI GHARABAGH, M. – Use of weapons upon civil aircraft: case study of Iran Air 655 in the light of international law. –
Diss. McGill, Montreal 1993

DOSWALD-BECK, L. – Vessels, aircraft and persons entitled to protection during armed conflicts at sea. –
65 *British Year Book of International Law* 1994, pp.211-301, at pp.269-276 and 294

211. Disarmament

HAECK, L. – Le survol libre dans les espaces aériens dits 'ouverts'. –
44 *RFDAS* 1991, pp.319-338

BENTZIEN, J. – Die luftrechtlichen Aspekte des Vertrags über den offenen Himmel. –
41 *ZLW* 1992, pp.327-348

FERRIER, J. – The Open Skies Treaty of 1992. –
18 *AASL* 1993, vol. I, pp.79-111

BAILER, St. – The treaty on open skies. –
SIPRI Yearbook 1995, pp.821-824

Chapter XVI. Miscellaneous

224. Flying shows

KRAATZ, H. – The NATO Status of Forces Agreement and the Supplementary Agreement. –
The Army Lawyer, Nov. 1990, pp.3-7

225. Training flights

JOHNSTON III, R.H. – Aviation. Duty of aviation safety inspectors and designated flight examiners. Hayes v. United States. –
57 *JALC* 1992, pp.1019-1032

FRANCHI, B. – Note sulla responsabilità dell'esercente di una scuola di pilotaggio per i danni arrecati a terzi dall'allievo pilota durante l'attività di prevolo. –
Trasporti 1994, no. 62-63, pp.169-198

Index des auteurs — Index of names — Indice de autores

Subject index

Index analytique

Índice analítico